D0709446

CALGARY PUBLIC LIBRARY

NOV   2013

MASTERING
FINANCIAL
MODELING

- *Colors.* Colors for a selected cell or block of cells can be set by clicking on the Fill Color icon (the icon is an inclined bucket). This icon is located within the Home tab in the ribbon. To change the current color, you need to click on the drop-down arrow; a set of colors to choose from is then displayed. This is shown in Figure 2.2.

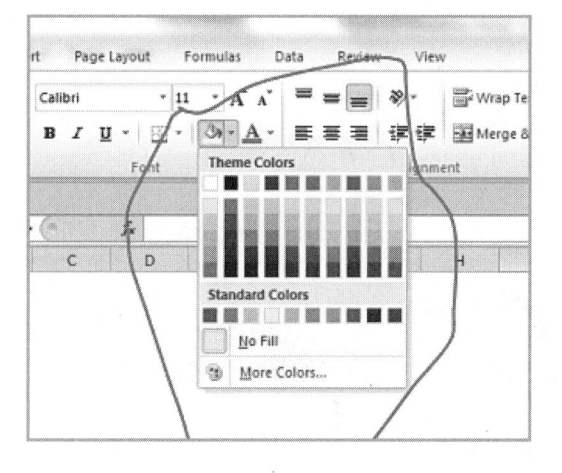

FIGURE 2.2 FILL COLOR (EXCEL)

- *Calculations settings.* These are available in Microsoft Excel 2010 by going to File>Options>Formulas. This then shows the window given in Figure 2.3.

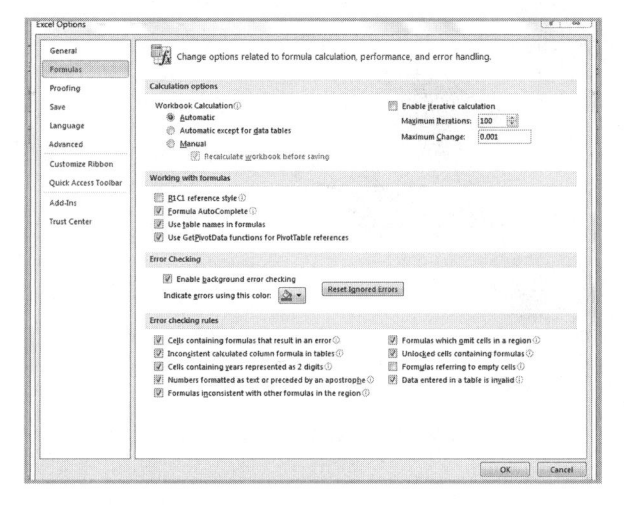

FIGURE 2.3 FORMULA OPTIONS (EXCEL)

2.3.2 Excel's Functions

- There are 408 functions in Microsoft Excel 2010 (343 in Microsoft Excel 2007 and 292 in Microsoft Excel 2003), thus providing plenty of scope for analytical computations. Of course, you do not need to familiarize yourself with all of these functions at once. Instead, as a starting point, it is okay for you to get to know these functions as and when you need them. In practice, the following functions tend to come back and again in many financial applications:
  - Logical functions (3): AND, IF, OR
  - Statistical functions (6): AVERAGE, COUNT, COUNTA, COUNTIF, MAX, MIN
  - Mathematical and trigonometric functions (7): INT, MOD, MROUND, ROUND, SUM, SUMIF, SUMPRODUCT
  - Financial functions (4): IRR, NPV, XIRR, XNPV
  - Text functions (4): LEFT, MID, RIGHT, TEXT
  - Information functions (4): ISBLANK, ISERROR, ISNUMBER, ISTEXT
  - Lookup functions (7): CHOOSE, HLOOKUP, INDEX, INDIRECT, MATCH, OFFSET, VLOOKUP
  - Date functions (8): DATE, YEAR, MONTH, DAY, EOMONTH, DAY360, NOW, DATEVALUE
- Microsoft Excel provides help regarding the use of all of its functions. This can be found by clicking on *fx* Insert Function (on the left-hand side of the edit bar).
- It is possible to combine different functions to yield even more modeling power, and there are numerous websites hosting discussions on these topics. For example, a simple Internet search for "Excel forums" will generate a list of such forums on the Internet.

2.4 THE ART OF MODELING

Ultimately, modeling is an art as much as it is a science. If two expert modelers are asked to build a model for doing a specific task, it is likely that the models that they will develop will be different. Both models might produce the same results and are likely to display a number of good practice features. But the two models are likely to look different, receive inputs differently, calculate differently, and so on. These differences between the models are a reflection of the different style used by each modeler.

Notwithstanding these differences in style, what should be found consistently in good models is the fact that good thinking and sound knowledge of the tools at hand were applied in order to develop such models.

By the end of this book, you too will be able to develop good models in your own style as long as you follow the steps given in this book. To this end, it is particularly important that you follow all the steps described in the first case study, which does not require any particular knowledge of accounting.

Part 2

Modeling Practice— Initial Case Studies

CHAPTER THREE

CASE STUDY 1:
The Phone Factory

3.1 INTRODUCTION

This case study has been designed to give a context for the teaching of financial modeling in Microsoft Excel. Case studies will be at the center of the reader's learning of modeling. For this first case study, you are asked to build a cash flow model only; that is, no income statement account and no balance sheet are required. Thus, little knowledge of accounting and finance is needed here.

Yet within this case study, a number of important financial and modeling concepts will be used; thus, completing the case study will teach you a number of useful and important techniques for building good models despite having little knowledge of accounting and finance.

3.2 FINANCIAL CONCEPTS COVERED

The following financial concepts are covered in this case study:

- Debt vs. equity
- Interest rate (compounded)

- Rolled-up interest
- Debt service coverage ratio
- Inflation
- Cash flows
- Internal rate of return (IRR and XIRR functions)
- Equity
- Cash waterfalls

3.3 MODELING CONCEPTS COVERED

The following modeling concepts are covered in this case study:

- Flags
- Conditional formatting
- The Goal Seek function
- SUMIF
- IRR, XIRR
- Grouping data
- Inputs, Calculations, and Outputs sheets

3.4 THE PHONE FACTORY

For this exercise, your manager has asked you to head up an exciting new project: setting up a mobile phone factory as part of your company's expansion into overseas markets.

Some preliminary work has already been done, and the following is some information about the project.

- The project development costs are estimated to be $1 million. This amount will be paid up front and includes land acquisition costs, local planning costs, and one-time fees payable to the local electricity, water, and telephone companies for bringing these utilities on site.
- Construction will last two years and will cost $1 million per year.
- For the purpose of this exercise, the factory's activities (that is, postconstruction) will run for eight years. This is known as the *period of operation*.

- Your company will sell the factory at the end of the eighth year of operation and has prudently assumed for now that it will get only the amount that it initially invested.
- During the operation period, the project will incur two types of costs (known as operating costs): fixed operating costs, estimated at $1 million per year, and variable operating costs, estimated at about $15 per mobile phone handset.
- Preliminary market studies suggest that the factory should manufacture about 12,000 handsets during the first year of operation. Thereafter, production should grow at 5 percent per year.
- In terms of financing this project (that is, providing the capital required for the project), your company will use a combination of its own money (this is known as *equity*, and investing this money in the project makes your company a shareholder of the project) and money borrowed from a bank (this is known as *debt*). The debt/equity ratio is assumed to be 2:1 (that is, two-thirds of the capital is debt and one-third is equity).
- Also the bank is flexible concerning the repayment of its debt as long as the overall debt service coverage ratio is at a minimum of 1.2 times (this means that for any given period, the cash available to pay interest and principal, known as debt service, must be greater than or equal to 1.2 times the debt service for that period). Basically, the bank wants to ensure that there is enough (or, more precisely, 20 percent more than enough) money in the project to cover the interest and principal payments for any given period.
- The drawdown of debt and equity is assumed to reflect the annual timing of construction costs.
- All costs are assumed to be incurred evenly over the year.
- Bank interest is 5 percent per annum.
- Inflation is assumed to be at 3 percent per year throughout the investment horizon period, that is, for the next 10 years.
- Your company has negotiated and the bank has agreed that, because of the lack of income generation during the construction period, bank interest incurred during construction will be added to the principal outstanding on the bank debt (this is known as a *roll-up*). This means that the project will still incur interest during the construction period, but it will not have to pay that interest. Instead, the interest that is incurred but

unpaid during construction will be *rolled up* or added to the balance of the debt outstanding at the end of each year during the construction period.

■ For the purpose of this exercise, you are asked to work on a semiannual basis and to aggregate the model's semiannual results into annual results.

Question: What is the minimum selling price per mobile phone handset if your company wants to achieve an annual IRR of 15 percent?

IRR stands for internal rate of return. It is basically the profit achieved on $100 after one year. For example, an IRR of 20 percent per year means that investing $100 will generate a profit of $20 after one year, and so the total money returned after one year will be $120.

CHAPTER FOUR

CASE STUDY 1:

Modeling the Front and Inputs Sheets

We will now apply the knowledge gained in Chapters 1 and 2 to build a financial model for the phone factory project.

4.1 STEP 1: SOME HIGH-LEVEL THINKING

We need to resist the temptation to go straight to our computer and start making calculations in Excel. Instead, let us try to draw a map of the model on paper to ensure that we have a good understanding of the requirements. But before we even do that, let us try to understand what we are being asked to do. Basically, we are planning to set up a business from scratch. The business requires some capital, say C, to get started. Once it is up and running, the business will incur running costs, say RC, but it will also generate some income, say I. The business will generate its income by selling mobile phone handsets. The income I will depend on the number of handsets sold, say N, and the unit selling price, say P. So $I = N \times P$. The question is what P should be to ensure that a certain measure of profitability, defined as the IRR, is achieved. We can calculate the profit for each year as $N \times P - RC$.

Adding up these annual profits over the eight-year operational period will give us the total amount of profit generated by this project. Against this total profit, there was an amount of $C outlaid initially.

4.2 STEP 2: HIGH-LEVEL MODEL MAP

This initial thinking, of course, is simplistic and will not give us the answer. The problem is a little bit more complicated than the way it was just described. The following issues arise as we start to think about the problem in further detail:

- The capital $C is not 100 percent equity. To determine the profitability of the equity investment, measured by the IRR, we need to calculate the IRR on the basis of one-third of $C.
- From the annual profit $N \times \$P - \$RC$, we need to deduct the amount paid to the bank. Whatever is left after that goes to us (that is, the shareholder/owner of the factory).
- The amount paid to the bank varies from one year to another. First of all, during the construction period, the interest is not paid, but the principal outstanding increases as a result of the interest roll-up. In fact, *the amount paid to the bank in any one year depends on the amount paid to the bank in previous years.*
- The annual profit varies from one year to another, driven by variable running costs and variable income. In fact, *the income generated in one year depends on the income generated in previous years* (we are told that production will increase by 5 percent per annum).

Despite these issues, the high-level thinking developed in Step 1, while simplistic, helps us to develop a framework for solving the problem, and thus we can draw up a simplistic map of what the model could do (see Figure 4.1).

Based on the map in Figure 4.1, we can envisage a Microsoft Excel file with four sheets: Inputs, Calculations, Outputs—Semiannual, and Outputs—Annual. The model will flow in that order, too.

Notes

- Steps 1 and 2 are often referred to as the *model scope*. For complex projects, the model scope can be a document in its own right. The model scoping document effectively describes *what*

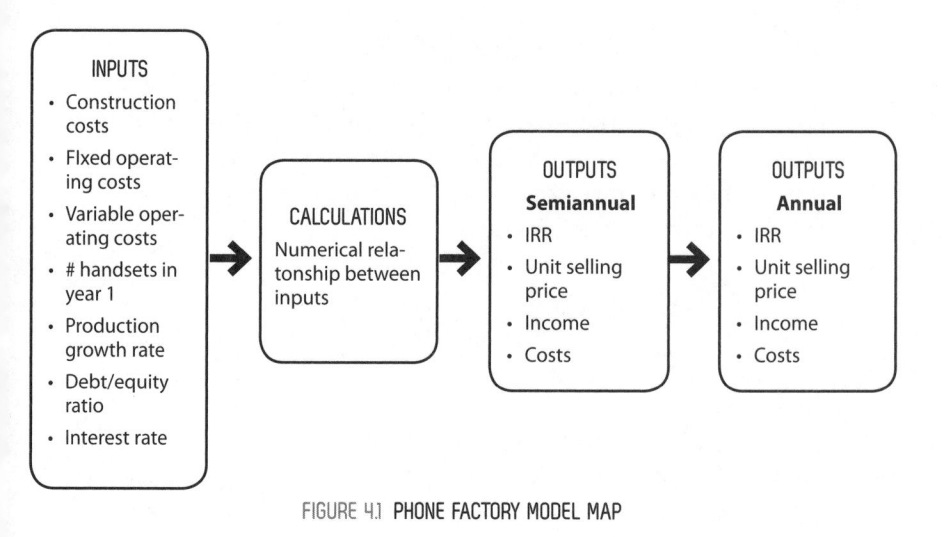

INPUTS
- Construction costs
- FIxed operating costs
- Variable operating costs
- # handsets in year 1
- Production growth rate
- Debt/equity ratio
- Interest rate

CALCULATIONS
Numerical relationship between inputs

OUTPUTS
Semiannual
- IRR
- Unit selling price
- Income
- Costs

OUTPUTS
Annual
- IRR
- Unit selling price
- Income
- Costs

FIGURE 4.1 PHONE FACTORY MODEL MAP

the model is *for* or *what* the model *does*. A second document, called the *model specification*, describes *how* the model works, or the model calculations. This is discussed further in the next chapter.

■ The issues discussed in Step 2 are indicative of a spreadsheet modeling approach to solving the case study (as opposed to, say, developing a closed-form solution by modeling the problem as a mathematical equation). A spreadsheet model is useful in situations where there is a time-dependence relationship between different elements of the problem at hand (for example, the amount paid to the bank in a given period depends on the amount paid in previous periods, or the cumulative amount of cash generated in one time period depends on the cumulative amount of cash generated in the previous period).

■ When a model is required to show different periodicities (for example, both annual and quarterly), it is recommended that you build the model using the most granular or shortest periods, then aggregate the results to the least granular or longest periods. In our case, this would mean working on a semiannual basis and then aggregating the results on an annual basis. The reason for this is that it is more accurate to aggregate results, such as income, from the shorter periods to the longer period than to, say, divide income from the longer period among the smaller periods. For example, it would almost certainly be inappropriate to assume that the income generated by a supermarket during the course of a year can be simply divided evenly between the first half of the year and the second half of the year. Supermarkets tend to make a substantial proportion of their money (sometimes up to 40 percent of annual revenue) during the Christmas/New Year's season (not surprisingly, this is referred to as seasonality).

4.3 STEP 3: CREATING A NEW BLANK WORKBOOK IN EXCEL

To create a new blank workbook in Microsoft Excel, simply open the Microsoft Excel program. If Microsoft Excel is already open, then a new blank workbook can be created through File>New>Blank Workbook.

4.4 STEP 4: CREATING THE FRONT SHEET

We will try to give the workbook a "book" feel, and as part of this, we will create a front sheet (just as a book has a front cover). We will call the front sheet Title.

By default, a new blank workbook includes three sheets named Sheet1, Sheet2, and Sheet3. Rename Sheet1 as Title. This can be done by double-clicking on the Sheet1 name and typing Title, then clicking outside of the Title area.

For now, we will just create a big rectangular frame within which the following information will be provided: Project Name, Subject, Date, and Developer.

Apply the following settings in the Title sheet:

- Column width at 8.43. (This can be set by right-clicking on the name of the column, selecting Column Width . . . from the pop-up menu, then entering the desired size; the default is 8.43.)
- Row height of 15. (This can be set by right-clicking on the row number, selecting Row Height . . . from the pop-up menu, then entering the desired size; the default is 15.)
- To create the frame, select the area F7:M18 and apply the Outside Borders button, which is located within the Home tab (see Figure 4.2). Then apply a grey background color to the selected area F7:M18. The background color is applied by using the bucket icon that is immediately to the right of the Outside Borders button.

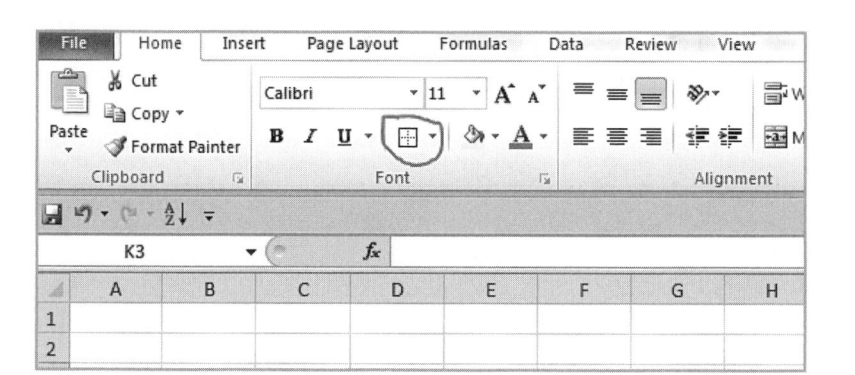

FIGURE 4.2 **BORDER (EXCEL)**

- In cell G8, type in "Case Study 1" with font size 12 and font style Arial.
- In cell G10, type in "The Mobile Phone Factory" with font size 18 and font style Arial.
- In cell G12, type in the formula "=now()" with font size 10 and font style Arial. Type Enter to confirm and right-click on that cell, then select Format Cells. . . . Then in the Number tab, select Custom at the bottom of the list. Then type "mmm yyyy" in the Type box and confirm by pressing the OK button (see Figure 4.3).

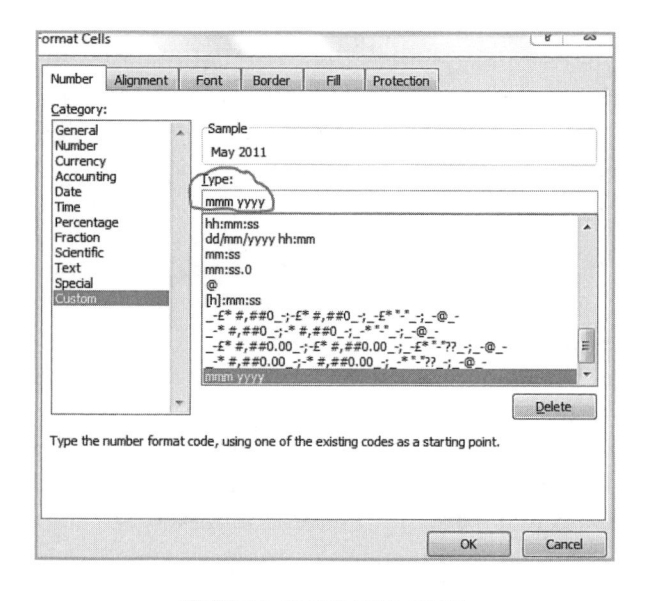

FIGURE 4.3 **FORMAT CELLS (EXCEL)**

- In cell G15, type in your first name and surname with font size 10 and font style Arial.
- The result should be as shown in Figure 4.4.

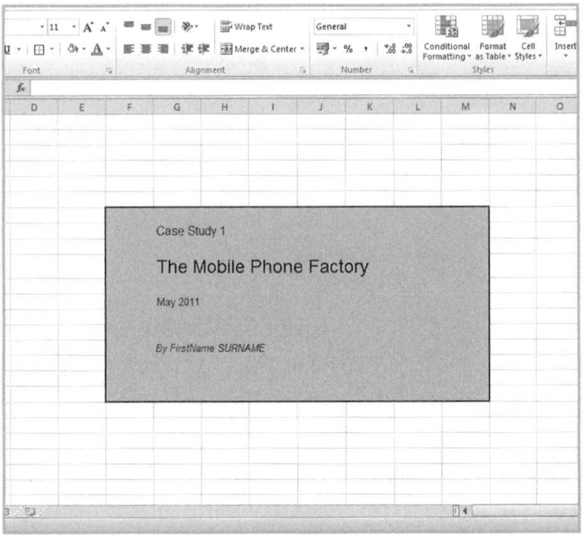

FIGURE 4.4 PHONE FACTORY MODEL TITLE

We have thus created a basic front sheet for our model. Of course, it is probably not the most beautiful front sheet in the world, and readers are encouraged to be as creative as they want for their own projects. But for now we have a basic working front sheet for our case study.

Finally, let us save our workbook as PhoneFactory_v1.

4.5 STEP 5: CREATING THE INPUTS SHEET

Now that we have created the front sheet, let us continue with the development of the model by creating the input sheet. Since the creation of the inputs sheet is an expansion of the PhoneFactory_v1 file built in the previous step, we will simply take a copy of that file and rename it as PhoneFactory_v2 (rather than starting from scratch again).

There are different ways of presenting inputs. One simple way of doing so is to present the inputs in the order in which they are introduced in the description of the problem at hand. However, we need to bear in mind that this model will be used to aid in making decisions regarding investing in the phone factory project. It is likely that, in these circumstances, the model will be referred to several times, updating selected inputs in the model, running it using different assumptions, and so on. As a result, it is better to try to group the inputs into a certain number of categories that would make sense for other people who are using the model (for example, senior managers who are approving the project). For example, we could group the inputs as shown in Table 4.1: general inputs, cost inputs, financing inputs, and opening balances (these inputs are needed to track the balance of debt, interest, and cash period by period).

TABLE 4.1 **INPUTS**

General Inputs

Number of semiannual periods in a year		2
Development years		1
Construction years		2
Operational years		8

Cost Inputs

Construction costs	$m	1
Development costs	$m	1
Fixed production costs	$m	1
Variable production costs	$	15
Number of phones produced during op yr 1	Nb	12,000
Growth in production (after op yr 1)		5.00%

Financing Inputs

Inflation		3.00%
Debt interest rate (annual)		5.00%
Debt/equity ratio		2/3
Target IRR (annual)		15.00%
Target debt service coverage ratio		1.20×

Opening Balances

Debt		0
Interest		0
Cash balance		0

Generally speaking, the Microsoft Excel sheet that we will be building here can be viewed as being a two-dimensional table (also known as a matrix) with information relating to a specific data item (such as variable production costs, income, cost, number of units, and so on) on each row and information relating to a specific time period (such as Year 2, Quarter 3, and so on) down each column.

- Open the file PhoneFactory_v2 and rename Sheet2 as Inputs, then click outside of the Inputs name to validate the name change.
- Change the color of the Inputs sheet to yellow (right-click on the Inputs name, click on Tab Color in the pop-up menu, then select the yellow color).
- For each input data item, it is good practice to write the description of the input data item in one column and then enter the data item in an adjacent column on the right-hand side (as intuitively presented in Table 4.1). For example, we will write the description of all input data in column D and the corresponding data items on the same row, but in column G. Labels for input categories will be written in column C.
- We will also use a yellow background color for all input cells so that inputs are easily recognizable.
- An illustration of how inputs are handled is given in Figure 4.5.

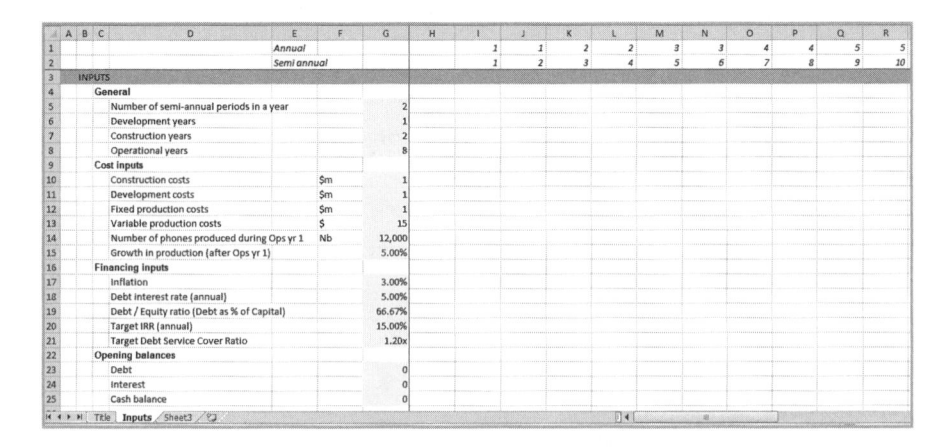

FIGURE 4.5 PHONE FACTORY MODEL INPUTS

- You might need to manually adjust the column widths as follows:
  - Columns A, B, and C widths: 2.5
  - Column D width: 32.3
  - Columns E onward: 8.43
- It is not critical that you have exactly the same column widths as in Figure 4.5, although you should try to use the same layout (that is, row and column positions) so that it is easier to follow the different modeling steps.
- Please also note that row 3 includes the overall title for the sheet, INPUTS. You should make the background color light blue.

4.6 STEP 6: MODEL TIMELINE

You will have also noticed in Figure 4.5 that the Input sheet includes the model timeline (see rows 1 and 2 for the annual and semiannual periods, respectively). As discussed in Step 2, when a model requires different periodicities, we should do all calculations in the smallest periods first (in this case study, the semiannual periods), then aggregate the results to the longer periods (that is, the annual periods). It is for this reason that the model shows two timelines, the semiannual and annual periods, one on top of the other so that for any given column, given one timeline, we know the equivalent position for the same column in the other timeline. For example, if semiannual period 4 is the fourth six-monthly period in the projection, then it must also be part of the second period in the annual timeline (that is, Year 2). This relationship between the semiannual and the annual periods is shown in Table 4.2.

TABLE 4.2

Semiannual	1	2	3	4	5	6	7	8	9	10
Annual	1	1	2	2	3	3	4	4	5	5

There are different ways of writing a formula in Microsoft Excel to generate this relationship.

For example, the semiannual period can be calculated as follows:

- Semiannual period 1: 1 (that is, a hard-coded input). In Figure 4.5, cell I2 contains 1.
- Semi-annual period 2 and all following cells: the number in the previous cell + 1. In Figure 4.5, cell J2 contains the formula "=I2+1". Then for all other cells along that row, simply copy cell J2 (shortcut: CTRL + C, meaning press and hold the CTRL key, then press key C) and paste it into the area K2:AB2 (short-cut: select cells K2 to AB2 and do CTRL + V). The shortcut for selecting adjacent cells is to click the top left cell of the area, press and hold the shift key, then click the bottom right cell of the area.

Once the semiannual timeline has been calculated, we calculate the annual period using the combination of two mathematical functions in Microsoft Excel as follows:

- INT(x) rounds the number x down to the nearest integer. Since one year includes two periods of six months, then conversely, given a number of six-month periods, we can obtain the year by dividing the number of semiannual periods by 2. If the number of semiannual periods is even, then our division gives a whole number; otherwise we get a fractional number. The INT function is applied to the result of dividing the number of semi-annual periods by 2.
- MOD(x, y) returns the remainder after the number x is divided by y. In our case, we apply the MOD function to x, where x is the number of semiannual periods and y is 2.
- INT(x) + MOD(x, y) then gives us the exact annual period number based on x being the semiannual period number and y being 2.
- Thus cell I1 contains the formula "=INT(I2/$G$5)+MOD(I2,$G$5)", where cell G5 contains the number 2.
- Then we simply copy cell I1 and paste it into all the other cells to the right of cell I1, that is, area J1:AB1.
- Note that we have applied the $ symbol to column G and row 5 so that when we copy the formula in cell I1 and paste it across row 1, all the formulas will continue to refer to cell G5.

Now that we have our model timeline ready in the inputs sheet, we will not need to create it again throughout the model. All we have to do is create links to the Inputs sheet from all other sheets requiring the model timeline, including the Calculation and Output sheets.

Save the file PhoneFactory_v2 again to make sure that Microsoft Excel has incorporated all the changes made since we first opened the file.

Note

- Another easier, but somewhat less elegant, approach to calculating the annual timeline formulas is as follows. Enter 1 in cells I1 and J1. Then enter the formula "=I1+1" in cell K1, then copy cell K1 and paste it into all cells to the right of cell K1, that is, the area L1:AB1.

CHAPTER FIVE

CASE STUDY 1:
Modeling the Calculations Sheet

In the previous chapter, we built the Front and Inputs sheets. We will now apply the knowledge gained in Chapters 1 and 2 to build the Calculations sheet for the financial model for the phone factory project.

5.1 STEP 1: WRITING MODEL SPECIFICATIONS

We already started thinking about the calculations in Steps 1 and 2 of the previous chapter. We now need to expand on this initial thinking so that we can start building the Calculations sheet. This detailed description of the calculations is often referred to as the *model specifications*, and for complex modeling projects, the model specifications can be a separate document in its own right. The model specifications describe the numerical relationships between the different inputs of the model. Whereas the model scope is concerned with *what* the model does (that is, its function or purpose), the model specifications are concerned with *how* the model works. We set out here an example of how the model would work. These specifications will form the basis for the Calculations sheet.

We envisage the following calculation modules.

5.1.1 Calculation Modules

An important best practice principle is the principle of modularization, that is, breaking the problem into smaller pieces. Here we consider the following calculation modules: a module for calculating funding requirements, a module for calculating operating costs, a debt module, an equity module, a revenue module, and an inflation module.

Funding Requirements Module

For each period of time:

- Calculate the development costs as $1 million per year for the first year (or $0.5 million per semiannual period for semiannual periods 1 and 2).
- Calculate the construction costs as $1 million per year for Years 1 and 2 (or $0.5 million per semiannual period for semiannual periods 1 to 4).
- Total funding requirement = construction cost + development costs.
- Debt requirement = 2/3 of funding requirement.
- Equity requirement = 1/3 of funding requirement.

Operating Costs Module

For each period of time:
- Calculate the fixed operating costs as $1 million per year during the operational phase (or $0.5 million per semiannual period during the operational period).
- Calculate the handset production volume as 12,000 during the first year of operations and growing at 5 percent per annum thereafter, meaning that Year 4 production is 5 percent higher than Year 3 production (or 6,000 per semiannual period for semiannual periods 5 and 6 and 5 percent growth per annum thereafter) (note that we are not assuming 2.5 percent growth per semiannual period, but rather 5 percent growth per year).
- Calculate the variable operating costs as $15 × production volume for the period (that is, $15 × number of handsets).

- Total operating costs = fixed operating costs + variable operating costs.

Inflation Module

Note that inflation must be factored into all the previous costs (that is, construction, development, and operating costs) and also into the income. And so we need to calculate the effect of inflation on $1 over time; this is known as the *inflation factor*. Once the inflation factor has been calculated for each period of time, it can then be multiplied by all amounts (whether cost or income) occurring in that period. The amount before adding the effect of inflation is known as the *real* amount, and the amount including the effect of inflation is known as the *nominal* amount.

For each period of time:

- Calculate the inflation factor as the inflation factor in the previous period × (1 + inflation rate %). Note that since we will be calculating on a semiannual basis, we will assume that the inflation factor is the inflation factor in the previous period × [1 + (annual inflation rate/2)].

Debt Module

It is best practice to calculate debt using a *control account*, which is basically a kind of "counter" or "meter" (such as one for tracking the usage or consumption of electricity, water, or gas in a house). A control account will normally include the following three items:

- *Opening position*, which states the usage of the item being tracked at the beginning of the period. In the case of debt, it will be the amount of debt outstanding at the start of the period. (The debt opening position is often referred to as the *balance brought forward*.)
- *Net change* during the period, which is the net increase or decrease in the usage of the item being tracked during that period with reference to the opening position. In our case, this will be the sum of any drawdown, repayment, or interest being rolled up to the debt amount during that period.
- *Closing position*, which states the usage of the item being tracked at the end of the period. In our case, it will be the amount of debt outstanding at the end of the period. (The

debt closing position is often referred to as the *balance carried forward.*)

There are two rules governing control accounts:

- The closing position at the end of any given period equals the opening position at the start of the period plus the net change during the period.
- The closing position at the end of any given period equals the opening position at the start of the following period.

Our debt module will include a control account for tracking or monitoring the principal and a control account for tracking or monitoring the interest on the debt.

- The debt control account will be calculated as follows:
  - Opening balance
  - Drawdown (increases balance)
  - Interest roll-up (increases balance)
  - Repayment (decreases balance)
  - Closing balance
- The interest control account will be calculated as follows:
  - Opening balance
  - Interest charge (increases balance)
  - Interest roll-up (decreases balance)
  - Interest paid (decreases balance)
  - Closing balance
- The interest charge will be calculated as (debt drawdown + debt opening balance) × annual interest rate/2.
- The interest roll-up is a negative number equivalent to the interest charge if we are in the construction phase; otherwise, the interest roll-up = 0.
- The interest paid is a negative number equivalent to the interest charge if we are in the operational phase and there is enough money to pay the total interest charge; otherwise, the interest paid = 0.

The money left after deducting all operating costs from the income generated—that is, the money available for paying interest charges and part or all of the principal outstanding—is known as the cash available for debt service (CFADS). CFADS = income – total operating costs, with total operating costs taken from the Operating Costs module just described and income taken from the Revenue module to be discussed later.

Interest paid can be calculated as the lower of CFADS or the interest charge if we are in the operational period and CFADS >0; otherwise, interest paid = 0.

- Interest closing balance = interest opening balance + interest charge + interest roll-up + interest paid. (Note that both interest roll-up and interest paid are negative numbers and therefore reduce the opening balance.)
- Debt drawdown = debt requirement; which has already been calculated in the Funding Requirements module. The debt drawdown increases the debt balance.
- Interest roll-up = interest roll-up as calculated in the interest control account.
- Debt repayment. To calculate debt repayment, let us remember that the bank requires the business to maintain a minimum debt service coverage ratio (DSCR) of 1.2 times. This means that the cash flow available for debt service (CFADS) divided by the debt service (that is, interest paid + debt repayment) must be greater than or equal to 1.2. Rewriting this mathematically, we get

CFADS/(interest paid + debt repayment) >= 1.2

which means

CFADS/1.2 >= interest paid + debt repayment

which means

(CFADS/1.2) – interest paid >= debt repayment

which means

Debt repayment <= (CFADS/1.2) – interest paid

In other words, as long as debt repayment = –[(CFADS/1.2) – interest paid], we will be within the bank's requirement. Note that we have calculated the debt repayment as a negative number, as this reduces the debt balance (unlike debt drawdown and interest roll-up, which increase the debt balance).

Debt closing balance = debt opening balance + debt drawdown +
interest roll-up + debt repayment
_−√e_

Revenue Module

For each period of time:

- Calculate income as the dollar unit price times the production volume.

The unit price is the amount we are being asked to determine such that the project achieves an internal rate of return (IRR) of 15 percent. As discussed in Steps 1 and 2 of the previous chapter, trying to find a closed-form solution to the case study is not straightforward, as we have different time dependencies that are best expressed using a spreadsheet tool like Excel. Indeed, it is much easier to change the value assigned to the unit price in a spreadsheet model so that the resulting IRR meets our requirement. Another advantage of this "trial-and-error" approach to finding the minimum unit selling price is that the user can "see" and better appreciate the effects on the IRR of changing the unit selling price, which is useful for discussion purposes (a closed-form approach would actually make the model more akin to a "black box" and would take away its transparency). Furthermore, Microsoft Excel enables the automation of trial and error by using the Goal Seek function. The Goal Seek function can find the unit price required to meet a given IRR target.

For now, let us use $300 as a unit price. When the model has been completed, we can then vary the unit price to support our discussions.

Main Module

For each period of time, the following summary is given, which also represents the cash waterfall (that is, the order in which the cash generated by the project is used):

- Opening cash balance
- Development costs
- Construction costs
- Debt drawdown
- Equity drawdown
- Income (positive)

- Total operating costs (negative)
- CFADS (calculated as income + total operating costs)
- Interest paid (negative)
- Debt repayment (negative)
- Cash available for shareholders (calculated as CFADS + interest paid + debt repayment)
- Dividend (a negative number equivalent to cash available for shareholders; also known as free cash flow)
- Closing cash balance

This cash waterfall assumes that the cash generated by the project is first used to meet operating costs, then any money left over is used to pay interest to the bank, then any money left over is used to repay the principal, then any money left over is freely available for shareholders. For each project, you will need to clarify the order of the use of cash with the people involved.

Equity Module

For each period of time:

- Equity outlay is a negative number equivalent to the equity requirement, which was already calculated in the Funding Requirements module.
- Return of capital (also known as capital redemption) is equal to the total equity requirement for the project if we are in the final semiannual period or 0 otherwise.
- Net cash flow from/to shareholders = equity outlay + dividend + capital redemption.
- IRR is calculated using the Microsoft Excel function and applied to the 10-year net cash flow to shareholders (that is, from the first to the last period).

5.2 STEP 2: MODEL CALCULATIONS MAP

It can be useful to draw a map of the model calculations showing how the different modules relate to one another. Figure 5.1 is an illustration of the model calculations map.

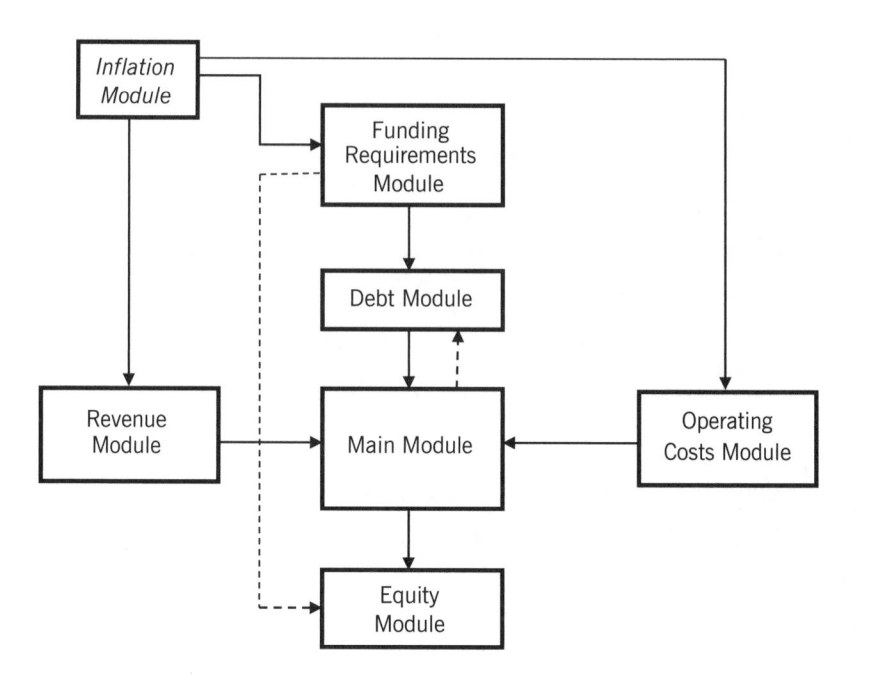

FIGURE 5.1 MODEL CALCULATIONS MAP

5.3 STEP 3: DOCUMENT THE MODEL ASSUMPTIONS _____

It is important to get into the habit of documenting the key assumptions used in the model. The model assumptions define the context in which the model should be used. For example, the following assumptions have been made (over time, further assumptions can be added to this list):

- Although we start generating money in Year 3, in practice, further short-term financing will probably be required to meet working capital needs, as it is likely that some payments will need to be made before any cash is received. For example, salaries will need to be paid at the end of each week or month, yet receipts from the sale of mobile phones may not arrive until after a couple of months. However, we will assume that cash receipts are sufficient to meet all payment obligations during the year.

- For handset production volume, we are not assuming 2.5 percent growth per semiannual period, but rather 5 percent growth per year.
- Since we will be calculating inflation on a semiannual basis, we will assume that the inflation factor equals the inflation factor in the previous period × (1 + annual inflation rate/2).
- The cash waterfall assumes that the cash generated by the project is first used to meet operating costs, then any money left over is used to pay interest to the bank, then any money left over is used to repay the principal, then any money left over is freely available for shareholders. For each project, you will need to clarify the order of the use of cash with the people involved.
- We have assumed equity capital redemption in the final semiannual period (that is, at the end of Year 10).

Now that we have specified *how* the model would work, let us move to the implementation.

5.4 STEP 4: CREATING THE CALCULATIONS SHEET _____

The Calculations sheet is where the numerical relationships among the different inputs are captured. To this end, it is useful—and is also best practice—to bring a copy of all inputs into the Calculations sheet so that these inputs are readily accessible within the Calculations sheet (through these copies) rather than your having to constantly refer to them in the Inputs sheet every time an input cell is required. A quick way of creating a copy of all inputs is to create a copy of the Inputs sheet and rename the copy as the Calculations sheet, then relink the input cells in the copy of the Inputs sheet to the original input cells in the original Inputs sheet. This can be done as follows.

- Create a copy of the PhoneFactory_v2 file.
- Rename the copy of the PhoneFactory_v2 file as PhoneFactory_v3.
- In PhoneFactory_v3, create a copy of the Inputs sheet. This can be done by right-clicking on the Inputs name. From the pop-up menu, select Move or Copy . . ., which brings up a pop-up window similar to the one in Figure 5.2.

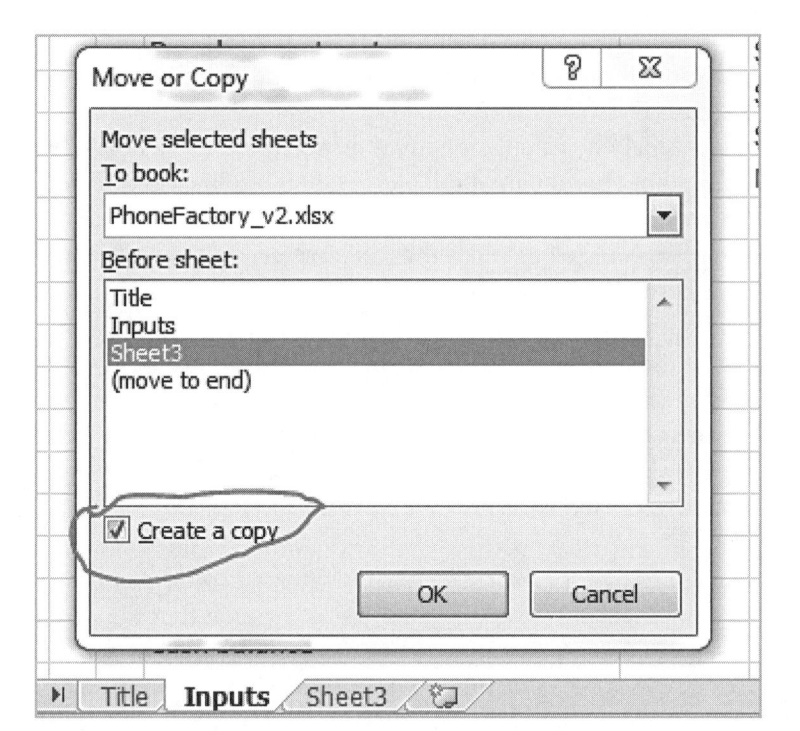

FIGURE 5.2 MOVE OR COPY SHEET (EXCEL)

- Select Sheet3 so that the copy is located immediately on the right-hand side of the Inputs sheet. Make sure the Create a copy box is checked; otherwise, no copy of the Inputs sheet will be created. Click OK. The copy version of the Inputs sheet is then created and is named by default as Inputs (2). Rename it as Calculations and set the tab color to red. This can be done by right-clicking on the Calculations name. From the pop-up menu, select Tab Color, which pops up the colors window.
- To relink all input cells in the Calculations sheet to the Inputs sheet, take one cell in the Calculations sheet at random, such as cell G5 and within it enter the formula "=Inputs!G5", which means that cell G5 in the Calculations sheet is linked to cell G5 in the Inputs sheet (and that the relationship is one of equality). Copy cell G5 in the Calculations sheet, and paste special formulas (a shortcut is pressing and holding ALT followed by pressing E and then S, from which you select formulas) into all other input cells in the Calculations sheet. Also paste in special

formulas for the timeline (a shortcut is to press F4, which is a repeat of the previous action, or pasting special formulas).

- Change the yellow background color to gray instead so that all cells that are linked to an external sheet are easily recognizable by the color convention.

5.5 STEP 5: CREATING FLAGS

A flag is a variable that takes one of two values: 0/1, TRUE/FALSE, or YES/NO. These are also known as switches, and they are effectively Boolean variables. We will create flags to indicate for any time period in the timeline whether the following events are happening during that period or not: the development phase, the construction phase, the operational phase, and the final year. The value of a flag is generally determined based on the fulfillment of certain conditions, and so a typical formula for a flag will contain an IF statement such that if a certain condition is met, then the flag takes the value corresponding to that condition. Otherwise, the flag takes the other value.

We will create the flags right below the general inputs section of the Calculations sheet. To do so, insert seven new blank lines in row 9 of the Calculations sheet (this is done by right-clicking row 9 and clicking Insert line seven times or by right-clicking rows 9 to 16 and clicking Insert line in the pop-up menu). Cells G9 to G16 contain the gray color. To remove this color, select the relevant cells and change their background color to No color.

- *Development flag.* Using the IF calculation, we can write in cell I11 the formula "=IF(I$2<=$G$6*$G$5,1,0)", which basically means that if the semiannual index is less than or equal to 2, then the flag shows 1 to reflect the fact that the development period lasts 1 year or for semiannual periods 1 and 2.
- *Construction flag.* Similarly using the IF calculation, we can write in cell I12 the formula "=IF(I$2<=$G$7*$G$5,1,0)", which basically means that if the semiannual index is less than or equal to 4, then the flag shows 1 to reflect the fact that the construction period lasts 2 years or the first 4 semiannual periods.
- *Operational flag.* Similarly using the IF calculation, we can write in cell I13 the formula "=IF(I$2<=$G$7*$G$5,0,1)", which

basically means that if the semiannual index is less than or equal to 4, then the flag shows 0 to reflect the fact that the construction period is outside of the operational period.

- *Final year flag.* Similarly using the IF calculation, we can write in cell I14 the formula "=IF(I$2=($G$8+$G$7)*$G$5,1,0)", which basically means that if the semiannual index is 20, then the flag shows 1 to reflect the fact that this is the final semiannual period.

- Copy cells I11 to I14 and paste them into the block J11:AB14.

Figure 5.3 gives an illustration of the Calculations sheet including the flags.

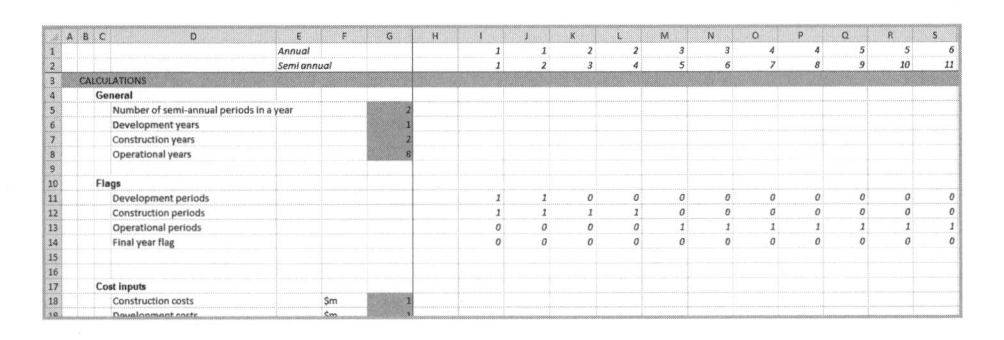

FIGURE 5.3 CALCULATIONS SHEET WITH FLAG

Notes

- There are other ways of writing these flags. For example, the formula for the operational flag can be defined to be the opposite of the construction flag, that is, operational flag = 1 – construction flag.

- The development flag can be defined as 1 if the semiannual period is 1 or 2, rather than if the semiannual period is less than or equal to 2.

- An important benefit of using flags is that they allow for the use of one formula per row, even though the condition driving the value of the flag may change within that row. We will see this benefit in the Funding Requirements module.

- The concept of a flag can be extended to cover more than two values (for example, a "flag" can take one of three values: Low, Medium, or High).

With the flags done, let us now turn to the implementation of the modules described earlier.

5.6 STEP 6: INFLATION MODULE

It is best practice to calculate the effect of inflation over time on $1 today. This is known as the *inflation factor*. Once the inflation factor for each period has been determined, it can be applied to any amount earned or spent during that period. For example, the effect of a 3 percent annual inflation rate on $1 today will be $1.03 in a year's time [that is, $1 × (1 + 3%)], $1.03 × 1.03, or $1.0609, in two years' time [that is, $1 × (1 + 3%) × (1 + 3%)], and so on. We can then write the inflation factor formula, say in cell I36, as (1 + annual inflation rate)^(semiannual period/number of semiannual periods in a year), or "=(1+$G$25)^(I$2/$G$5)", where cell G25 contains the annual inflation rate of 3 percent, I2 is the period index, and G5 is the number 2. Copy cell I36 and paste it into the block I36:AB36.

Microsoft Excel calculates the inflation factor and gives the results shown in Table 5.1.

TABLE 5.1

Semiannual Period	1	2	3	4	5	6	7	8	9	10
Inflation factor (3% annual inflation rate)	1.015	1.030	1.045	1.061	1.077	1.093	1.109	1.126	1.142	1.159

5.7 STEP 7: FUNDING REQUIREMENTS MODULE

The development cost is $1 million per year for the duration of 1 year. Assuming that these costs are incurred evenly over time, we will incur $0.5 million in each of semiannual periods 1 and 2.

Construction costs are $1 million per year for 2 years, or $0.5 million per semiannual period (assuming that costs are incurred evenly over time).

These costs exclude the effects of inflation and are referred to as *real costs*. To include the effects of inflation, we simply need to multiply the real costs by the corresponding inflation factor in each period. The costs including inflation are known as *nominal costs*.

Since these costs occur during specific periods (the first year for the development costs and the first two years for the construction costs), we will also need to apply the corresponding flag that automatically tells us when these costs occur.

5.7.1 Real Costs

We can write the real development and construction costs on rows 39 and 40, respectively.

- *Real development costs.* The formula for the first period will be Development flag times (development cost divided by the number of semiannual periods in a year). This translates into "=I$11*$G$19/$G$5".
- *Real construction costs.* The formula for the first period will be Construction flag times (Construction cost divided by the number of semiannual periods in a year). This translates into "=I$12*$G$18/$G$5".
- *Total funding requirement.* This is calculated by adding the development and construction costs period by period. The formula for the first period can be written as "=SUM(I39:I40)".
- Copy the block I39:41 and paste it into rows 39 to 41 (that is, I39:AB41).

5.7.2 Nominal Costs

We can write the nominal development and construction costs on rows 43 and 44, respectively.

- *Nominal development costs.* The formula for the first period will be the inflation factor times real development cost. This translates into "=I39*I$36".
- *Nominal construction costs.* The formula for the first period will be the inflation factor times real construction cost. This translates into "=I40*I$36".
- *Total funding requirement.* This is calculated by adding the development and construction costs period by period. The formula in the first period can be written as "=SUM(I43:I44)".
- Copy the block I43:45 and paste it into rows 43 to 45 (that is, I43:AB45).

5.7.3 Debt and Equity Funding

The total nominal funding required is split into two-thirds debt and one-third equity. Therefore, we can write the debt and equity formulas on rows 48 and 49, respectively, as follows:

- Debt funding is 2/3 of the total nominal funding requirement. The formula for the first period can be written as "=$G$27*I45".

- Equity funding is 1/3 of the total nominal funding requirement, or the total nominal funding requirement minus the amount of debt funding. The formula in the first period can be written as "=I45-I48".

An illustration of the Funding Requirements module is given in Figure 5.4.

		D	E	F	G	H	I	J	K	L	M	N	O	P	Q	R	S
1			Annual				1	1	2	2	3	3	4	4	5	5	6
2			Semi annual				1	2	3	4	5	6	7	8	9	10	11
34																	
35																	
36		Inflation factor					1.015	1.030	1.045	1.061	1.077	1.093	1.109	1.126	1.142	1.159	1.177
37																	
38		Costs at real prices															
39		Development costs					0.50	0.50	0.00	0.00	0.00	0.00	0.00	0.00	0.00	0.00	0.00
40		Construction costs					0.50	0.50	0.50	0.50	0.00	0.00	0.00	0.00	0.00	0.00	0.00
41		Total					1.00	1.00	0.50	0.50	0.00	0.00	0.00	0.00	0.00	0.00	0.00
42		Costs at nominal prices															
43		Construction costs					0.51	0.52	0.00	0.00	0.00	0.00	0.00	0.00	0.00	0.00	0.00
44		Development costs					0.51	0.52	0.52	0.53	0.00	0.00	0.00	0.00	0.00	0.00	0.00
45		Total					1.01	1.03	0.52	0.53	0.00	0.00	0.00	0.00	0.00	0.00	0.00
46																	
47		Funding requirements															
48		Debt					0.68	0.69	0.35	0.35	0.00	0.00	0.00	0.00	0.00	0.00	0.00
49		Equity					0.34	0.34	0.17	0.18	0.00	0.00	0.00	0.00	0.00	0.00	0.00

FIGURE 5.4 FUNDING REQUIREMENTS MODULE

Notes

- Thanks to the use of flags, we were able to write just one formula for calculating nominal costs by simply applying the flag to the real cost. Without using a flag mechanism, it would have been necessary to break down the formula into at least two subformulas, one for each of the two values that a flag can take.
- Instead of calculating the total funding requirement using the SUM function, we could have simply used the + operator, given that there were only two rows being added. However, the SUM function is useful when more than two components are being added.
- When calculating subtotals or totals, it can be useful to include a line separating the components making up the total (that is,

those above the line) from the total itself (that is, the number below the line).

■ In order to have the timeline displayed permanently on the screen regardless of how far one scrolls down, you can freeze rows 1 and 2. Likewise, you can freeze columns A to G. To do this in Microsoft Excel 2010, simply select cell H3, then, in the View tab of the ribbon, click Freeze Panes (see Figure 5.5). Then select the option at the top of the pop-up menu. This option reads Freeze Panes if no pane has been frozen or Unfreeze Panes if a pane has already been frozen. Microsoft Excel freezes all rows above the active cell and all columns to the left of the active cell.

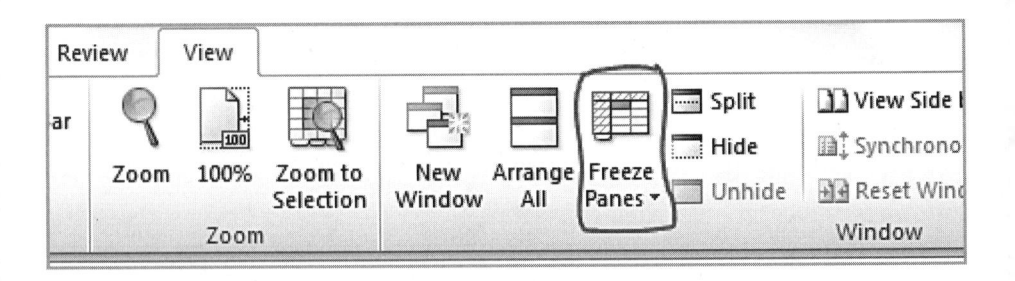

FIGURE 5.5 FREEZE PANES (EXCEL)

5.8 STEP 8: DEBT MODULE

5.8.1 Debt Control Account

The elements of the debt control account are given in Table 5.2.

TABLE 5.2 DEBT CONTROL ACCOUNT

Balance brought forward
Drawdown
Interest rolled up
Repayment
Debt carried forward

We can write these items on rows 52 to 56, respectively, as follows:

- *Balance brought forward (or opening balance).* At the start of semiannual period 1, the balance brought forward is 0, as given in the inputs. Thereafter, the balance brought forward at the start of each period equals the balance carried forward at the end of the previous period. The formula for the first period would be "=IF(I$2=1,G31,H56)".
- *Drawdown.* This is the debt requirement as determined in the Funding Requirements module. The formula for the first period would be "=I48".
- *Interest rolled up.* This row is left empty for now, as we haven't calculated the interest control account.
- *Repayment.* This row is left empty for now, as we haven't yet calculated CFADS (see the discussion of the Main module in Step 11).
- *Debt carried forward (or closing balance).* This number equals the sum of the four previous items. The formula for the first period would be "=SUM(I52:I55)".
- Copy the block I52:I56 and paste it into rows 52 to 56 (that is, I52:AB56).

5.8.2. Interest Control Account

The elements of the interest control account are given in Table 5.3.

TABLE 5.3 INTEREST CONTROL ACCOUNT

| Balance brought forward |
| Interest charge |
| Interest rolled up |
| Interest paid |
| Interest carried forward |

We can write these items on rows 59 to 63, respectively, as follows:

- *Balance brought forward (or opening balance).* At the start of semiannual period 1, the balance brought forward is 0, as given in the inputs. Thereafter, the balance brought forward at the start of each period equals the balance carried forward at the end of the previous period. The formula for the first period would be "=IF(I$2=1,G32,H63)".

- *Interest charge.* This equals (the debt balance brought forward plus the debt drawdown) times (annual interest rate divided by the number of semiannual periods in the year). The formula for the first period would be "=SUM(I52:I53)*($G$26/$G$5)".

- *Interest rolled up.* This is the interest charge if we are in the construction period; otherwise, it is 0. The formula for the first period would be "=IF(I12=1,-I60,0)".

- *Interest paid.* This row is left empty for now, as we haven't yet calculated CFADS.

- *Interest carried forward (or closing balance).* This is the sum of the previous four items. The formula for the first period would be "=SUM(I59:I62)".

- Copy the block I59:I63 and paste it into rows 59 to 63 (that is, I59:AB63).

An illustration of the Debt module is given in Figure 5.6.

	A	B	C	D	E	F	G	H	I	J	K	L	M	N	O	P	Q	R	S
1					Annual				1	1	2	2	3	3	4	4	5	5	6
2					Semi annual				1	2	3	4	5	6	7	8	9	10	11
50																			
51			Debt control account																
52				Opening balance					0.00	0.69	1.41	1.81	2.21	2.21	2.21	2.21	2.21	2.21	2.21
53				Drawdown					0.68	0.69	0.35	0.35	0.00	0.00	0.00	0.00	0.00	0.00	0.00
54				Interest rolled-up					0.02	0.03	0.04	0.05	0.00	0.00	0.00	0.00	0.00	0.00	0.00
55				Repayment															
56				Closing balance					0.69	1.41	1.81	2.21	2.21	2.21	2.21	2.21	2.21	2.21	2.21
57																			
58			Interest control account																
59				Opening balance					0.00	0.00	0.00	0.00	0.00	0.06	0.11	0.17	0.22	0.28	0.33
60				Interest charge					0.02	0.03	0.04	0.05	0.06	0.06	0.06	0.06	0.06	0.06	0.06
61				Interest rolled up					(0.02)	(0.03)	(0.04)	(0.05)	0.00	0.00	0.00	0.00	0.00	0.00	0.00
62				Interest paid															

FIGURE 5.6 DEBT MODULE

Note

- You will notice in Figure 5.6 that the interest rolled up line has been filled in. When the debt control account was calculated, the interest rolled up line was left empty. However, now that the interest rolled up has been calculated in the interest control account, we can go back to the debt control account and complete the interest rolled up line as the negative of the interest rolled up number in the interest control account. In Figure 5.6, the formula for the first period (that is, cell I54) is "=-I61". Then copy cell I54 and paste it into the block I54:AB54.

5.9 STEP 9: OPERATING COSTS MODULE _____

Variable costs are driven by the number of handsets, and so we first need to calculate the volume of production.

5.9.1 Real Costs

- Production starts at 12,000 handsets during the first year of production, or 6,000 each in semiannual periods 5 and 6. Then production increases at 5 percent per annum. We can take the previous year's production volume and multiply by 1 + 5%.
- We can write the production level on row 66, with the formula for the first period (that is, in cell I66) written as follows: "=IF(OR(I2=5,I2=6),$G$22/$G$5,G66*(1+$G$23))", which means that if we are in semiannual period 5 or 6, then production is 12,000 divided by the number of semiannual periods in the year. Otherwise, take the production from two semiannual periods earlier (that is, from the previous year) and multiply it by (1 + 5%).
- Variable production cost in millions of dollars is calculated as $15 divided by 1,000,000. This is shown in cell G67 in Figure 5.7, and the formula reads "=G21/1000000".
- Real variable production cost is calculated as $15 multiplied by the number of handsets. We can write the production cost on row 68, with the formula for the first period (that is, in cell I68) being written as follows: "=I66*$G$67".
- Real fixed production cost is given as $1 million per year or $0.5 million per semiannual period, although this is applicable only during the production period. We can write the fixed production cost on row 69, with the formula for the first period (that is, in cell I69) being written as follows: "=I13*$G$20/$G$5", where I13 is the operational flag.
- Real total production costs can be calculated as the sum of fixed and variable production costs. We can write the total production cost on row 70, with the formula for the first period (that is, in cell I70) being written as follows: "=SUM(I68:I69)".
- Copy cells I66:I70 and paste them into the block I66:AB70.

5.9.2 Nominal Costs

The costs just calculated are real. Next, we calculate the same costs, taking into account the effects of inflation.

- The nominal variable production cost is calculated as the inflation factor times the real variable production cost. We can write the nominal production cost on row 73, with the formula for the first period (that is, in cell I73) being written as follows: "=I68*I$36".
- The nominal fixed production cost is calculated as the inflation factor times the real fixed production cost. We can write the nominal production cost on row 74, with the formula for the first period (that is, in cell I74) being written as follows: "=I69*I$36".
- Total nominal production costs can be calculated as the sum of fixed and variable nominal production costs. We can write the total production cost on row 75, with the formula for the first period (that is, in cell I75) being written as follows: "=SUM(I73:I74)".
- Copy cells I73:I75 and paste them into the block I73:AB75.

An illustration of the operating Cost module is given in Figure 5.7.

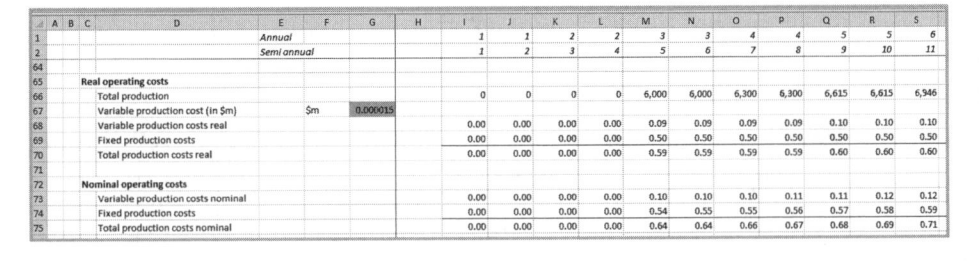

	A	B	C	D	E	F	G	H	I	J	K	L	M	N	O	P	Q	R	S
1					Annual				1	1	2	2	3	3	4	4	5	5	6
2					Semi annual				1	2	3	4	5	6	7	8	9	10	11
64																			
65			Real operating costs																
66			Total production						0	0	0	0	6,000	6,000	6,300	6,300	6,615	6,615	6,946
67			Variable production cost (in $m)		$m	0.000015													
68			Variable production costs real						0.00	0.00	0.00	0.00	0.09	0.09	0.09	0.09	0.10	0.10	0.10
69			Fixed production costs						0.00	0.00	0.00	0.00	0.50	0.50	0.50	0.50	0.50	0.50	0.50
70			Total production costs real						0.00	0.00	0.00	0.00	0.59	0.59	0.59	0.59	0.60	0.60	0.60
71																			
72			Nominal operating costs																
73			Variable production costs nominal						0.00	0.00	0.00	0.00	0.10	0.10	0.10	0.11	0.11	0.12	0.12
74			Fixed production costs						0.00	0.00	0.00	0.00	0.54	0.55	0.55	0.56	0.57	0.58	0.59
75			Total production costs nominal						0.00	0.00	0.00	0.00	0.64	0.64	0.66	0.67	0.68	0.69	0.71

FIGURE 5.7 OPERATING COSTS MODULE

Note

- Strictly speaking, production volume must be an integer; however, we have simply set the number of decimal places to 0. This will do for the purpose of the exercise.

5.10 STEP 10: REVENUE MODULE

- Revenue is driven by the number of handsets together with the unit selling price. It is calculated as the unit price in dollars times production volume.
- As previously discussed in the model specifications, unit price is defined as an input that will be made to vary, and so for now we assign it the value of $300.
- In cell G79, we convert the unit selling price to millions of dollars by dividing cell G78 by 1,000,000 as follows: "=G78/1000000".

5.10.1 Real Revenue

- We can write the real revenue formula on row 80, with the formula for the first period (that is, in cell I80) being written as follows: "=$G$79*I66", with G79 being the unit selling price in millions of dollars and I66 being the number of handsets manufactured in semiannual period 1.

5.10.2 Nominal Revenue

- We can write the nominal revenue formula on row 81, with the formulae for the first period (that is, in cell I81) being written as follows: "=I80*I36", with I80 being the real revenue in semiannual period 1, and I36 being the inflation factor in semiannual period 1.
- Copy cells I80:I81 and paste them into the block I80:AB81.

An illustration of the revenue module is given in Figure 5.8.

	A	B	C	D	E	F	G	H	I	J	K	L	M	N	O	P	Q	R	S
1						Annual			1	1	2	2	3	3	4	4	5	5	6
2						Semi annual			1	2	3	4	5	6	7	8	9	10	11
76																			
77		Revenue																	
78			Unit selling price		$		300												
79			Unit selling price		$m		0.0003												
80			Real revenue						0.00	0.00	0.00	0.00	1.80	1.80	1.89	1.89	1.98	1.98	2.08
81			Nominal revenue						0.00	0.00	0.00	0.00	1.94	1.97	2.10	2.13	2.27	2.30	2.45

FIGURE 5.8 REVENUE MODULE

5.11 STEP 11: MAIN MODULE

The Main module brings together the different modules that have already been developed. The cash waterfall was already described in the model specifications section as follows:

- *Opening cash balance* (developed through the control account mechanism)
- Development costs (negative, taken from the Funding Requirements module)
- Construction costs (negative, taken from the Funding Requirements module)
- Equity drawdown (positive, taken from the Funding Requirements module)
- Debt drawdown (positive, taken from the Funding Requirements module)
- Nominal revenue (positive, taken from the Revenue module)
- Total nominal operating costs (negative, taken from the Operating Costs module)
- CFADS (calculated as income plus total operating costs)
- Interest paid (negative), taken as the lower of CFADS and interest charge during the operational period if CFADS is greater than 0; otherwise taken to be 0.
- Cash available after interest payment (calculated as CFADS plus interest paid)
- Debt repaid (negative), taken as the lowest of CFADS less interest paid, balance brought forward, and (CFADS divided by 1.2) less interest paid.
- Cash available for shareholders (calculated as CFADS plus interest paid plus debt repaid)
- Dividends (the negative of the cash available for shareholders)
- *Closing cash balance* (developed through the control account mechanism)

We can write the Main module beginning on line 84 as follows:

- *Opening cash balance* (line 84). The source of this figure is given at the end of the discussion of the Main module.
- Development costs. The formula for the first period (that is, in cell I85) can be written as follows: "=-I43".

- Construction costs. The formula for the first period (that is, in cell I86) can be written as follows: "=-I44".
- Equity drawdown. The formula for the first period (that is, in cell I87) can be written as follows: "=I49".
- Debt drawdown. The formula for the first period (that is, in cell I88) can be written as follows: "=I48".

We skip the next line and write the remainder of the Main module starting on line 90 as follows:

- Nominal revenue. The formula for the first period (that is, in cell I90) can be written as follows: "=I81".
- Total production costs nominal. The formula for the first period (that is, in cell I91) can be written as follows: "=-I75".
- CFADS. The formula for the first period (that is, in cell I92) can be written as follows: "=SUM(I90:I91)".
- Interest paid. The formula for the first period (that is, in cell I93) can be written as follows: "=IF(AND(I$13=1,I92>0),-MIN(I92,I60),0).
- Cash available after interest payment. The formula for the first period (that is, in cell I94) can be written as follows: "=I92+I93".
- Debt repaid. In order to calculate the amount of debt repaid, we need to have available the target amount of debt repaid, which was given in the model specifications. To this end, we do the following side calculation, which is placed below the Main module on line 101 as follows.
  - The target debt service is equal to CFADS divided by 1.2. The formula for the first period (that is, in cell I101) would read "=IF(I92>0,I92/$G$29,0)".
  - The target debt repaid is target debt service less interest paid. The formula for the first period (that is, in cell I102) would read "=I101+I93".
- Once we have the target debt repaid in line 102, we return to the debt repayment on line 95 and write for the first period (that is, in cell I95) the formula "=IF(AND(I$13=1,I94>0),-MIN(I94,I52,I102),0)".
- Cash available for shareholders. The formula for the first period (that is, in cell I96) can be written as follows: "=I95+I94".

- Dividend. The formula for the first period (that is, in cell I97) can be written as follows: "=Max(0,I96)".

We can then complete the cash flow in the Main module with a cash balance control account. The opening cash balance is written at the top of the waterfall, and the closing cash balance is written at the bottom.

- *Opening cash balance.* The formula for the first period (that is, in cell I84) can be written as follows: "=IF(I2=1,$G$33,H98)", with G33 being the opening cash balance and H98 being the closing cash balance from the previous period.
- *Closing cash balance.* The formula for the first period (that is, in cell I98) can be written as follows: "=SUM(I84:I88,I96:I97)".
- Copy cells I80:I102 and paste them into the block I80:AB102.

Notes

- With the Main module now completed, we return to the Debt module to complete the debt repayment line, which was left empty.
- The debt repayment line on row 55 will have the formula "=I95" in its first period. This can then be copied and pasted into the entire block I55:AB55.
- Likewise, the interest paid line on row 62 will have the formulae "=I93" in its first period. This can then be copied and pasted into the entire block I62:AB62.

The Main module is illustrated in Figure 5.9.

	A	B	C	D	E	F	G	H	I	J	K	L	M	N	O	P	Q	R	S
1					Annual				1	1	2	2	3	3	4	4	5	5	6
2					Semi annual				1	2	3	4	5	6	7	8	9	10	11
82																			
83			Main Module																
84			Opening cash balance						0.00	0.00	0.00	0.00	0.00	0.00	0.00	0.00	0.00	0.00	0.00
85			Development costs						(0.51)	(0.52)	0.00	0.00	0.00	0.00	0.00	0.00	0.00	0.00	0.00
86			Construction costs						(0.51)	(0.52)	(0.52)	(0.53)	0.00	0.00	0.00	0.00	0.00	0.00	0.00
87			Debt drawdown						0.68	0.69	0.35	0.35	0.00	0.00	0.00	0.00	0.00	0.00	0.00
88			Equity drawdown						0.34	0.34	0.17	0.18	0.00	0.00	0.00	0.00	0.00	0.00	0.00
89																			
90			Nominal revenue						0.00	0.00	0.00	0.00	1.94	1.97	2.10	2.13	2.27	2.30	2.45
91			Total production costs nominal						0.00	0.00	0.00	0.00	(0.64)	(0.64)	(0.66)	(0.67)	(0.68)	(0.69)	(0.71)
92			CFADS						0.00	0.00	0.00	0.00	1.30	1.32	1.44	1.46	1.58	1.61	1.74
93			Interest paid						0.00	0.00	0.00	0.00	(0.06)	(0.03)	(0.00)	0.00	0.00	0.00	0.00
94			Cash available after interest payment						0.00	0.00	0.00	0.00	1.25	1.29	1.43	1.46	1.58	1.61	1.74
95			Debt repaid						0.00	0.00	0.00	0.00	(1.03)	(1.07)	(0.11)	0.00	0.00	0.00	0.00
96			Cash available for shareholders						0.00	0.00	0.00	0.00	0.22	0.22	1.32	1.46	1.58	1.61	1.74
97			Dividends						0.00	0.00	0.00	0.00	(0.22)	(0.22)	(1.32)	(1.46)	(1.58)	(1.61)	(1.74)
98			Closing cash balance						0.00	0.00	0.00	0.00	0.00	0.00	0.00	0.00	0.00	0.00	0.00
99																			
100																			
101			Target debt service						0.00	0.00	0.00	0.00	1.09	1.10	1.20	1.22	1.32	1.34	1.45
102			Target debt to repay						0.00	0.00	0.00	0.00	1.03	1.07	1.18	1.22	1.32	1.34	1.45

FIGURE 5.9 MAIN MODULE

5.12 STEP 12: EQUITY MODULE

The Equity module includes just three data items and calculations based on them:

- Drawdown (negative, taken from the Funding Requirements module)
- Dividends (positive, taken from the Main module)
- Redemption (positive, calculated as total equity cost received at the end of the 10 years)
- Net cash flow, calculated as the sum of the previous three lines
- IRR, calculated as XIRR applied to the net cash flows at the dates when these cash flows occur

We can write the Equity module starting on line 105 as follows:

- Drawdown. The formula for the first period (that is, the value in cell I105) can be written as follows: "=-I87".
- Dividends. The formula for the first period (that is, the value in cell I106) can be written as follows: "=-I97".
- Redemption. The formula for the first period (that is, the value in cell I107) can be written as follows: "=SUM($I$87:$L$87)*I14", with SUM($I$87:$L$87) being the total equity outlay and I14 being the final period flag.
- Net cash flow. The formula for the first period (that is, the value in cell I108) can be written as follows: "=SUM(I105:I107)".
- Copy cells I105:I108 and paste them into the block I105:AB108 .IRR.
    - Although there is an IRR function in Microsoft Excel, applying it directly to semiannual cash flows would not give an annual IRR figure, but rather would give an IRR for semiannual flows. Therefore, we use the XIRR function, which calculates the annual IRR regardless of the timing of cash flows. The XIRR function requires at least two parameters, namely, the cash flows and the dates on which these cash flows occur. To this end we write in row 110 assumptions regarding dates. Suppose the project starts on July 1, 2011, and so the end of the first semiannual period would be December 31, 2011. We write in cell I110 the formula "=DATE(2011,12,31)", which gives the December 31, 2011,

date. Then in cell J110, we write "=I110+(365/2)", which means add half a year to the previous date. Copying cell J110 and pasting it across the block J110:AB110 gives the entire timeline of the cash flows.

- With the dates now calculated, we can calculate the XIRR of the project in cell G111 with the formula "=XIRR(I108:AB108,I110:AB110)", which is the application of the XIRR function to the cash flows on line 108 together with the dates of these cash flows on line 110.
- This gives an IRR of 101.8 percent based on the unit selling price of $300.
- We can then change the unit selling price by changing the value in cell G78. For example, for a unit selling price of $150, the IRR would be only 35.2 percent.
- Rather than manually changing the unit selling price to get the target IRR of 15 percent, it is possible to use Excel's Goal Seek function, which determines the unit selling price such that the target IRR is reached.
- To use Goal Seek, click on the What-If Analysis button on the ribbon. This brings up a small pop-up window; click on the Goal Seek . . . item. This further brings up a small dialogue box in which the Goal Seek parameters need to be entered. The first data point to enter at the top is the Set cell point. We want to set cell G111 (which is the XIRR result cell) to the value of 15 percent, which is the second data point. And we want this to happen by changing cell G78, which is the unit selling price (please note that cell G78 must be an input cell so that Microsoft Excel can overwrite it). The Goal Seek dialogue box is illustrated in Figure 5.10. After you click OK to confirm the parameter settings, Microsoft Excel runs different values of the unit selling price and comes up with the unit selling price of $118.31 per handset, which results in an IRR of 15 percent.

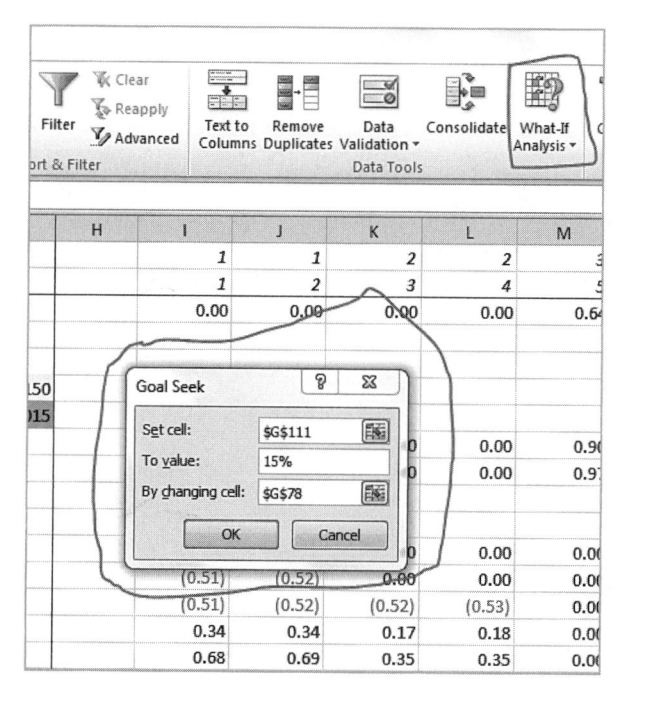

FIGURE 5.10 GOAL SEEK (EXCEL)

An illustration of the Equity module is given in Figure 5.11.

A	B	C	D	E	F	G	H	I	J	K	L	M	N	O	P	Q	R
				Annual				1	1	2	2	3	3	4	4	5	5
				Semi annual				1	2	3	4	5	6	7	8	9	10
		Equity module															
		Drawdown						(0.34)	(0.34)	(0.17)	(0.18)	0.00	0.00	0.00	0.00	0.00	0.00
		Dividend paid						0.00	0.00	0.00	0.00	0.02	0.02	0.03	0.03	0.03	0.04
		Redemption						0.00	0.00	0.00	0.00	0.00	0.00	0.00	0.00	0.00	0.00
		Net cash flow						(0.34)	(0.34)	(0.17)	(0.18)	0.02	0.02	0.03	0.03	0.03	0.04
		Dates for XIRR function						31/12/11	30/06/12	30/12/12	30/06/13	30/12/13	30/06/14	30/12/14	30/06/15	30/12/15	29/06/16	29
		IRR				15.0%											

FIGURE 5.11 EQUITY MODULE

CHAPTER SIX

CASE STUDY 1:

Modeling the Outputs Sheets

Having completed all the necessary calculations, we are now ready to bring together the key results from our calculations in the Outputs sheets.

6.1 STEP 1: DECIDING ON THE CONTENT OF THE OUTPUTS SHEETS

Since we are looking to summarize the key results from the Calculations sheet, the first thing we must do is to decide what information and/or data should be included in such a summary. To this end, we refer to what we were asked to do in this case study, a question that we already dealt with during the project scoping stage (see Chapter 4).

The case study is about putting together a financial model for the construction and operation of a mobile phone factory. Given *construction and operating costs*, all funded by a combination of *debt and equity*, and given *production volumes*, we are asked to determine the *unit selling price* of a handset such that the project achieves an *equity IRR* of at least 15 percent.

The Outputs sheets should include, at a minimum, the information in italics in the previous paragraph. Furthermore, key assumptions should be included as well. Including key assumptions helps give context to the results summarized in the Outputs sheets.

With this in mind, Table 6.1 gives an outline of what the Outputs sheets could look like.

TABLE 6.1

Key Assumptions

	Value
Development years	
Construction years	
Operational years	
Construction costs	
Development costs	
Fixed production costs	
Variable production costs	
Number of phones produced during operational year 1	
Growth in production (after operational year 1)	
Inflation	
Debt interest rate (annual)	
Debt/equity ratio (debt as % of capital)	
Target IRR (annual)	
Target debt service coverage ratio	

Cash Waterfall

Semiannual period	1	2	3	4	5	6	...	19	20
Cash waterfall									
Opening cash balance									
Development costs									
Construction costs									
Equity drawdown									
Debt drawdown									
Unit selling price									
Revenue									
Operating costs									
Cash available for debt service									

Semiannual period	1	2	3	4	5	6	...	19	20
Interest on debt									
Debt paid									
Cash available for shareholders									
Dividends									
Closing cash balance									
Equity IRR									
Drawdown									
Dividend paid									
Redemption									
Net equity cash flow									

IRR	Calculated
Target IRR	Input
Is target IRR condition met?	Yes or no

Apart from the last row in Table 6.1 ("Is target IRR condition met?"), everything in the table has already been calculated in the Calculations sheet, and therefore we simply pull the relevant data from the Calculations sheet into the Outputs sheets.

6.2 STEP 2: CREATING THE OUTPUTS SHEET (SEMIANNUAL)

To create the semiannual Outputs sheet in such a way as to keep the same column width and same layout as in the Calculations sheet, make a copy of the Calculations sheet. Microsoft Excel automatically names the copied sheet Calculations (2).

- Rename the sheet as Outputs_Semiannual and change the tab color to green. Then, working your way from the top down, do the following:
  - Change the content of cell B3 to "OUTPUTS_Semiannual."
  - Write "Key assumptions" in cell C4.
  - Delete the row "Number of semiannual periods in a year"

- Keep the cost inputs and the financing inputs and delete everything below the line "Target debt service coverage ratio." This can be done by selecting all rows below the row "Target debt service coverage ratio" and clearing them. The Clear All button clears not only cell values, but also cell formulas and cell formats. It is available within the Clear button in the toolbar, as shown in Figure 6.1.

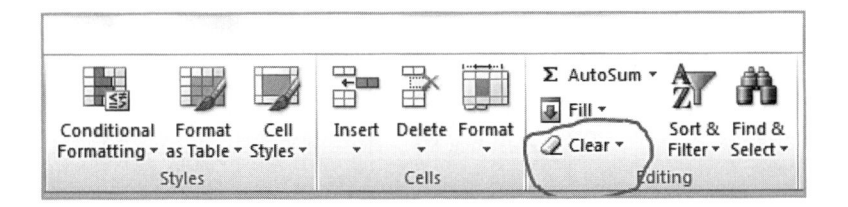

FIGURE 6.1 CLEAR (EXCEL)

6.2 STEP 2: SUMMARY OF KEY ASSUMPTIONS

The Key assumptions box can be arranged as follows.

- Development years: the formula can be written as "=Inputs!G6".
- Construction years: the formula can be written as "=Inputs!G7".
- Operational years: the formula can be written as "=Inputs!G8".
- Construction costs: the formula can be written as "=Inputs!G10".
- Development costs: the formula can be written as "=Inputs!G11".
- Fixed production costs: the formula can be written as "=Inputs!G12".
- Variable production costs: the formula can be written as "=Inputs!G13".
- Number of phones produced during operational year 1: the formula can be written as "=Inputs!G14".
- Growth in production (after operational year 1): the formula can be written as "=Inputs!G15".
- Inflation: the formula can be written as "=Inputs!G17".

- Debt interest rate (annual): the formula can be written as "=Inputs!G18".
- Debt/equity ratio (debt as % of capital): the formula can be written as "=Inputs!G19".
- Target IRR (annual): the formula can be written as "=Inputs!G20".
- Target debt service coverage ratio: the formula can be written as "=Inputs!G21".

The assumptions box is illustrated in Figure 6.2.

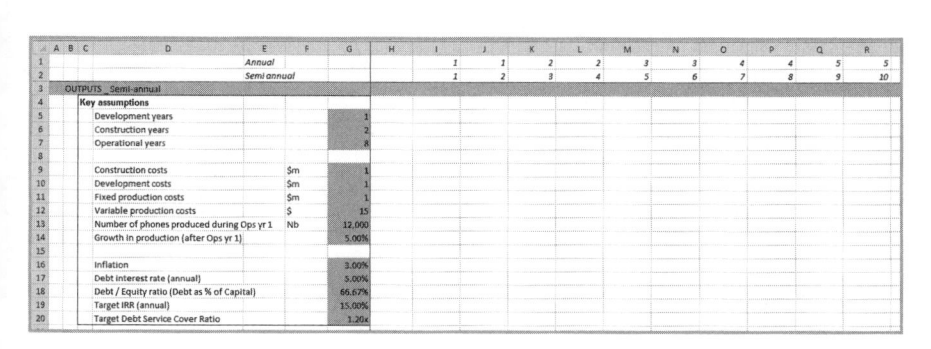

FIGURE 6.2 KEY ASSUMPTIONS (OUTPUTS)

Note:

Instead of writing the formulas in rows 5 to 20 one by one, it is faster to copy cell G5 and paste it into the block G5:G7; copy cell G9 and paste it into the block G9:G14; then copy cell G16 and paste it into the block G16:G20.

6.3 STEP 3: CASH WATERFALL (SEMIANNUAL) _____

The cash waterfall box can be arranged as follows:

- *Opening cash balance.* The formula for the first period (that is, the value in cell I24) can be written as follows: "=Calculations!I84".
- Development costs. The formula for the first period (that is, the value in cell I25) can be written as follows: "=Calculations!I85".
- Construction costs. The formula for the first period (that is, the value in cell I26) can be written as follows: "=Calculations!I86".

- Equity drawdown. The formula for the first period (that is, the value in cell I27) can be written as follows: "=Calculations!I87".
- Debt drawdown. The formula for the first period (that is, the value in cell I28) can be written as follows: "=Calculations!I88".
- Unit selling price. The formula (that is, the value in cell G29) can be written as follows: "=Calculations!G78".
- Revenue. The formula for the first period (that is, the value in cell I30) can be written as follows: "=Calculations!I90".
- Operating costs. The formula for the first period (that is, the value in cell I31) can be written as follows: "=Calculations!I91".
- Cash available for debt service. The formula for the first period (that is, the value in cell I32) can be written as follows: "=Calculations!I92".
- Interest on debt. The formula for the first period (that is, the value in cell I34) can be written as follows: "=Calculations!I93".
- Debt repaid. The formula for the first period (that is, the value in cell I35) can be written as follows: "=Calculations!I95".
- Cash available for shareholders. The formula for the first period (that is, the value in cell I36) can be written as follows: "=Calculations!I96".
- Dividends. The formula for the first period (that is, the value in cell I37) can be written as follows: "=Calculations!I97".
- *Closing cash balance.* The formula for the first period (that is, the value in cell I38) can be written as follows: "=Calculations!I98".
- Copy cells I24:I38 and paste them into the block I24:AB38.

The cash waterfall box is shown in Figure 6.3.

A B C	D	E	F	G	H	I	J	K	L	M	N	O	P	Q	R
		Annual				1	1	2	2	3	3	4	4	5	5
		Semi annual				1	2	3	4	5	6	7	8	9	10
Cash waterfall															
Opening cash balance						0.00	0.00	0.00	0.00	0.00	0.00	0.00	0.00	0.00	0.00
Development costs						(0.51)	(0.52)	0.00	0.00	0.00	0.00	0.00	0.00	0.00	0.00
Construction costs						(0.51)	(0.52)	(0.52)	(0.53)	0.00	0.00	0.00	0.00	0.00	0.00
Equity drawdown						0.34	0.34	0.17	0.18	0.00	0.00	0.00	0.00	0.00	0.00
Debt drawdown						0.68	0.69	0.35	0.35	0.00	0.00	0.00	0.00	0.00	0.00
Unit selling price			$	118.3											
Revenue						0.00	0.00	0.00	0.00	0.76	0.78	0.83	0.84	0.89	0.91
Operating costs						0.00	0.00	0.00	0.00	(0.64)	(0.64)	(0.66)	(0.67)	(0.68)	(0.69)
Cash available for debt service						0.00	0.00	0.00	0.00	0.13	0.13	0.17	0.17	0.21	0.21
Interest on debt						0.00	0.00	0.00	0.00	(0.06)	(0.05)	(0.05)	(0.05)	(0.05)	(0.05)
Debt paid						0.00	0.00	0.00	0.00	(0.05)	(0.06)	(0.09)	(0.09)	(0.13)	(0.13)
Cash available for shareholders						0.00	0.00	0.00	0.00	0.02	0.02	0.03	0.03	0.03	0.04
Dividends						0.00	0.00	0.00	0.00	(0.02)	(0.02)	(0.03)	(0.03)	(0.03)	(0.04)
Closing cash balance						0.00	0.00	0.00	0.00	0.00	0.00	0.00	0.00	0.00	0.00
Equity IRR															
Drawdown						(0.34)	(0.34)	(0.17)	(0.18)	0.00	0.00	0.00	0.00	0.00	0.00
Dividend paid						0.00	0.00	0.00	0.00	0.02	0.02	0.03	0.03	0.03	0.04
Redemption						0.00	0.00	0.00	0.00	0.00	0.00	0.00	0.00	0.00	0.00
Net equity cash flow						(0.34)	(0.34)	(0.17)	(0.18)	0.02	0.02	0.03	0.03	0.03	0.04
IRR				15.0%											

FIGURE 6.3 CASH WATERFALL (SEMIANNUAL)

6.4 STEP 4: EQUITY IRR (SEMIANNUAL)

The equity IRR box can be arranged as follows:

- Drawdown. The formula for the first period (that is, the value in cell I40) can be written as follows: "=Calculations!I105".
- Dividend paid. The formula for the first period (that is, the value in cell I41) can be written as follows: "=Calculations!I106".
- Redemption. The formula for the first period (that is, the value in cell I42) can be written as follows: "=Calculations!I107".
- Net equity cash flow. The formula for the first period (that is, the value in cell I43) can be written as follows: "=SUM(I40:I42)".
- Copy cells I40:I43 and paste them into the block I40:AB43.
- IRR. The formula (in cell G45) can be written as follows: "=Calculations!G111".
- Target IRR. The formula (in cell G46) can be written as follows: "=G19".
- Is target IRR condition met? The formula (in cell G47) can be written as follows: "=IF(G45>G46,"Yes", "No")".

The equity box is illustrated in Figure 6.4.

		Annual				1	1	2	2	3	3	4	4	5	5
2		Semi annual				1	2	3	4	5	6	7	8	9	10
26	Construction costs				(0.51)	(0.52)	(0.52)	(0.53)	0.00	0.00	0.00	0.00	0.00	0.00
27	Equity drawdown				0.34	0.34	0.17	0.18	0.00	0.00	0.00	0.00	0.00	0.00
28	Debt drawdown				0.68	0.69	0.35	0.35	0.00	0.00	0.00	0.00	0.00	0.00
29	Unit selling price	$	118.3											
30	Revenue				0.00	0.00	0.00	0.00	0.76	0.78	0.83	0.84	0.89	0.91
31	Operating costs				0.00	0.00	0.00	0.00	(0.64)	(0.66)	(0.66)	(0.67)	(0.68)	(0.69)
32	Cash available for debt service				0.00	0.00	0.00	0.00	0.13	0.13	0.17	0.17	0.21	0.21
34	Interest on debt				0.00	0.00	0.00	0.00	(0.06)	(0.05)	(0.05)	(0.05)	(0.05)	(0.05)
35	Debt paid				0.00	0.00	0.00	0.00	(0.05)	(0.06)	(0.09)	(0.09)	(0.13)	(0.11)
36	Cash available for shareholders				0.00	0.00	0.00	0.00	0.02	0.02	0.03	0.03	0.03	0.04
37	Dividends				0.00	0.00	0.00	0.00	(0.02)	(0.02)	(0.03)	(0.03)	(0.03)	(0.04)
38	Closing cash balance				0.00	0.00	0.00	0.00	0.00	0.00	0.00	0.00	0.00	0.00
39	Equity IRR													
40	Drawdown				(0.34)	(0.34)	(0.17)	(0.18)	0.00	0.00	0.00	0.00	0.00	0.00
41	Dividend paid				0.00	0.00	0.00	0.00	0.02	0.02	0.03	0.03	0.03	0.04
42	Redemption				0.00	0.00	0.00	0.00	0.00	0.00	0.00	0.00	0.00	0.00
43	Net equity cash flow				(0.34)	(0.34)	(0.17)	(0.18)	0.02	0.02	0.03	0.03	0.03	0.04
45	IRR		15.0%											
46	Target IRR		15.00%											
47	Is target IRR condition met?		Yes											

FIGURE 6.4 EQUITY OUTPUT (SEMIANNUAL)

Note

Cell G47 features a special format called *conditional format* such that if its value is "Yes," then the cell's background color turns green, and if the cell's value is "No," then the cell turns red. This is known as *conditional formatting*.

a. To apply a conditional formatting, select the relevant cells (in this case, cell G47) and click on Conditional Formatting in the toolbar (see Figure 6.5).

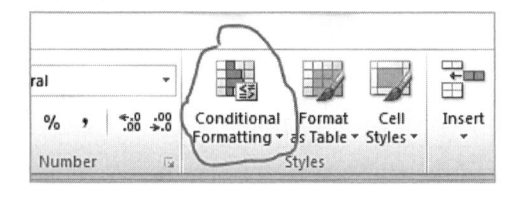

FIGURE 6.5 CONDITIONAL FORMATTING (PART 1)

b. Then select Highlight Cells Rules.
c. Select Equal To. This opens a pop-up window entitled Equal To.
d. Enter "Yes" in the "Format cells that are EQUAL TO:" box, then click on the black arrow situated on the right-hand side of the pop-up window (see Figure 6.6).
e. Click on Custom Format. This opens another window entitled Format Cells.
f. Click on the Fill tab and select the green color (circled in the last line of colors), then click OK. The Format Cells tab window closes.
g. Click OK on the Equal To window.

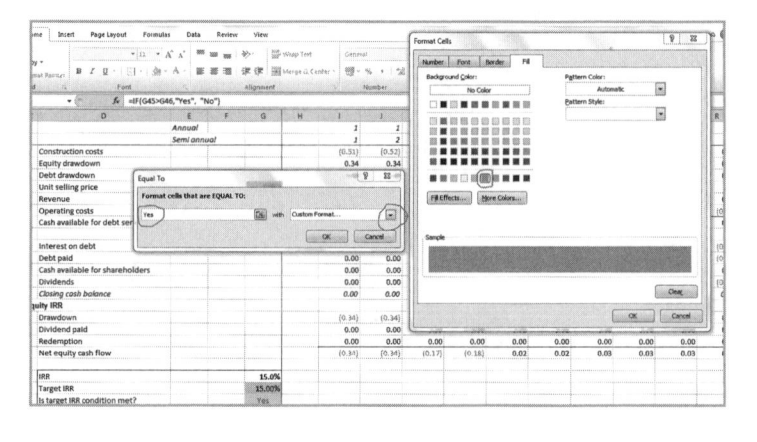

FIGURE 6.6 CONDITIONAL FORMATTING (PART 2)

Repeat Steps a to h, only this time enter "No" in step d and select the red color in step f.

6.5 STEP 5: CREATING THE OUTPUTS SHEET (ANNUAL) ____

To create the annual Outputs sheet in such a way as to keep the same column width and same layout as in the semiannual Outputs sheet, make a copy of the semiannual Outputs sheet. Microsoft Excel automatically names the copied sheet as Outputs_SemiAnnual (2).

- Rename the sheet as Outputs_Annual.
- Then, working your way from the top down, do the following:
  - Delete E1:AB1 and use row 2 instead as the annual timeline.
  - Rename E2 as "Annual" and delete columns S:AB (since we are now working on an annual basis and the model runs for 10 years).
  - Change the content of cell B3 to "OUTPUTS_Annual."
  - Keep the Key assumptions box as is, since this information is still correct.

6.6 STEP 6: CASH WATERFALL (ANNUAL) ____

The cash waterfall box can be arranged as follows:

- *Opening cash balance.* The formula for the first period (that is, the value in cell I24) can be written as follows: "=IF(I$2= 1,Calculations!I84,H38)"—that is, the opening cash balance for the first period is taken from the semiannual output sheet, but thereafter the opening cash balance for any period is the closing cash balance at the end of the previous period.
- Development costs. We use the SUMIF function to aggregate the results of semiannual periods into annual periods. The formula for the first period (that is, the value in cell I25) can be written as follows: "=SUMIF(Outputs_SemiAnnual!$I$1:AB 1,I$2,Outputs_SemiAnnual!$I25:$AB25)". The first parameter is referred to as the *range* and is the array of annual periods in the semiannual output sheet. The second parameter is referred to as the selection *criterion*, and this indicates which indexes in

the range will be selected for the purpose of the SUMIF. The third parameter is referred to as the *SUM range* and is the range of numbers over which the SUM (or addition) is to be applied. Thus the formula for the first period tells Microsoft Excel to look within the annual indexes range in the semiannual output sheet for indexes matching the criterion *annual period 1* (as taken in the annual Outputs sheet, row 1), and where such a match is found, to include the corresponding development cost for that semiannual period in the addition.

- Construction costs. Copy the formula for development costs and paste it into cell I26. The resulting formula is "=SUMIF(Outputs_SemiAnnual!$I$1:$AB$1,I$2, Outputs_SemiAnnual!$I26:$AB26)".
- Equity drawdown. Paste the same formula into cell I27. The resulting formula is "=SUMIF(Outputs_SemiAnnual!$I$1:$AB $1,I$2,Outputs_SemiAnnual!$I40:$AB40)".
- Debt drawdown. Paste the same formula into cell I28.
- Revenue. Paste the same formula into cell I30.
- Operating costs. Paste the same formula into cell I31.
- Interest on debt. Paste the same formula into cell I34.
- Debt repaid. Paste the same formula into cell I35.
- Dividends. Paste the same formula into cell I37.
- Unit selling price. The formula in cell G29 is still valid.
- Cash available for debt service/The formula for the first period (that is, the value in cell I32) can be written as follows: "=SUM(I30:I31)".
- Cash available for shareholders. The formula for the first period (that is, the value in cell I36) can be written as follows: "=SUM(I32,I34:I35)".
- *Closing cash balance.* The formula for the first period (that is, the value in cell I38) can be written as follows: "=SUM(I24,I36:I37)".
- Copy cells I24:I38 and paste them into the block I24:R38.

6.7 STEP 7: EQUITY IRR (ANNUAL)

The equity IRR box can be arranged as follows:

- Drawdown. Copy the formula for development costs from the cash waterfall and paste it into cell I40. The resulting formula is "=SUMIF(Outputs_SemiAnnual!\$I\$1:\$AB\$1,I\$2, Outputs_SemiAnnual!\$I40:\$AB40)".

- Dividend paid. Paste the same formula into cell I41. The resulting formula is "=SUMIF(Outputs_SemiAnnual!\$I\$1:\$AB\$1,I\$2,Outputs_SemiAnnual!\$I41:\$AB41)".
- Redemption. Paste the same formula into cell I42.
- Net equity cash flow. The formula for the first period (that is, the value in cell I43) can be written as follows: "=SUM(I40:I42)".
- Copy cells I40:I43 and paste them into the block I40:R43.
- IRR. The formula (in cell G45) can be written as follows: "=IRR(I43:R43,0.1)".
- Target IRR. The formula (in cell G46) can be left as is.
- Is target IRR condition met? The formulae (in cell G47) can also be left as is.

The cash waterfall and equity boxes are illustrated in Figure 6.7.

B C	D	E	F	G	H	I	J	K	L	M	N	O	P	Q	R
		Annual				1	2	3	4	5	6	7	8	9	10
	Development costs					(1.02)	0.00	0.00	0.00	0.00	0.00	0.00	0.00	0.00	0.0
	Construction costs					(1.02)	(1.05)	0.00	0.00	0.00	0.00	0.00	0.00	0.00	0.0
	Equity drawdown					0.68	0.35	0.00	0.00	0.00	0.00	0.00	0.00	0.00	0.0
	Debt drawdown					1.36	0.70	0.00	0.00	0.00	0.00	0.00	0.00	0.00	0.0
	Unit selling price		$	118.3											
	Revenue					0.00	0.00	1.54	1.67	1.80	1.95	2.11	2.28	2.46	2.6
	Operating costs					0.00	0.00	(1.28)	(1.33)	(1.38)	(1.43)	(1.49)	(1.55)	(1.61)	(1.67
	Cash available for debt service					0.00	0.00	0.26	0.34	0.42	0.52	0.62	0.73	0.86	0.9
	Interest on debt					0.00	0.00	(0.11)	(0.10)	(0.09)	(0.08)	(0.06)	(0.04)	(0.01)	0.0
	Debt paid					0.00	0.00	(0.11)	(0.18)	(0.26)	(0.35)	(0.46)	(0.57)	(0.29)	0.0
	Cash available for shareholders					0.00	0.00	0.04	0.06	0.07	0.09	0.10	0.12	0.56	0.9
	Dividends					0.00	0.00	(0.04)	(0.06)	(0.07)	(0.09)	(0.10)	(0.12)	(0.56)	(0.9
	Closing cash balance					0.00	0.00	0.00	(0.00)	0.00	(0.00)	(0.00)	0.00	0.00	0.0
Equity IRR															
	Drawdown					(0.68)	(0.35)	0.00	0.00	0.00	0.00	0.00	0.00	0.00	0.0
	Dividend paid					0.00	0.00	0.04	0.06	0.07	0.09	0.10	0.12	0.56	0.9
	Redemption					0.00	0.00	0.00	0.00	0.00	0.00	0.00	0.00	0.00	1.0
	Net equity cash flow					(0.68)	(0.35)	0.04	0.06	0.07	0.09	0.10	0.12	0.56	2.0
	IRR			15.2%											
	Target IRR			15.00%											
	Is target IRR condition met?			Yes											

FIGURE 6.7 CASH WATERFALL AND EQUITY OUTPUT (ANNUAL)

Note

- The IRR for the annual period (15.2 percent) is slightly different from the IRR for the semiannual period (15 percent). This is to be expected, as the IRR, which is a function of time (given the time value of money), applied in the annual model is based on annualized cash flows rather than on the exact semiannual cash flows. That said, the differences between the two IRR figures are small.

CHAPTER SEVEN

CASE STUDY 2:
Options Appraisal

In this chapter, we will focus on an options appraisal case study. In this case study, you have been hired to advise the Department of Education on a pilot project. Across the country, getting young people between the ages of 16 and 18 to remain interested in attending school and preparing for college is a big challenge. The department is concerned that this limited interest in schooling on the part of 16- to 18-year-old youths will have a negative impact on the country's long-term development prospects, including a shortage of the skills needed by industry that will lead to reduced economic growth and increased poverty. In an attempt to encourage learning among people in this age group, the department has developed a new business model for learning that is specifically targeted to these youngsters. The new model of learning is designed to entice 16- to 18-year-olds to remain in school and has been advertised extensively in the media. It has also been branded and is called Cool Learning (this is a fictitious name). However, before rolling out Cool Learning across the country, the department would like to pilot it in two areas. The pilot will start in the coming academic year and will cover the selected two areas,whereas in all other areas, the current format (the Base Case model) of teaching will continue to be used.

7.1 BASE CASE

The Base Case model is the current approach to learning, in which students attend high school for three or four years. We are specifically interested in what happens during the last two years of high school (the 16 to 18 year olds); at the end of which students who pass their final exams graduate and go on to college. The Base Case model has been used for years, and we know both average pass rates and the cost (to the government) per student. The cost is measured in terms of the amount of money spent by the government on providing learning. The benefit is measured in terms of the number of students and the pass rate (defined as the number of students who qualify to go on to college divided by the number of students).

The Base Case key inputs are:

- Cost per student in previous academic year
- Pass rate

7.2 COOL LEARNING PROGRAM

The Cool Learning model does not change either the content of the learning or the time it takes to complete it (two years). It simply repackages the learning in order to make it more attractive to the students or learners. It involves giving each student or learner an account with the department (similar to having a bank account) that keeps track of which subjects the student has enrolled in, the course work status, and other such information. The student's account is available on the Internet. The student is also given a card, similar to a credit card, that shows his name and a unique number. Providing the student with an online account and a card lets him feel empowered (have a sense of being in control of his learning), and it is expected that this feeling of empowerment will result in a greater desire to learn. Thus, the aim of the Cool Learning program is to achieve greater learning participation among 16- to 18-year-olds. This will be tested in the Cool Learning pilot project.

The Cool Learning pilot key inputs are:

- Learning cost in pilot area A.
- Learning cost in pilot area B.

- Additional costs. These are costs that are not going into learning. They would not be incurred under the Base Case model, so they are indeed additional. They include the following:
  - Additional spending in each of the pilot areas
  - Finance
  - IT systems for the online platform
  - Evaluation
  - Marketing and communications

7.3 REQUIREMENTS

As an advisor, your job is to help the department appraise the Cool Learning pilot and compare it with the Base Case option (that is, the last two years of high school). The key question for the department is as follows: should we invest in Cool Learning, or should we put the money into the existing Base Case model? What would it take for Cool Learning to be a worthwhile investment?

7.4 FINANCIAL MODELING

This case study is what is often referred to as an options appraisal case, in which we are comparing multiple options or scenarios. In our case, we have two options to compare: Base Case and Cool Learning. Please note that the Base Case option is often referred to as the Do Nothing option and is always a possibility. Indeed, the Department of Education could decide that Cool Learning is not an option and so carry on with its current approach to learning.

For each option, we need to evaluate the cost of that option, the number of students involved, and, based on an assumed pass rate, the number of students qualified for admission to college. Once these results are known, it will be easier to make an informed comparison of the two options.

7.4.1 Base Case Model

The Base Case is the way learning at the high school level (that is, for students aged 16 to 18) has been carried out in the country for many years. Good statistical data are available, and based on this, the average cost per student for the previous academic year is known. We also know the success rate during that academic year, which is in line with historical pass-rate levels.

Inputs

- *Cost per learner.* Based on inflation forecasts, it is possible to project the historical cost per learner for Years 1 and 2.
- *Success rate.* This is assumed to be equal to the pass rate for the previous academic year.
- *Funds available for learning.* The budget that would have been spent on providing learning to the students using the Base Case model in those two areas is known. However, to ensure that we are comparing both options on the same basis, we will take the funds available for learning in the Base Case model as being those available with the Cool Learning model (discussed in the next section).

Specifications

- *Number of learners.* This is calculated as funds available for learning divided by the projected cost per learner.
- *Number of high school qualifications (or number of students qualified for admission to college).* This is calculated as number of learners times the success rate.
- *Cost per high school qualification.* This is calculated as funds available for learning divided by number of high school qualifications.

7.4.2 Cool Learning Pilot

The Cool Learning model is the new approach to learning.

Inputs

- *Number of learners budgeted for Cool Learning.* This is known, since these are the students between the ages of 16 and 18 in the two pilot areas. It is just that instead of enrolling under the Base Case model, these students will enroll through Cool Learning.
- *Cost of learning.* Likewise, the budget that would have been spent on providing learning to these students using the Base Case model will be used to fund the new Cool Learning model in those two areas.

- *Additional implementation costs.* In addition to the standard amount of funds provided for Cool Learning in each of the two areas, the department has provided further funding for additional costs required to implement the new scheme.
- *Success rate.* This is assumed to be equal to the pass rate for the previous academic year. Note that Cool Learning is expected to increase students' interest in learning, and so the pass rate should increase. But to be conservative, the pass rate is assumed to be identical to that of the Base Case model.

Specifications

- *Funds available for learning.* This is calculated as the sum of the cost of learning and additional implementation costs, and it represents the total amount available for spending under Cool Learning. Since we are comparing the Base Case model with the Cool Learning model, both options will use the same funds available for learning.
- *Cost per learner.* This is calculated as the cost per learner under the Base Case plus the additional implementation costs budgeted for Cool Learning divided by the number of learners.
- *Number of learners.* This is calculated as funds available for learning divided by the projected cost per learner.
- *Number of high school qualifications.* This is calculated as the number of learners times the success rate.
- *Cost per high school qualification.* This is calculated as funds available for learning divided by number of high school qualifications.
- *Break-even success rate.* One of the key questions you must help the department answer is what it would take for Cool Learning to be a worthwhile investment. One way of approaching this question is to think in terms of the number of qualifications achieved under the Cool Learning pilot. Ultimately, the department is looking to achieve a large number of high school graduates who are eligible to go on to college. And so in order for the Cool Learning pilot to be worthwhile, it will have to achieve at least the same number of high school qualifications as the Base Case. But we know that the cost per student for Cool Learning is higher than that for the Base Case because in addition to the Base Case cost per student, we have to add the additional Cool Learning implementation cost per student. Therefore, in order to achieve at least the same number of

qualifications in Cool Learning as in the Base Case, the success rate with Cool Learning must be higher than the success rate with the Base Case model.

7.5 BUILDING THE FINANCIAL MODEL

We will create a new workbook in which we will build the Cool Learning financial model. The model will be annual, with two projection years: Year 1 and Year 2, focusing on the last two years of high school. There will be two groups of inputs: Base Case inputs and Cool Learning inputs, as described previously. The model itself is not too big, and so we will build the inputs, calculations, and outputs in the same sheet.

7.5.1 Timeline

- We will assume that we are nearing the end of academic year 2012. The Cool Learning pilot will start in the next academic year, 2013, and will run for two academic years: 2013 and 2014.
- We have two complete historical academic years, 2010 and 2011, and one almost-complete academic year, 2012.
- We can write the timeline in row 3. Let us say that cell J3 contains academic year 2010, cell K3 contains academic year 2011, cell L3 contains academic year 2012, cell M3 contains academic year 2013, and cell N3 contains academic year 2014.

7.5.2 Inputs

- *Inflation rate.* We can write the historical and forecasted inflation rates on row 8 as follows: the historical inflation rate for 2010, 2011, and 2012 was 5 percent, and the forecasted inflation rate for 2013 and 2014 is also 5 percent.

Base Case Inputs

- *Cost per learner ($).* In cell J11, we write the cost per learner as $1,500.
- *High school success rate.* In cell J12, we write the high school success rate as 40 percent.
- *Number of high school learners budgeted for in the pilot areas (A and B).* In cell J13, we write the number 2,000, which represents the number of high school learners budgeted for in the pilot areas (A and B).

Cool Learning Inputs

- *Learning cost in pilot area A, $000.* In cells M16 and N16, we write the figure $2,600.
- *Learning cost in pilot area B, $000.* In cells M17 and N17, we write the figure $2,600.
- *Total cost of learning.* In cell M18, we write the formula "=SUM(M16:M17)". Copy cell M18 and paste the formula into cell N18.
- *Additional pilot costs, $000:*
  - Area A. In cells M21 and N21, we write the additional pilot cost as $200.
  - Area B. In cells M22 and N22, we write the additional pilot cost as $100.
  - Finance. In cells M23 and N23, we write the additional pilot cost as $70.
  - Systems. In cells M24 and N24, we write the additional pilot cost as $50.
  - Evaluation. In cells M25 and N25, we write the additional pilot cost as $50.
  - Marketing and communications. In cells M26 and N26, we write the additional pilot cost as $280.
  - Total additional costs. In cell M27, we write the formula "=SUM(M21:M26)". Copy cell M27 and paste the formula into cell N27.

The Inputs section of the Cool Learning model is illustrated in Figure 7.1.

7.5.3 Calculations—Base Case

Projected Cost per Learner ($)

In cell K32, we can write the formula "=IF(K3=2011,J11*(1+K8),J32 *(1+K8))", which calculates cost per learner after inflation for 2011 as being equal to cost per learner in 2010 times 1 plus the 2011 inflation rate if we are in 2011. Otherwise, cost per learner after inflation in Year t is equal to the cost per learner after inflation in Year t - 1 times 1 plus the inflation rate.

Copy cell K32 and paste the formula into the block K32:N32.

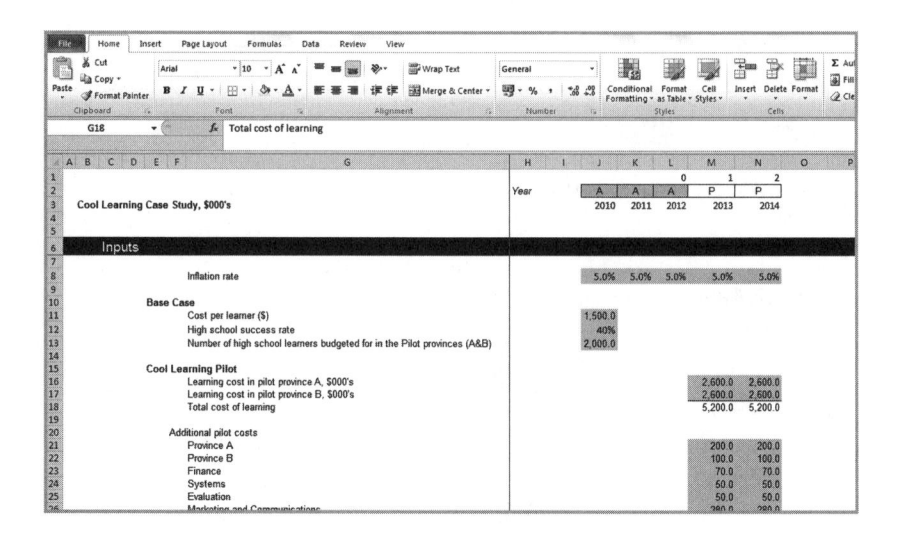

FIGURE 7.1 COOL LEARNING (INPUTS)

Learning Cost in Pilot Area A, $000

In cell M34, we write the formula "=M16", which picks up the learning cost in pilot area A from the Inputs section.

Copy cell M34 and paste the formula into the block M34:N34.

Learning Cost in Pilot Area B, $000

In cell M35, we write the formula "=M17", which picks up the learning cost in pilot area B from the Inputs section.

Copy cell M35 and paste the formula into the block M35:N35.

Total Additional Costs

In cell M36, we write the formula "=M27", which picks up the additional costs from the Inputs section.

Copy cell M36 and paste the formula into the block M36:N36.

Total Funds Available Under Base Case

In cell M37, we write the formula "=SUM(M34:M36)", which calculates the total funds available under the Base Case as the sum of the learning cost in pilot area A, the learning cost in pilot area B, and total additional costs.

Copy cell M37 and paste the formula into the block M37:N37.

Number of Learners

Assume that the same cohort moves from Year 1 to Year 2.

In cell M39, we write the formula "=SUM(M37:N37)*1000/N32", which calculates the number of learners as total funds available under the Base Case times 1,000 divided by the after-inflation projected cost per learner in 2014.

High School Success Rate

In cell M40, we write the formula "=J12", which picks up the high school success rate from the Inputs section.

Number of High School Qualifications

In cell M41, we write the formula "=M40*M39", which calculates the number of high school qualifications as equal to the high school success rate times the number of learners.

Cost per Qualification ($)

In cell M42, we write the formula "=SUM(M37:N37)*1000/M41", which calculates the cost per qualification ($) as equal to the sum of the total funds available under the Base Case for both Year 1 and Year 2 times 1,000 divided by the number of high school qualifications.

The Base Case model is illustrated in Figure 7.2.

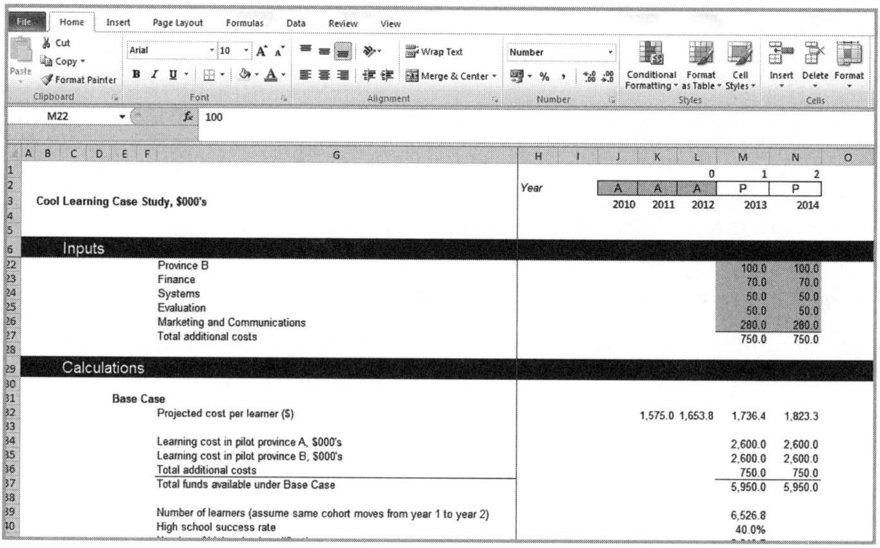

FIGURE 7.2 COOL LEARNING (BASE CASE)

7.5.4 Calculations—Cool Learning Pilot

Projected Cost per Learner ($)

In cell M45, we write the formula "=M32", which picks up cost per learner after inflation from the Base Case calculations.

Number of High School Learners Budgeted
For in the Pilot Areas (A and B)

In cell M46, we write the formula "=J13", which picks up the number of high school learners budgeted for in the pilot areas (A and B) from the Inputs section.

Cool Learning Additional Costs

In cell M47, we write the formula "=M27", which picks up the Cool Learning additional costs from the Inputs section.

Copy cell M47 and paste the formula into the block M47:N47.

Estimated Cost per Learner (Cool Learning)

In cell M48, we write the formula "=SUM(M47:N47)*1000/ M46+M45", which calculates the estimated cost per learner as the sum of the Cool Learning additional costs in Year 1 and Year 2 times 1,000 divided by the number of high school learners budgeted for in the pilot areas (A and B) *plus* the projected cost per learner ($).

Total Funds Available Under Cool Learning

In cell M50, we write the formula "=M37", which picks up the total funds available under Cool Learning from the Base Case.

Copy cell M50 and paste the formula into the block M50:N50.

Number of Learners in the Pilot

Assume that the same cohort moves from Year 1 to Year 2.

In cell M52, we write the formula "=SUM(M50:N50)*1000/M48", which calculates the number of learners in the pilot areas as the sum of the total funds available under Cool Learning for Years 1 and 2 times 1,000 divided by the estimated cost per learner (Cool Learning).

High School Success Rate

We assume that this is the same as in the Base Case. Therefore, in cell M53, we write the formula "=M40", which picks up the high school success rate from the Base Case model.

Number of High School Qualifications

In cell M54, we write the formula "=M53*M52", which calculates the number of high school qualifications as the number of learners in the pilot areas times the high school success rate.

Cost per Qualification ($)

In cell M55, we write the formula "=SUM(M50:N50)*1000/M54", which calculates the cost per qualification ($) as equal to sum of the total funds available under Cool Learning for both Year 1 and Year 2 times 1,000 divided by the number of high school qualifications.

Next, we need to calculate the minimum pass rate required in the pilot areas to achieve the same number of qualifications as in the Base Case.

Number of High School Qualifications in the Base Case

In cell M59, we write the formula "=M41", which picks up the number of high school qualifications in the Base Case from the Base Case section.

Number of Learners in the Pilot Areas

Assume that the same cohort moves from Year 1 to Year 2.

In cell M60, write the formula "=M52", which picks up the number of learners in the pilot areas from the Cool Learning pilot section.

Minimum Pass Rate Required in Pilot to Break Even

In cell M61, we write the formula "=M59/M60", which calculates the minimum pass rate required in the pilot to break even as being equal to the number of high school qualifications in the Base Case divided by the number of learners in the pilot areas (assume that the same cohort moves from Year 1 to Year 2).

The Cool Learning pilot is illustrated in Figure 7.3.

7.5.5 Outputs

We will present the model output in a simple summary table showing side-by-side key results from the Base Case and the Cool Learning pilot. Key results we will show include the following:

- Learning costs ($000)

For the Base Case model, in cell I67, we write the formula "=M37+N37", which aggregates the learning costs across Years 1 and 2 in the Base Case.

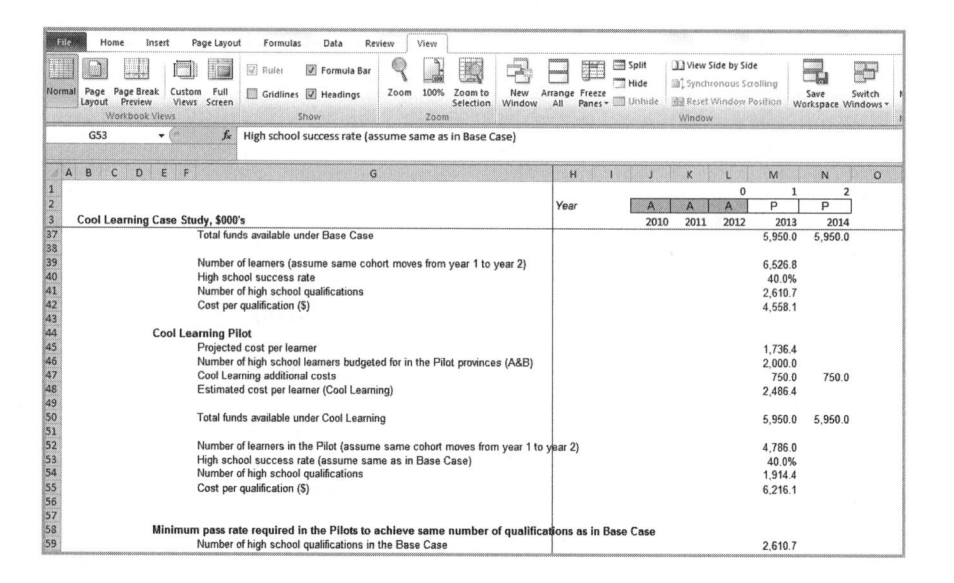

FIGURE 7.3 COOL LEARNING PILOT

For the Cool Learning pilot, in cell L67, we write the formula "=I67", which picks up the same learning costs from the Base Case.

- Number of learners

For the Base Case model, in cell I69, we write the formula "=M39", which picks up the number of learners under the Base Case from the Base Case section.

For the Cool Learning pilot, in cell L69, we write the formula "=M52", which picks up the same number of learners from the Cool Learning section.

- Pass rate

For the Base Case model, in cell I70, we write the formula "=J12", which picks up the pass rate from the Input section.

For the Cool Learning pilot, in cell L70, we write the formula "=I70", which picks up the same pass rate as for the Base Case.

- Number of qualifications

For the Base Case model, in cell I71, we write the formula "=M41", which picks up the number of qualifications under the Base Case from the Base Case section.

For the Cool Learning pilot, in cell L71, we write the formula "=M54", which picks up the number of qualifications from the Cool Learning section.

- Cost per qualification ($)

For the Base Case model, in cell I72, we write the formula "=M42", which picks up the cost per qualification ($) under the Base Case from the Base Case section.

For the Cool Learning pilot, in cell L72, we write the formula "=M55", which picks up the cost per qualification ($) from the Cool Learning section.

- Pass rate required in pilot to break even (same number of qualifications as in the Base Case)

For the Base Case model, in cell I73, we write the formula "n/a" to indicate that this is not applicable under the Base Case.

For the Cool Learning pilot, in cell L73, we write the formula "=M61", which picks up the pass rate required in the pilot to break even (same number of qualifications as in the Base Case) from the Cool Learning section.

The Outputs section is illustrated in Figure 7.4.

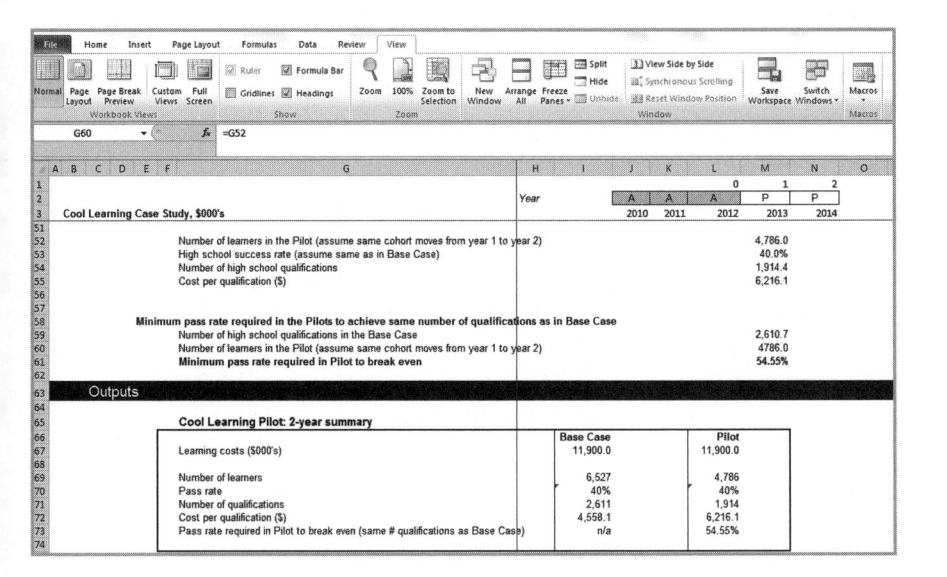

FIGURE 7.4 COOL LEARNING OUTPUTS

However, for presentational reasons, we will move the Outputs section to the top. To this end, we need to do the following:

- Cut rows 63 to 76.
- Insert the cut rows in row 5.

The result is now as shown in Figure 7.5.

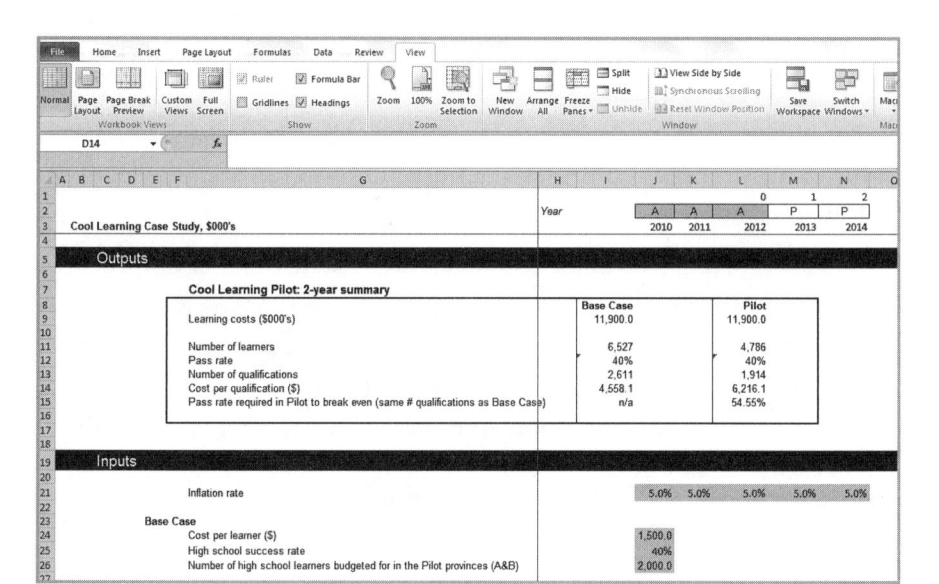

FIGURE 7.5   COOL LEARNING FINAL OUTPUTS

7.6 ANALYSIS

- In total, the department has a budget of $11.9 million to spend on high school learning (that is, for 16- to 18-year-old students) in the pilot areas A and B. The money is currently earmarked for the Cool Learning pilot. However, if the department were to carry on with the Base Case approach, it would expect to train 6,527 students across these two areas. Assuming a 40 percent pass rate, then 2,611 qualifications would be achieved, giving a cost per qualification of $4,558.

- If the $11.9 million were to be spent on implementing the Cool Learning pilot, then the cost per student would be higher because a portion of the $11.9 million ($1.5 million across Years 1 and 2) would be used to set up IT accounts, finance, and so on. As a result of the higher cost per student, the number of students is lower than under the Base Case, 4,786 students. Therefore, at the same pass rate of 40 percent as in the Base Case, Cool Learning would achieve fewer qualifications, 1,914.

- In order for Cool Learning to achieve the same number of qualifications as in the Base Case (which is 2,611), it would need to achieve a 54.55 percent success rate, which is higher than the historical 40 percent success rate. Given the historical 40 percent success rate, one can wonder whether a 54.55 percent success rate is realistic. This is a judgment call that the financial model cannot answer. But at least the model can inform the Department of Education what it would take for the Cool Learning scheme to be worth the investment.

Part 3

Modeling Practice—Further Case Studies

CHAPTER EIGHT

CASE STUDY 3:
The Phone Factory Revisited

8.1 INTRODUCTION

Let us fast-forward the Phone Factory case study by two years. The plant has now been built, and we are ready to start operations. The market for mobile phones has turned out to be much larger than we had initially anticipated (two years ago). As a result, the factory has been built with a much bigger production capacity. Furthermore, demand for mobile phone handsets is so strong that the starting selling price is 50 percent higher than we had initially forecast. Sales are forecast to reach $6 million for the first year (about 30,000 handsets sold at an average of $200).

With the factory now up and running, your manager has asked for a revised 10-year financial model setting out projections for the profit and loss, balance sheet, and cash flow for the Phone Factory. The model will be presented to the board of your company.

In this chapter, you will learn to build an *integrated financial model*, which is basically a financial model in which the profit and loss, balance sheet, and cash flow statements are *interlinked* in a *consistent* manner.

Here are the main model assumptions.

8.2 MODEL ASSUMPTIONS _____

8.2.1 Operational Assumptions

The operational assumptions are given in Table 8.1.

TABLE 8.1 OPERATIONAL ASSUMPTIONS

	Year 1	Year 2	Year 3	Year 4	Year 5	Year 6	Year 7	Year 8	Year 9	Year 10
Sales ($ millions)	6									
Sales growth (%)		150.0%	100.0%	50.0%	30.0%	20.0%	10.0%	8.0%	8.0%	8.0%
Gross profit (%)	80.0%	80.0%	80.0%	80.0%	80.0%	80.0%	80.0%	80.0%	80.0%	80.0%
EBITDA (%)	45.0%	45.0%	40.0%	35.0%	30.0%	30.0%	30.0%	30.0%	30.0%	30.0%
Capex as % of sales	5.0%	5.0%	5.0%	5.0%	5.0%	5.0%	5.0%	5.0%	5.0%	5.0%
Working capital as % of sales	20.0%	20.0%	20.0%	20.0%	20.0%	20.0%	20.0%	20.0%	20.0%	20.0%

- *Sales growth %.* The sales growth percentage is quite high, particularly in the first few years. This reflects the strong unmet demand for mobile phone handsets in the target overseas market. Sales are projected to grow throughout the projected period, although at a gradually slower pace, stabilizing at 8 percent per annum from Year 8 onward.
- *Gross profit %.* This is assumed to be 80 percent throughout the projected period.
- *EBITDA %.* This is assumed to be 45 percent during Years 1 and 2 and gradually comes down to 30 percent from Year 5 onward.
- *Capex as % of sales.* Once the factory has been built, capital expenditure requirements are minimal. They are projected at 5 percent of sales throughout the period and reflect the need to hire more staff as the business grows.
- *Working capital as % of sales.* Working capital here includes stock (inventory, in American usage), trade debtors (accounts receivable), and trade creditors (accounts payable). Working capital is projected at 20 percent of sales throughout the period and reflects the fact that the business will require a larger amount of stock, trade debtors, and trade creditors as the business grows.

8.2.2 Opening Balance Sheet (in Millions of Dollars)

The opening balance sheet, shown in Table 8.2, is the balance sheet at the end of the two years of construction (in other words, the balance sheet at the start of operations).

TABLE 8.2

Fixed assets	8.0
Working capital	0.0
Cash	1.0
Debt	(6.0)
Net assets	3.0
Share capital	3.0
Retained profit	0.0
Net worth	3.0

- *Fixed assets.* Fixed assets include property, plant, and equipment (PPE) and are valued at cost, $8 million, which is how much it cost to build the factory.
- *Working capital.* The opening working capital is assumed to be 0, reflecting the fact that at the start of operations, there is no stock (inventory), trade debtors (accounts receivable), or trade creditors (accounts payable).
- *Cash.* The opening cash balance is assumed to be $1 million; in other words, the business begins operations with $1 million of cash available to fund working capital (for example, to purchase inventory).
- *Debt.* The factory has been built at a cost of $8 million and also has $1 million of cash, creating total capital of $9 million. Of the $9 million of capital, $6 million is debt.
- *Share capital.* Of the $9 million of capital, $3 million is equity. The factory has total capital of $9 million. Since $6 million of the $9 million of capital is debt, $3 million is equity.
- *Retained profit (retained earnings, in American usage).* This is assumed to be 0, reflecting the fact that the business has not begun operating to generate any profit.
- *Net assets.* This is calculated as the sum of fixed assets, working capital, cash, and debt and equals $3 million.

- *Net worth.* This is calculated as the sum of share capital and retained profit and equals $3 million.
- Net assets must be equal to net worth. This is the case here, and therefore the balance sheet balances.

Balance Sheet Format

The balance sheet can be presented in a variety of ways. In this book, the balance sheet is laid out as shown on the left-hand side of Table 8.3. The right-hand side of the table shows a balance sheet layout that is often encountered in the United States. The difference between the two formats occurs in the upper part of the balance sheet. In the format used throughout this book, the upper part of the balance sheet gives long-term assets, then current assets, then cash, whereas the format commonly used in the United States starts with cash, followed by current assets and then long-term assets.

The format used in this book lends itself to calculating the balance sheet as net assets being funded by the shareholders' funds, or, put differently, net assets = net worth. The format often encountered in the United States lends itself to calculating the balance sheet as assets = liabilities.

TABLE 8.3

Balance Sheet Format Used Throughout the Book	Balance Sheet Format Often Encountered in the United States
Long-term assets	Cash
Current assets	Current assets
Cash	Long-term assets
Current liabilities	Current liabilities
Long-term liabilities (excluding equity)	Long-term liabilities (excluding equity)
Equity	Equity
Net assets = long-term assets + current assets + cash – current liabilities – long-term liabilities (excluding equity)	Assets = cash + current assets + long-term assets
	Liabilities = current liabilities + long-term liabilities (excluding equity) + equity
Balance sheet equation: Net assets = equity	*Balance sheet equation: Assets = liabilities*

Note that mathematically the equation assets = liabilities is equivalent to the equation net assets = equity. Indeed, assets = liabilities means cash + current assets + long-term assets = current liabilities + long-term liabilities (excluding equity) + equity, which can be rewritten as cash +

current assets + long-term assets − current liabilities − long-term liabilities (excluding equity) = equity, which means that net assets = equity. Therefore, while the layout is different, the balance sheet remains the same.

In the balance sheet example shown in Table 8.2, we do not show current assets and current liabilities separately, but instead show working capital.

8.2.3 Debt Assumptions

- Interest rate: 6%

TABLE 8.4 AMORTIZATION SCHEDULE

	Year 1	Year 2	Year 3	Year 4	Year 5	Year 6
Amortization	0.5	0.5	1.0	1.0	1.5	1.5

- *Interest rate.* This is assumed to be 6 percent per annum.
- *Amortization schedule.* The assumed amortization schedule is such that the loan is fully repaid in six years (see Table 8.4). However, the repayment is not in equal amounts. Instead, the amount repaid in the earlier years is small, with a bigger proportion of the loan being repaid in later years. This is often referred to as a *back-ended* amortization schedule, and it gives the business more breathing space in earlier years when cash generation is low.

8.2.4 Dividend Assumptions

- Dividend payout as a percentage of profit after tax (PAT) is 50 percent.
- Dividends are payable once debt has been fully repaid.
- *Dividend payout.* This is assumed to be 50 percent of profit after tax (PAT). In other words, half of the profit after tax is paid to the shareholders (who are the owners of the business), with the other half being reinvested in the business.
- *Timing of dividend.* The dividend will not be paid until the debt has been fully repaid. This reflects the fact that the debt provider wants to ensure that the free cash generated by the business is used first and foremost to repay the debt.

8.2.5 Other Assumptions

- Tax rate: 30%
- Depreciation: straight-line depreciation, assuming that the factory has a useful economic life of 20 years with a nil residual value.

TABLE 8.5 OTHER ASSUMPTIONS

	Year 1	Year 2	Year 3	Year 4	Year 5	. . .	Year 20
Depreciation	8/20 or 0.4	8/20 or 0.4	8/20 or 0.4	8/20 or 0.4	8/20 or 0.4		8/20 or 0.4

- *Tax rate.* This is assumed to be 30 percent of earnings before tax (EBT).
- *Depreciation.* The useful economic life of the factory is assumed to be 20 years with no residual value. Depreciation is assumed to be on a straight-line basis. Thus the book value of the factory is decreased by 1/20 of its original cost each year, or $8/20 (see Table 8.5).

8.3 HIGH-LEVEL MODEL MAP

As in Case Study 1 (Chapters 4 and 5), let us once again resist the temptation to jump straight to building the model in Excel. Instead, let us think through what is required here and plan the model accordingly.

We need to build an *integrated* financial model including the profit and loss statement, the balance sheet, and the cash flow statement. The model will take inputs, make calculations, and produce the required outputs in the form of a profit and loss statement, a balance sheet, and a cash flow statement.

The map in Figure 8.1 describes the model.

The model will be relatively simple, and so based on the map in Figure 8.1, we can envisage a Microsoft Excel file with two sheets: Inputs & Workings, and Outputs.

8.4 CREATING THE FRONT SHEET

Let us create a new workbook. In Sheet1, we create a front sheet similar to that in Chapter 4 (see Figure 8.2).

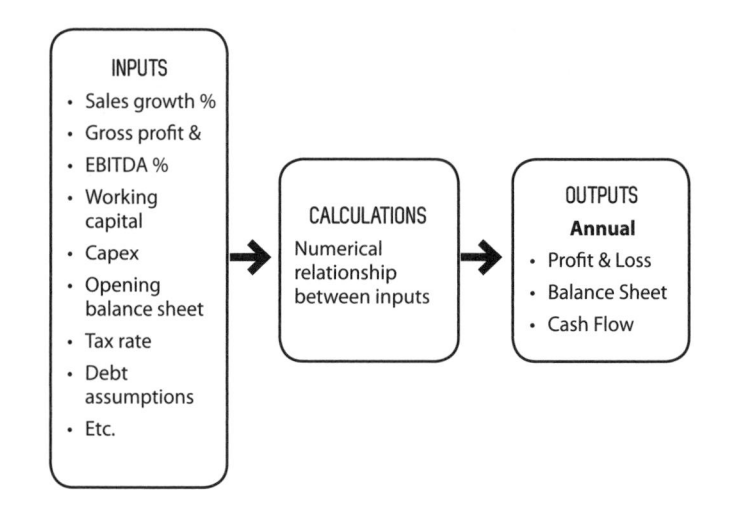

FIGURE 8.1 HIGH-LEVEL MODEL MAP

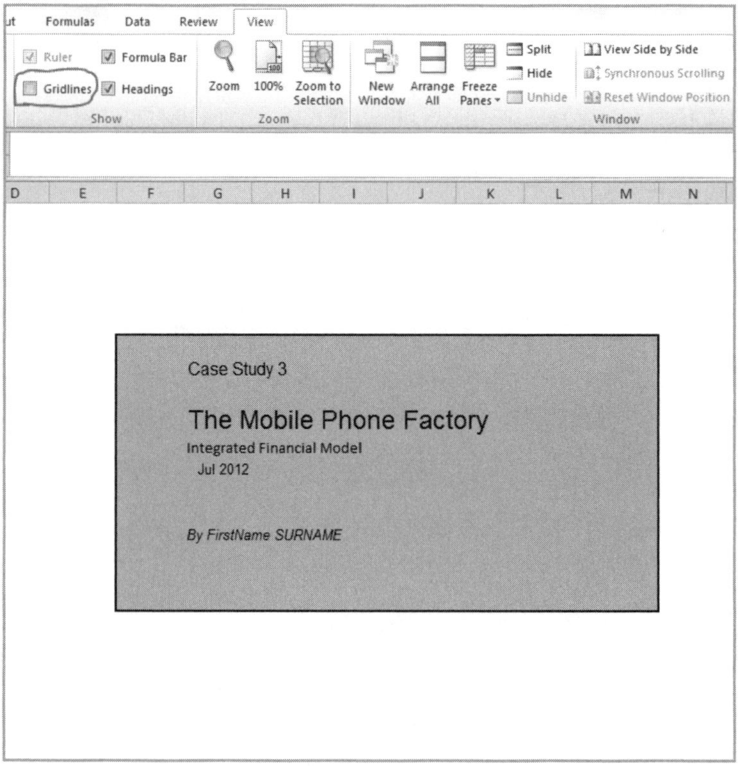

FIGURE 8.2 FRONT COVER OR TITLE

Note that the sheet does not show any gridlines. This was achieved by turning off the Gridlines tick box within the View tab of the ribbon.

8.5 CREATING THE INPUTS & WORKINGS SHEET

We rename Sheet2 as "Inputs & Workings" and color it as yellow. Then we enter the assumptions provided in Section 8.2 into the sheet as shown in Figures 8.3 and 8.4.

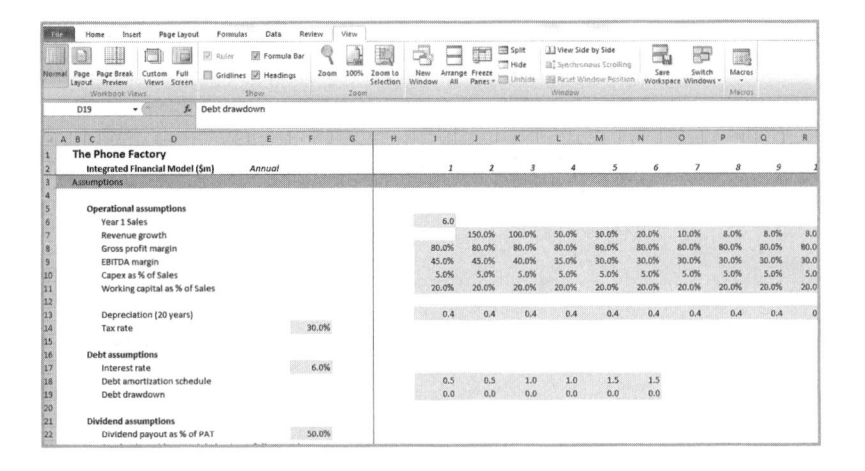

FIGURE 8.3 ASSUMPTIONS—PART 1

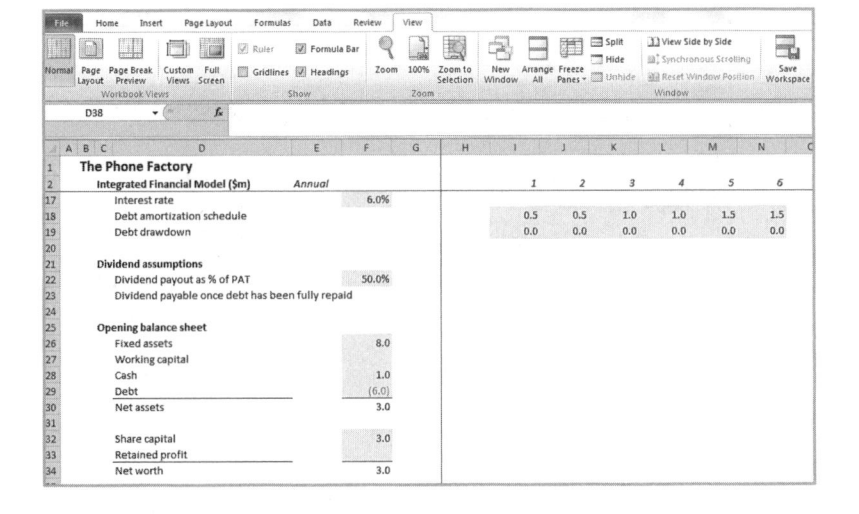

FIGURE 8.4 ASSUMPTIONS—PART 2

- Set the width for columns A, B, and C to 2.57, and set the column D width to 32.29.
- Freeze the pane at cell H3.
- Enter the title "The Phone Factory" in cell B1, and enter the subtitle "Integrated Financial Model ($m)" in cell C2.
- Enter the timeline on row 2 as illustrated.

8.6 WRITING MODEL SPECIFICATIONS

Following the principle of modularization explained in Chapter 5, we consider the following modules: Profit and Loss, Debt, Fixed Assets, Balance Sheet, and Cash Flow.

8.6.1 Profit and Loss Module

Sales
- Year 1 sales are given.
- Year-over-year sales growth is given.
- For each period of time t, calculate sales_t as sales_t–1 times (1 + sales growth_t).

Gross Profit
- For each period of time t, calculate gross profit_t as gross profit margin_t times sales_t.

Earnings Before Interest, Taxes, Depreciation, and Amortization (EBITDA)
- For each period of time t, calculate EBITDA_t as EBITDA margin_t times sales_t.

Depreciation
- This is given.

Earnings Before Interest and Taxes (EBIT)
- For each period of time t, calculate EBIT_t as EBITDA_t minus depreciation_t.

Interest
- For each period of time t, the interest charge will be calculated in the Debt module (discussed in the next section).

Earnings Before Tax (EBT)

- For each period of time t, calculate EBT_t as EBIT_t minus interest_t.

Tax

- For each period of time t, calculate tax_t as tax rate times EBT_t if EBT_t is positive. Otherwise, tax_t = 0.

Profit After Tax (PAT)

- For each period of time t, calculate PAT_t as EBT_t minus tax_t.

Dividend

- For each period of time t, calculate dividend_t as dividend payout ratio times PAT_t if there is no debt outstanding. Otherwise, dividend_t = 0.

Net Profit

- For each period of time t, calculate net profit_t as PAT_t minus dividend_t.

Retained Profit (Retained Earnings)

- This will be calculated using a control account whereby retained profit carried forward_t = retained profit brought forward_t plus net profit_t.
- Retained profit brought forward_t = retained profit carried forward_t–1.
- Retained profit brought forward_year 1 = retained profit carried forward in the opening balance sheet.

8.6.2 Debt Module

As in Chapter 5, our Debt module will include a control account for "tracking" or monitoring the principal and a control account for tracking or monitoring the interest on the debt.

The debt control account will be calculated as follows:

- Debt opening balance_t = debt closing balance_t–1, with debt opening balance_year 1 = debt balance in opening balance sheet.
- Debt drawdown_t = 0.

- Debt repayment_t is given by the amortization schedule.
- Debt closing balance_t = debt opening balance_t plus debt drawdown_t plus debt repayment_t.

The interest control account will be calculated as follows:

- Interest opening balance_t = interest closing balance_t–1, with interest opening balance_year 1 = 0.
- Interest charge_t = interest rate times (debt opening balance_t + debt drawdown_t).
- Interest paid_t = – interest charge_t.
- Interest closing balance_t = interest opening balance_t plus interest charge_t plus interest paid_t.

8.6.3 Fixed Assets Module

As in Chapter 5, it is best practice to calculate fixed assets using a control account for tracking or monitoring the book value of fixed assets. The fixed assets control account will be calculated as follows:

- Fixed assets opening balance_t = fixed assets closing. balance_t–1, with fixed assets opening balance_year 1 = fixed assets balance in opening balance sheet.
- Capital expenditures (capex) increase the book value of fixed assets. Capex_t = capex as % of sales_t times sales_t.
- Depreciation decreases the book value of fixed assets. Depreciation_t is already given.
- Fixed assets closing balance_t = fixed assets opening balance_t plus capex_t minus depreciation_t.

8.6.4 Balance Sheet Module

- Fixed assets closing balance_t is calculated in the fixed assets module just discussed.
- Working capital_t = working capital as percent of sales_t times sales_t.
- Closing cash balance_t is calculated in the Cash Flow module (discussed later).
- Closing debt balance_t is calculated in the Debt module (discussed earlier).
- Net assets_t = fixed assets closing balance_t plus working capital_t plus closing cash balance_t minus debt closing balance_t.

- Share capital_t = share capital in opening balance sheet.
- Retained profit carried forward_t is calculated in the Profit and Loss module (discussed earlier).
- Net worth_t = share capital_t plus retained profit carried forward_t.

Since net worth must equal net assets, let us add at the bottom of the balance sheet a balance sheet check that checks whether the balance sheet balances in each period. To this end, we include two additional lines as follows:

- Balance_t = net assets_t minus net worth_t.
- Check_t = if (ABS (Balance_t) <= 0.01, TRUE, FALSE), where Abs(x) is the absolute value of x, a Microsoft Excel function retuning the magnitude of a number regardless of its sign. The way the formula has been expressed means that as long as the absolute value of the difference between net assets_t and net worth_t is within 0.01, we consider such a difference to be immaterial.

8.6.5 Cash Flow Module

As already discussed, there are three elements in an integrated financial model: the profit and loss statement, the balance sheet, and the cash flow statement. With the profit and loss statement and the balance sheet now established, the cash flow statement can be derived from the other two statements in such a way that the resulting financial model is integrated. Indeed, if the financial model is integrated, then a change in any element of the financial model will result in a change elsewhere in the financial model. For example, an increase in working capital in the balance sheet will result in a cash outflow in the cash flow statement, resulting in a reduction in the closing cash balance. As another example, a decrease in net profit (in the profit and loss statement) will result in a decrease in net worth (in the balance sheet). Another example: debt repayment (a cash outflow in the cash flow statement) will result in a reduced debt balance in the balance sheet.

Deriving the cash flow statement based on the profit and loss statement and the balance sheet is known as the *indirect method* of calculating the cash flow statement. This is in contrast to the *direct method* of calculating the cash flow statement, in which a summary of receipts and payments is given. The latter is more useful in the context of a financial controller monitoring cash receipts and cash payments for a given business. The former is more useful for building an integrated financial model.

In this book, we will use the indirect method for calculating cash flows. The indirect cash flow statement starts with EBITDA as the top line and flows down the waterfall to get to net cash flow as follows:

- EBITDA_t. This is calculated in the profit and loss module.
- Movement in working capital_t. This equals working capital_t–1 minus working capital_t, or working capital at the start of the year minus working capital at the end of the year.
- Operating cash flow_t. This equals EBITDA_t plus movement in working capital_t.
- Capex_t. This is calculated in the Fixed Asset module.
- Cash flow before taxation and financing_t. This equals operating cash flow_t minus capex_t.
- Tax_t. This is calculated in the Profit and Loss module.
- Cash flow available for debt service_t. This equals cash flow before taxation and financing_t minus tax_t.
- Interest paid_t. This is calculated in the Debt module.
- Debt repayment_t. This is calculated in the Debt module.
- Cash flow available for shareholders_t. This equals cash flow available for debt service_t minus interest paid_t minus debt repayment_t.
- Dividend_t. This is calculated in the Profit and Loss module.
- Net cash flow_t. This equals cash flow available for shareholders_t minus dividend_t.

We also need to include a control account calculating the closing cash balance_t.

- The closing cash balance_t equals the opening cash balance_t plus net cash flow_t.
- The opening cash balance_t equals the closing cash balance_t–1, with the opening cash balance_year 1 given in the opening balance sheet.

8.7 MODEL CALCULATIONS MAP

As in Chapter 4, a high-level map of the model calculations can be useful for illustrating how the different modules relate to one another. Figure 8.5 is an illustration of the model calculations map.

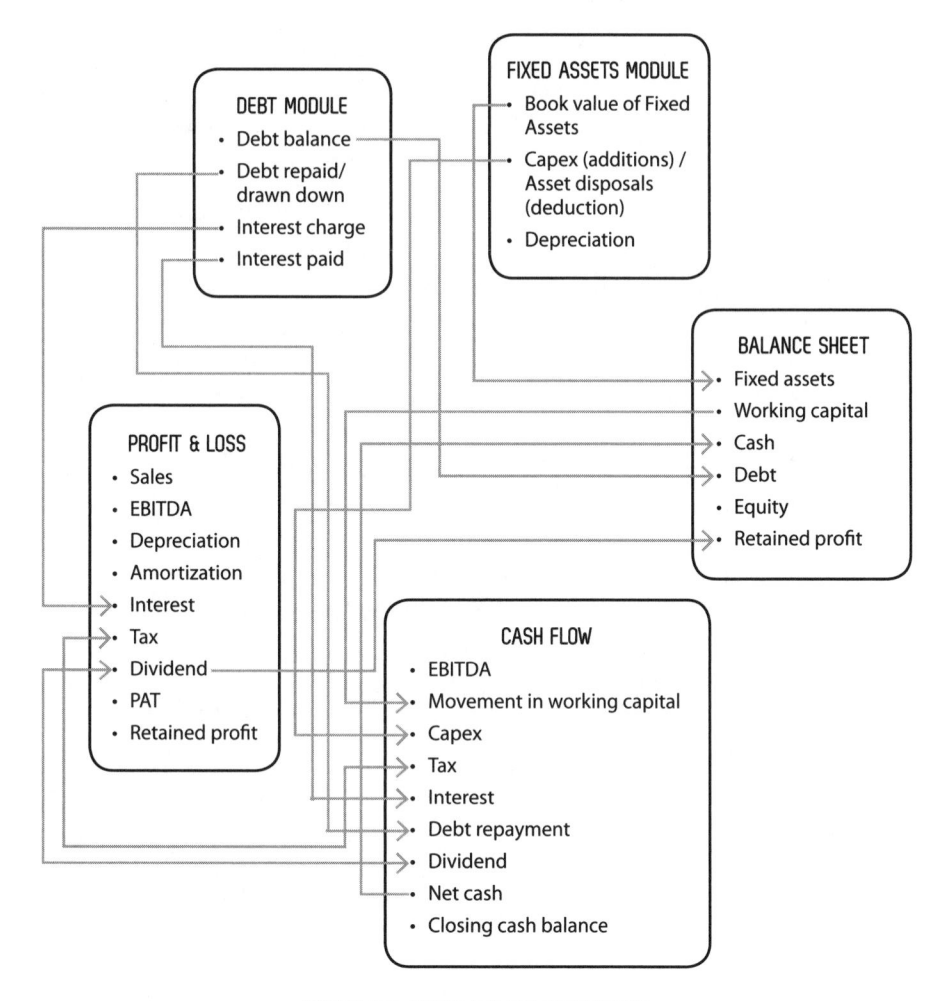

FIGURE 8.5 MODEL CALCULATIONS MAP

8.8 MODEL ASSUMPTIONS

It is useful to state all the key assumptions made in the model. These include the following:

- Interest charge is paid the same year.
- Tax charge is paid the same year.
- Dividend charge is paid the same year.
- There are no increases or reductions in share capital.
- There is no disposal of assets.
- There are no intangibles (and therefore no amortization thereof).

8.9 ADDING THE CALCULATION MODULES TO THE INPUTS & WORKINGS SHEET _____

The Inputs & Workings sheet contains the inputs already. Having gone through *how* the model calculations would work, we can now add the different calculation modules to the Inputs & Workings sheet.

8.9.1 Profit and Loss Module

Let's create the Profit and Loss section right below the Assumptions section in the Inputs & Calculations sheet, say on row 36. We can now add the different lines of the Profit and Loss statement following the specifications described earlier.

Sales

- We can write in cell I38 (column I is the column for the first period, or Year 1) the formula "=IF(I$2=1,I6,H38*(1+I7))", which basically means that if we are in Year 1, then sales = sales_ year 1 (which is $6 million); otherwise, sales = sales from the previous year times (1 + sales growth % for the current year).

Gross profit

- We can write in cell I39 the formula "=I$38*I8", which is saying that gross profit equals sales times gross profit margin.

EBITDA

- We can write in cell I40 the formula "=I$38*I9", which says that EBITDA equals sales times the EBITDA margin.

EBITDA growth

- We can write in cell I41 the formula "=IF(I$2=1,"",I40/H40–1)", which calculates the year-over-year annual growth from Year 2 onward. The IF formula ensures that if we are in Year 1, then the year-over-year growth is not applicable, and so the answer is "", which is Excel's formula for an empty cell.

Depreciation

- We can write in cell I42 the formula "= –I13", which picks up the opposite of the corresponding value of depreciation from row 13, hence the negative sign. This reminds us that whereas sales and gross profit are positive in that they increase the profitability of the project, depreciation goes in the opposite direction (that is, it is a cost to the project).

EBIT

- We can write in cell I43 the formula "=I40+I42", which calculates the profit (or earnings) before interest and taxes as EBITDA less depreciation. Note that EBIT is defined as EBITDA less depreciation and amortization. Since there is no amortization, EBIT is simply EBITDA less depreciation.

Interest

- As illustrated in the model calculation map in Figure 8.5, the interest charge is calculated in the Debt module. So we skip the interest line for now.

EBT

- We can write in cell I45 the formula "=I43+I44", which calculates EBT as EBIT less interest (note that interest will be negative, as it reduces profit—that is, it is a cost to the business).

Taxes

- We can write in cell I46 the formula "=–IF(I45>0,$F$14*I45,0)", which calculates the taxes as tax rate times EBT if EBT is positive. In other words, taxes are incurred only if the project recorded a profit.

PAT

- We can write in cell I47 the formula "=I46+I45", which calculates PAT as EBT less taxes.

Dividend

- We can skip the formula for now, as the dividend is applicable only after the debt has been fully repaid. We will update the dividend line once the Debt module has been completed.

Net profit

- We can write in cell I49 the formula "=I47+I48", which calculates net profit as PAT less dividend.

Retained profit b/f

- We can write in cell I50 the formula "=IF(I$2=1,$F$33,H51)", which means that if we are in Year 1, then the retained profit brought forward equals the retained profit from the opening balance sheet. Otherwise, retained profit brought forward equals the retained profit carried forward at the end of the previous period.

Retained profit c/f

- We can write in cell I51 the formula "=I50+I49", which calculates the retained profit carried forward as the retained profit brought forward plus net profit.

Copy cells I38:I51 and paste them into the block I38:R51. The Profit and Loss module is illustrated in Figure 8.6.

					1	2	3	4	5	6	7	8	9	10
The Phone Factory														
Integrated Financial Model ($m)	Annual													
Net assets		3.0												
Share capital		3.0												
Retained profit														
Net worth		3.0												
Profit and Loss														
Sales					6.0	15.0	30.0	45.0	58.5	70.2	77.2	83.4	90.1	97.3
Gross profit					4.8	12.0	24.0	36.0	46.8	56.2	61.8	66.7	72.1	77.8
EBITDA					2.7	6.8	12.0	15.8	17.6	21.1	23.2	25.0	27.0	29.2
EBITDA growth						150%	78%	31%	11%	20%	10%	8%	8%	8%
Depreciation					(0.4)	(0.4)	(0.4)	(0.4)	(0.4)	(0.4)	(0.4)	(0.4)	(0.4)	(0.4)
EBIT					2.3	6.4	11.6	15.4	17.2	20.7	22.8	24.6	26.6	28.8
Interest														
EBT					2.3	6.4	11.6	15.4	17.2	20.7	22.8	24.6	26.6	28.8
Tax					(0.7)	(1.9)	(3.5)	(4.6)	(5.1)	(6.2)	(6.8)	(7.4)	(8.0)	(8.6)
PAT					1.6	4.4	8.1	10.7	12.0	14.5	15.9	17.2	18.6	20.1
Dividend														
Net profit					1.6	4.4	8.1	10.7	12.0	14.5	15.9	17.2	18.6	20.1
Retained profit b/f					0.0	1.6	6.1	14.2	24.9	36.9	51.4	67.3	84.6	103.2
Retained profit c/f					1.6	6.1	14.2	24.9	36.9	51.4	67.3	84.6	103.2	123.3

FIGURE 8.6 PROFIT AND LOSS MODULE

Note that the profit and loss figures in Figure 8.6 are not yet final, as the interest and dividend lines have not been completed.

8.9.2 Debt Module

Let's create the Debt module right below the Profit and Loss module in the Inputs & Workings sheet, say on row 53. We can now run a control account for the principal and a control account for the interest in line with the specifications described earlier.

Debt Control Account

Debt balance b/f

- In cell I56, we can write the formula "=IF(I$2=1,–$F$29,H59)", which basically means that if we are in Year 1, then the debt brought forward is equal to the debt amount in the opening balance sheet (which is in cell F29). Otherwise, debt brought forward is equal to debt carried forward from the previous year.

Debt drawdown

- In cell I57, we can write the formula "=I19", which basically picks up the debt drawdown amount from row 19.

Debt repayment

- In cell I58, we can write the formula "=–I18", which basically picks up the opposite of the entry in row 18 (debt repaid). Note the importance of including the negative sign for debt repayment. Whereas debt drawdown increases the debt balance outstanding, debt repaid will reduce the debt balance outstanding; hence the need to use a negative sign.
- Debt balance c/f
    - In cell I59, we can write the formula "=SUM (I56:I58)", which basically calculates the debt carried forward as debt brought forward plus debt drawdown less debt repaid.

Interest Control Account

Interest b/f

- In cell I62, we can write the formula "=H65", which basically means that interest brought forward equals interest carried forward from the previous year.

Interest charge

- In cell I63, we can write the formula "=SUM(I56:I57)*$F$17", which calculates the interest charge as the sum of the debt balance brought forward plus the debt drawdown times the annual interest rate (which is in cell F17).

Interest paid

- In cell I64, we can write the formula "=–I63", which reflects our assumption that interest charged (or incurred) is paid in the same year. Note the importance of including the negative sign for interest paid. Like debt repayment in the debt control account, the effect of interest paid on the interest balance is the opposite of that of the interest charge.

Interest c/f

- In cell I65, we can write the formula "=SUM(I62:I64)", which basically calculates interest carried forward as interest brought forward plus interest charge less interest paid.

Copy cells I56:I65 and paste them into the block I56:R65.

8.9.3 Fixed Assets Module

Let's create the Fixed Assets module right below the Debt module, say on row 67. We can now run a control account for the fixed assets in line with the specifications described earlier.

Fixed Assets Control Account

Fixed assets balance b/f

- In cell I68, we can write the formula "=IF(I$2=1,$F$26,H71)", which basically means that if we are in Year 1, then fixed assets brought forward is equal to the fixed assets amount in the opening balance sheet (which is in cell F26). Otherwise, fixed assets brought forward equals fixed assets carried forward from the previous year.

Capex

- In cell I69, we can write the formula "=I10*I38", which basically calculates capex as capex as a percent of sales times the sales figure.

Depreciation

- In cell I70, we can write the formula "=I42", which basically picks up the depreciation amount from the Profit and Loss module. Note the importance of including the negative sign for depreciation. Whereas capex increases the book value (value on the balance sheet) of the fixed assets, depreciation has the opposite effect on their book value. Because the content of cell I42 is already a negative number, there is no need to add another negative sign to it (if we did, we would count depreciation as positive for the book value of fixed assets, which would be incorrect).

Fixed assets balance c/f

▪ In cell I71, we can write the formula "=SUM(I68:I70)", which basically calculates fixed assets carried forward as being equal to fixed assets brought forward plus capex less depreciation.

Copy cells I68:I71 and paste them into the block I68:R71. The Debt and Fixed Assets modules are illustrated in Figure 8.7.

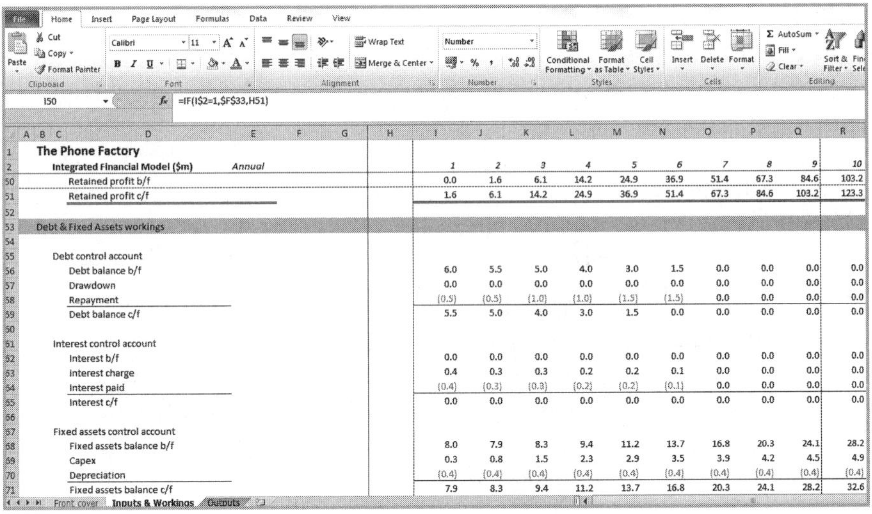

FIGURE 8.7 DEBT AND FIXED ASSETS MODULES

Note:

Now that the Debt module has been completed, we can go back to the Profit and Loss module and complete the interest and dividend lines as follows:

Interest

▪ In cell I44, we can write the formula "=−I63", which picks up the interest charge from the Debt module. Interest is a cost in the Profit and Loss module; hence the negative sign.

Dividend

- In cell I48, we can write the formula "=–IF(I56>0,0,I47*$F$22)", which means that the dividend is 0 if the debt balance is positive. Otherwise, the dividend equals PAT times the dividend payout. Just like interest, the dividend is a cost in the Profit and Loss module; hence the negative sign.
- Copy cell I44 and paste it into the block I44:R44 for interest. Copy cell I48 and paste it into the block I48:R48 for dividend.
- This portion of the revised Profit and Loss module is illustrated in Figure 8.8.

The Phone Factory										
Integrated Financial Model ($m)	Annual	1	2	3	4	5	6	7	8	9	10
Interest		(0.4)	(0.3)	(0.3)	(0.2)	(0.2)	(0.1)	0.0	0.0	0.0	0.0
EBT		1.9	6.0	11.3	15.1	17.0	20.6	22.8	24.6	26.6	28.8
Tax		(0.6)	(1.8)	(3.4)	(4.5)	(5.1)	(6.2)	(6.8)	(7.4)	(8.0)	(8.6)
PAT		1.4	4.2	7.9	10.6	11.9	14.4	15.9	17.2	18.6	20.1
Dividend		0.0	0.0	0.0	0.0	0.0	0.0	(8.0)	(8.6)	(9.3)	(10.1)
Net profit		1.4	4.2	7.9	10.6	11.9	14.4	8.0	8.6	9.3	10.1
Retained profit b/f		0.0	1.4	5.6	13.5	24.1	35.9	50.3	58.3	66.9	76.2
Retained profit c/f		1.4	5.6	13.5	24.1	35.9	50.3	58.3	66.9	76.2	86.3
Debt & Fixed Assets workings											
Debt control account											
Debt balance b/f		6.0	5.5	5.0	4.0	3.0	1.5	0.0	0.0	0.0	0.0
Drawdown		0.0	0.0	0.0	0.0	0.0	0.0	0.0	0.0	0.0	0.0
Repayment		(0.5)	(0.5)	(1.0)	(1.0)	(1.5)	(1.5)	0.0	0.0	0.0	0.0
Debt balance c/f		5.5	5.0	4.0	3.0	1.5	0.0	0.0	0.0	0.0	0.0
Interest control account											
Interest b/f		0.0	0.0	0.0	0.0	0.0	0.0	0.0	0.0	0.0	0.0
Interest charge		0.4	0.3	0.3	0.2	0.2	0.1	0.0	0.0	0.0	0.0
Interest paid		(0.4)	(0.3)	(0.3)	(0.2)	(0.2)	(0.1)	0.0	0.0	0.0	0.0
Interest c/f		0.0	0.0	0.0	0.0	0.0	0.0	0.0	0.0	0.0	0.0

FIGURE 8.8 PORTION OF THE REVISED PROFIT AND LOSS MODULE

8.9.4 Balance Sheet Module

Let's create the Balance Sheet module right below the Debt and Fixed Assets modules in the Inputs & Workings sheet, say on row 73. We can now add the different lines of the balance sheet following the specifications described earlier.

Fixed assets

- In cell I75, we can write the formula "=I71", which picks up the book value of fixed assets from the Fixed Assets module.

Working capital

- In cell I76, we can write the formula "=I11*I38", which calculates working capital as working capital as a percentage of sales times sales.

Cash

- We skip cash for now, as we have yet to complete the Cash Flow module.

Debt

- In cell I78, we can write the formula "= –I59", which picks up the opposite of the debt balance carried forward from the Debt module. Note that debt is shown as negative, as it is a liability, whereas fixed assets is shown as positive, as it is an asset.

Net assets

- In cell I79, we can write the formula "=SUM(I75:I78)", which calculates net assets as equal to fixed assets plus working capital plus cash less debt.

Share capital

- In cell I81, we can write the formula "=$F$32", which picks up share capital from the opening balance sheet.

Retained profit c/f

- In cell I82, we can write the formula "=I51", which picks up retained profit (retained earnings) carried forward from the Profit and Loss module.

Net worth

- In cell I83, we can write the formula "=SUM(I81:I82)", which calculates net worth as equal to share capital plus retained profit carried forward.

Balance

- In cell I85, we can write the formula "=I79–I83", which calculates the difference between net assets and net worth. This is for the purpose of checking whether the balance sheet balances.

Balance sheet error check

- In cell I86, we can write the formula "=IF(ABS(I85)<=0.01, TRUE,FALSE)", which shows TRUE if the absolute value of the difference between net assets and net worth is less than or equal to 0.01. Otherwise, the formula shows FALSE.
- In addition to calculating the balance sheet check in cell I86, we also run a conditional formatting in cell I86 such that the cell takes on a green background when the value of the cell is TRUE. Otherwise, the cell's background is red. An example of conditional formatting is given in Chapter 6 (Section 6.4).

Copy cells I75:I86 and paste them into the block I75:R86. The Balance Sheet module is illustrated in Figure 8.9.

	1	2	3	4	5	6	7	8	9	10
The Phone Factory										
Integrated Financial Model ($m)	*Annual*									
Fixed assets control account										
Fixed assets balance b/f	8.0	7.9	8.3	9.4	11.2	13.7	16.8	20.3	24.1	28.2
Capex	0.3	0.8	1.5	2.3	2.9	3.5	3.9	4.2	4.5	4.9
Depreciation	(0.4)	(0.4)	(0.4)	(0.4)	(0.4)	(0.4)	(0.4)	(0.4)	(0.4)	(0.4)
Fixed assets balance c/f	7.9	8.3	9.4	11.2	13.7	16.8	20.3	24.1	28.2	32.6
Balance Sheet										
Fixed assets	7.9	8.3	9.4	11.2	13.7	16.8	20.3	24.1	28.2	32.6
Working capital	1.2	3.0	6.0	9.0	11.7	14.0	15.4	16.7	18.0	19.5
Cash										
Debt	(5.5)	(5.0)	(4.0)	(3.0)	(1.5)	0.0	0.0	0.0	0.0	0.0
Net assets	3.60	6.25	11.35	17.20	23.93	30.88	35.74	40.75	46.18	52.09
Share capital	3.00	3.00	3.00	3.00	3.00	3.00	3.00	3.00	3.00	3.00
Retained profit c/f	1.4	5.6	13.5	24.1	35.9	50.3	58.3	66.9	76.2	86.3
Net worth	4.4	8.6	16.5	27.1	38.9	53.3	61.3	69.9	79.2	89.3
Balance										
	(0.8)	(2.3)	(5.1)	(9.9)	(15.0)	(22.5)	(25.6)	(29.2)	(33.1)	(37.2)
	FALSE	*FALSE*	*FALSE*	*FALSE*	*FALSE*	*FALSE*	*FALSE*	*FALSE*	*FALSE*	*FALSE*

FIGURE 8.9 BALANCE SHEET MODULE

Note:

The balance sheet figures are not yet final, as the cash line has not yet been completed.

8.9.5 Cash Flow Module

Let's create the Cash Flow module right below the Balance Sheet module in the Inputs & Workings sheet, say on row 88. We can now add the different lines of the Cash Flow module following the specifications described earlier.

EBITDA

- In cell I90, we can write the formula "=I40", which picks up the EBITDA figure from the Profit and Loss module.

Movement in working capital

- In cell I91, we can write the formula "=H76–I76", which calculates the movement in working capital as working capital at the end of the previous period (H76) less working capital at the end of the current period (I76).

Operating cash flow

- In cell I92, we can write the formula "=I91+I90", which calculates the operating cash flow as EBITDA (I90) plus movement in working capital (I91).

Capex

- In cell I93, we can write the formula "= –I69", which picks up capex as the opposite of the capex figure in the Fixed Assets module.

Cash flow before taxation and financing

- In cell I94, we can write the formula "=I93+I92", which calculates cash flow before taxation and financing as operating cash flow plus capex. Note that since capex is shown in the Cash Flow module as a negative number (that is, a cash outflow), the capex figure is added to (hence the + sign), rather than deducted from, operating cash flow.

Taxes

- In cell I95, we can write the formula "=I46", which picks up taxes from the Profit and Loss module. We assume that taxes are paid the year in which they are incurred.

Cash flow available for debt service

- In cell I96, we can write the formula "=I95+I94", which calculates cash flow available for debt service as cash flow before taxation and financing plus taxes.

Interest

- In cell I97, we can write the formula "=I64", which picks up interest from the Debt module.

Debt repayment

- In cell I98, we can write the formula "=I58", which picks up the amount of debt repaid from the Debt module.

Cash flow available for shareholders

- In cell I99, we can write the formula "=SUM(I96:I98)", which calculates cash flow available for shareholders as cash flow available for debt service plus interest plus debt repayment. Note that since debt repayment and interest are shown as negative numbers (cash outflows), they are added to (hence the + sign), rather than deducted from, cash flow available for debt service.

Dividend

- In cell I100, we can write the formula "=I48", which picks up the dividend from the Profit and Loss module.

Net cash flow

- In cell I101, we can write the formula "=I100+I99", which calculates net cash flow as cash flow available for shareholders plus dividend. Note that since the dividend, when it is not zero, is shown as a negative number (a cash outflow), it is added to (hence the + sign), rather than deducted from, cash flow available for shareholders.

Cash balance b/f

- In cell I102, we can write the formula "=IF(I$2=1,$F$28,H103)", which calculates cash balance brought forward as the cash balance in the opening balance sheet (F28) if we are in period 1. Otherwise, cash balance brought forward is equal to the cash balance carried forward in the previous period.

Cash balance c/f

- In cell I103, we can write the formula "=I102+I101", which calculates the cash balance carried forward as the cash balance brought forward plus net cash flow.

Copy cells I90:I103 and paste them into the block I90:R103. The Cash Flow module is illustrated in Figure 8.10.

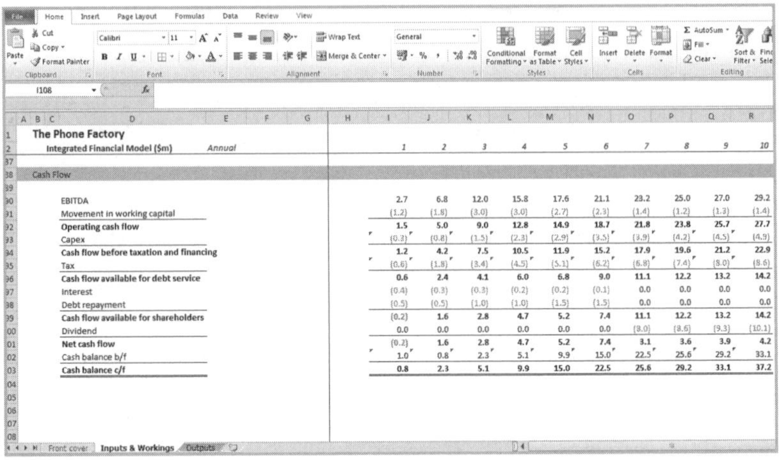

The Phone Factory
Integrated Financial Model ($m) — Annual

Cash Flow	1	2	3	4	5	6	7	8	9	10
EBITDA	2.7	6.8	12.0	15.8	17.6	21.1	23.2	25.0	27.0	29.2
Movement in working capital	(1.2)	(1.8)	(3.0)	(3.0)	(2.7)	(2.3)	(1.4)	(1.2)	(1.3)	(1.4)
Operating cash flow	1.5	5.0	9.0	12.8	14.9	18.7	21.8	23.8	25.7	27.7
Capex	(0.3)	(0.8)	(1.5)	(2.3)	(2.9)	(3.5)	(3.9)	(4.2)	(4.5)	(4.9)
Cash flow before taxation and financing	1.2	4.2	7.5	10.5	11.9	15.2	17.9	19.6	21.2	22.9
Tax	(0.6)	(1.8)	(3.4)	(4.5)	(5.1)	(6.2)	(6.8)	(7.4)	(8.0)	(8.6)
Cash flow available for debt service	0.6	2.4	4.1	6.0	6.8	9.0	11.1	12.2	13.2	14.2
Interest	(0.4)	(0.3)	(0.3)	(0.2)	(0.2)	(0.1)	0.0	0.0	0.0	0.0
Debt repayment	(0.5)	(0.5)	(1.0)	(1.0)	(1.5)	(1.5)	0.0	0.0	0.0	0.0
Cash flow available for shareholders	(0.2)	1.6	2.8	4.7	5.2	7.4	11.1	12.2	13.2	14.2
Dividend	0.0	0.0	0.0	0.0	0.0	0.0	(8.0)	(8.6)	(9.3)	(10.1)
Net cash flow	(0.2)	1.6	2.8	4.7	5.2	7.4	3.1	3.6	3.9	4.2
Cash balance b/f	1.0	0.8	2.3	5.1	9.9	15.0	22.5	25.6	29.2	33.1
Cash balance c/f	0.8	2.3	5.1	9.9	15.0	22.5	25.6	29.2	33.1	37.2

FIGURE 8.10 CASH FLOW MODULE

Note:

With the Cash Flow module now completed, we can go back to the Balance Sheet module and complete the cash line as follows:

Cash

- In cell I77, we can write the formula "=I103", which picks up the cash balance carried forward from the Cash Flow module.

  Copy cell I77 and paste it into the block I77:R77.

Overall balance sheet check

- Since we are in the Balance Sheet module, let us create an overall balance sheet check in the frozen pane area of the Inputs & Workings sheet, say in row 1.

  Write "Balance sheet check" in cell P1. Copy any cell in the block I86:R86 and paste it into cell R1. This copies the conditional formatting in the block I86:R86 as well as the formula in the selected cell in the block I86:R86. Then write in cell R1 the formula "=AND(I86:R86)", which calculates the Boolean value of applying the AND function on cells I86 through R86. If all these cells have a value of TRUE, then AND(I86:R86) will also be TRUE. However, if at least one of these cells has a value of FALSE, then AND(I86:R86) will be FALSE.

Having the balance sheet check located in the frozen pane area means that we have a permanent display of the balance sheet status. The revised Balance Sheet module is shown in Figure 8.11.

FIGURE 8.11 REVISED BALANCE SHEET

Notes:

- The balance sheet balances can be seen in the block I86:R86.
- The balance sheet check also shows this in cell R1.

8.10 CREATING THE OUTPUTS SHEET

Having completed all the necessary calculations, we are now ready to bring together the key results from our calculations into the Outputs sheet.

The key outputs are the profit and loss statement, the balance sheet, and the cash flow statement.

- Copy the "Inputs & Workings" sheet, rename it Outputs, and color it green. This way, the Outputs sheet initially has the same content as the Inputs & Workings sheet. We will then delete the elements of the Inputs & Workings sheet that are not going to be included in the Outputs sheet.
- Since the main outputs are the profit and loss statement, the balance sheet, and the cash flow statement, we will link the Profit and Loss, Balance Sheet, and Cash Flow modules in the Outputs sheet to the corresponding Profit and Loss, Balance Sheet, and Cash Flow modules in the Inputs & Workings sheet.

To do the linking, we can select the first cell in the Profit and Loss module, cell I38, in the Outputs sheet and write in it the formula "='Inputs & Workings'!I38".

- Link the Profit and Loss module in the Outputs sheet to the corresponding Profit and Loss module in the Inputs & Workings sheet. To do this, copy cell I38 and paste its formula into the block I38:R51. This can be done using the following keyboard short cut:

  - Select cell I38 and type CTRL+C (that is, press and hold the CTRL key, then, with CTRL pressed down, type C). This copies cell I38.
  - Select block I38:R51 and type ALT, then E, then S. This pops the Paste Special window, which is shown in Figure 8.12.
  - Select the Formulas option, circled in Figure 8.12, using the down arrow on the keyboard.
  - Confirm the selected option by typing the ENTER or RETURN key or clicking the OK button.

- Link the Balance Sheet module in the Outputs sheet to the corresponding Balance Sheet module in the Inputs & Workings sheet. To do this, copy cell I75 and paste its formula into block I75:R79, block I81:R83, and block I85:R86.

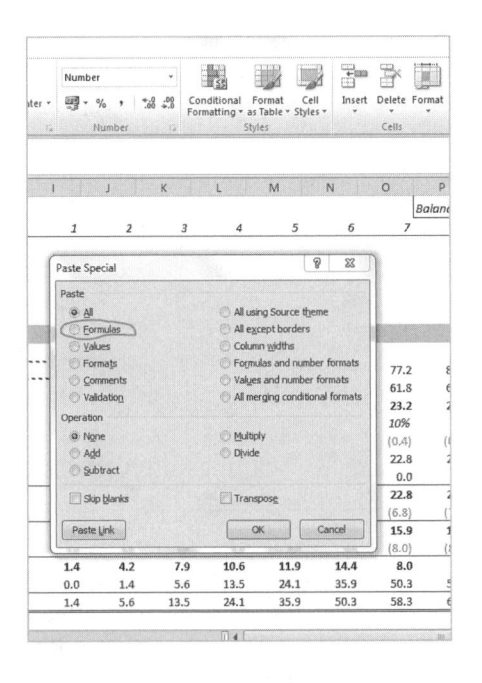

FIGURE 8.12 PASTE SPECIAL FORMULA

- To link the Cash Flow module in the Outputs sheet to the corresponding Cash Flow module in the Inputs & Workings sheet, paste the formula (note that the formula in cell I75 is still in Copy) into the block I90:R103.
- Select rows 3 to 35 and delete the entire block. This now brings the Profit and Loss module right to the top at row 3.
- Delete the Debt and Fixed Assets modules by selecting and deleting rows 20 to 39. This now brings the Balance Sheet module to row 20 with the Cash Flow module starting in row 35.

Let us make a few minor adjustments to make the Outputs sheet more user friendly.

- Add an "end of sheet" divider at the bottom of the Cash Flow module. To do this, copy row 35 (the row with the Cash Flow title) and insert it in row 52. Then rename the title as End of Sheet.
- We also include a sales growth line, a gross profit margin line, and an EBITDA margin line in the profit and loss section of the Outputs sheet. To this end, we need to insert a row below sales, a row below gross profit, and a row below EBITDA, which we name "Sales growth", "Gross profit margin", and "EBITDA margin", respectively.
- For sales growth, in cell I6, we write the formula "=IF(I2=1,"",'Inputs & Workings'!I7)", which copies the corresponding sales growth figure from the Inputs & Workings sheet.
- Furthermore, we write in cell S6 formula "=(R5/I5)^(1/R2)–1", which calculates the compounded annual growth rate (CAGR) for sales from Year 1 to Year 10.
- Similarly, for gross profit margin, we write in cell I8 the formula "='Inputs & Workings'!I8".
- And similarly, for EBITDA margin, we write in cell I10 the formula "='Inputs & Workings'!I9".
- Furthermore, we write in cell S11 the formula "=(R9/I9)^(1/R2)–1" to calculate the CAGR of EBITDA from Year 1 to Year 10.

Copy cell I6 and paste it into the block I6:R6. Copy cell I8 and paste it into the block I8:R8. Copy cell I10 and paste it into the block I10:R10.

The resulting Outputs sheet is shown in Figures 8.13 through 8.15. First we show the profit and loss statement (Figure 8.13).

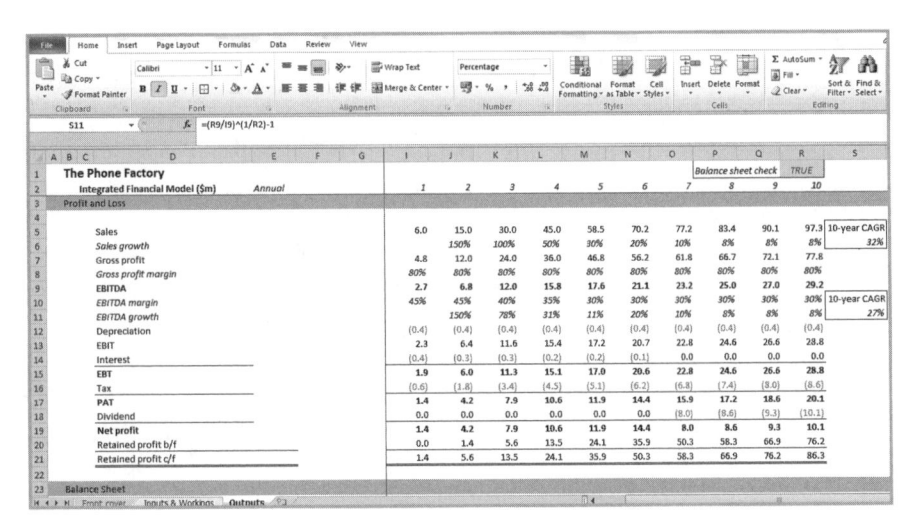

FIGURE 8.13 PROFIT AND LOSS OUTPUT

Next we show the balance sheet (Figure 8.14).

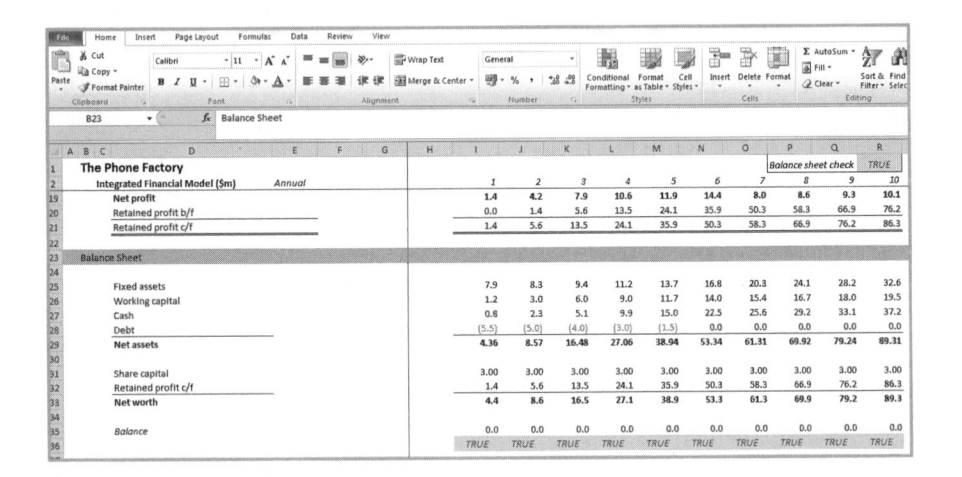

FIGURE 8.14 BALANCE SHEET OUTPUT

Finally, we show the cash flow statement (Figure 8.15).

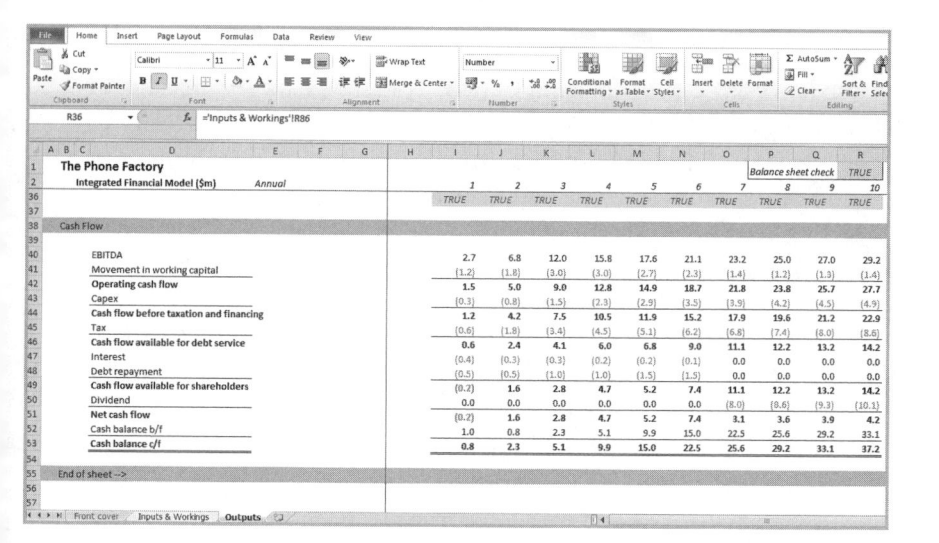

FIGURE 8.15 CASH FLOW OUTPUT

8.11 ANALYSIS

8.11.1 Profit and Loss

- The projections reflect a business that is growing fast, with sales projected to grow at a compounded annual growth rate of 32 percent from Year 1 to Year 10.
- The business is projected to be profitable as well, with an average EBITDA margin of 35 percent over the projection period (that is, the EBITDA margins for Year 1 through to Year 10 average at 35 percent).
- EBITDA is projected to grow at a CAGR of 27 percent over the projection period.

8.11.2 Balance Sheet

- Debt is repaid within five years.
- Net worth builds up well over the projected period to reach $89.3 million at the end of Year 10.

8.11.3 Cash Flow

- The business is projected to be very cash generative. Total operating cash flow generated over the 10-year period is projected to amount to $160.7 million (that is, the sum of operating cash flows from Year 1 through to Year 10 equals $160.7 million).
- Free cash flow available for shareholders totals $72.2 million over the 10-year period. However, please note that there is insufficient cash generation in Year 1 to meet all cash expenditures that year, resulting in –$0.2 million. This cash shortfall of $0.2 million is met by drawing down from the opening cash balance of $1 million. As a result, the closing cash balance at the end of Year 1 is $0.8 million.
- The closing cash balance at the end of Year 10 is projected to reach $37.2 million.

CHAPTER NINE

CASE STUDY 4:

Growth Capital

Let us take our model building one step further. In this chapter, we introduce our fourth case study, investing money in a growth business. This is often known as a growth equity, a growth capital, or a development capital story. A number of investors focus on investment opportunities of this type. In such an investment opportunity, the investor is looking for businesses that require additional development capital to fully realize their growth potential. The business might be at a stage where it is profitable, but further capital is needed in order to scale the business up.

Such businesses can be found in a variety of sectors. Our particular case study involves a textile manufacturing company.

Having built the business from scratch four years ago, the founder has taken it to a point where it is now profitable. Demand for the company's textile products is very strong, and the company needs further capital to pay down a burdensome debt that was initially provided by a nonbank third party and was taken on to finance the early-stage development of the business. Further capital is also required to repay a bank overdraft facility and endow the business with much-needed cash in the short term.

The founder has invited your investment firm to consider financing the next phase of growth of the business and has provided key inputs concerning operational assumptions (revenue; earnings before interest, taxes, depreciation, and amortization [EBITDA]; working capital;

and capital expenditures). You have been leading discussions with the founder on behalf of your firm, and the key terms of your proposed investment have been agreed upon. The inputs are summarized here, and you will need to build a five-year integrated financial model that includes the profit and loss statement, the balance sheet, and the cash flow statement. In addition to this, you'll need to calculate the initial financial returns on your proposed investment to see whether the project makes financial sense for your firm.

9.1 KEY INPUTS

Operational inputs are given in Table 9.1.

TABLE 9.1 OPERATIONAL INPUTS

Year	0	1	2	3	4	5	6	7	8	9	10
Sales	57.0										
EBITDA	9.5										
Sales growth %		10%	10%	8%	8%	8%	4%	4%	4%	4%	4%
EBITDA margin		16%	17%	18%	18%	18%	18%	18%	18%	18%	18%
Stock (inventory in U.S. usage) as % of sales		10%	10%	10%	10%	10%	10%	10%	10%	10%	10%
Trade debtors (accounts receivable) as % of sales		17%	17%	17%	17%	17%	17%	17%	17%	17%	17%
Trade creditors (accounts payable) as % of sales		20%	20%	20%	20%	20%	20%	20%	20%	20%	20%
Other creditors as % of sales		8%	8%	8%	8%	8%	8%	8%	8%	8%	8%
Capex as % of sales		5%	5%	5%	5%	5%	4%	4%	3%	3%	3%
Corporation (corporate) tax		28%	28%	28%	28%	28%	28%	28%	28%	28%	28%
Depreciation		–1.5	–1.5	–1.5	–1.5	–1.5	–1.5	–1.5	–1.5	–1.5	–1.5
Term loan A (TLA) repayment		–1.0	–1.0	–1.0	–1.0	–1.0					

- *Historical Sales and EBITDA.* For now, limited historical financial information has been provided, namely the most recent historical sales and EBITDA.

- *Sales growth %.* Sales growth projections have been provided for the next five years, after which revenue is projected to grow with inflation.
- *EBITDA %.* EBITDA margin is projected to improve over the next two years and stabilize thereafter at 18 percent.
- *Stock.* This is projected to be 10 percent of sales.
- *Trade debtors.* This is projected to be 17 percent of sales.
- *Trade creditors.* This is projected to be 20 percent of sales.
- *Other creditors.* This is projected to be 8 percent of sales.
- *Capex.* This is projected to be 5 percent of sales.
- *Corporation tax.* This is projected to be 28 percent of profit before tax.
- *Depreciation.* This is assumed to be $1.5 million annually.
- *Term loan A.* There is an existing term loan balance (see sources and uses inputs in Table 9.2) that will be paid down using part of the proceeds from the new investment. Assuming that the balance remaining after paying down the term loan is $5 million, then the proposed amortization schedule is $1 million per year for the next five years (that is, the loan is projected to be fully repaid in five years).

TABLE 9.2 SOURCES AND USES (S&U) INPUTS

Uses	
Excess cash	10.00
Refinancing existing TLA	22.00
Fees	1.00
Total	33.00
Sources	
Ordinary shares	15.00
Loan stock	18.00
Total	33.00

- *Uses of funds.* The proposed investment is estimated at $33 million and would be used to:
  - Provide cash of $10 million to the business.
  - Pay down $22 million of the existing debt of $27 million (see balance sheet inputs in Figure 9.1).
  - Pay fees totaling $1 million related to processing the transaction to the investor.

- *Sources of funds.* The proposed investment would come from the following sources of funds:
  - Ordinary equity investment of $15 million (see the later discussion of the postmoney equity valuation).
  - Loan stock of $18 million (see the later discussion of the terms of the instruments).

Based on the predeal balance sheet and the sources and uses of funds, it is possible to determine the postdeal balance sheet. The predeal balance sheet is the balance sheet immediately prior to the transaction, and the postdeal balance sheet is the balance sheet immediately after the transaction. The postdeal balance sheet is the starting balance sheet for the financial projections. In particular, the projected balance sheet at the end of Year 1 depends on the postdeal balance sheet. Likewise, the Year 2 balance sheet will in turn depend on the Year 1 balance sheet. And so on and so forth.

The predeal balance sheet is presented on the left-hand side of Figure 9.1. Manual adjustments to the predeal balance sheet are made to reflect the sources and uses of funds. Then the postdeal balance sheet is calculated for each line of the predeal balance sheet by adding the adjustments to the predeal number. The adjustments are made as follows.

- *Uses of funds.* The proposed investment is estimated at $33 million and would be used to:
  - Provide cash of $10 million to the business. An amount of $10 million is included in the cash balance line. This amount will be added to the predeal cash balance of –$2.4 million to result in a postdeal cash balance of $7.6 million.
  - Pay down $22 million of the existing debt of $27 million. An amount of $22 million is included in the term loan A line. This amount will be deducted from the predeal term loan A balance of –$27 million to result in a postdeal term loan A balance of –$5 million.
  - Pay fees totaling $1 million related to processing the transaction to the investor. The transaction fees are capitalized (that is, they are added to the long-term assets of the company). An amount of $1 million is included in the transaction costs line. This amount will be added to the predeal transaction costs balance of 0 to result in a postdeal transaction costs balance of $1 million.
- *Sources of funds.* The proposed investment would come from the following sources of funds:

- Ordinary equity investment of $15 million. An amount of $15 million is included in the ordinary shares line. This amount will be added to the predeal ordinary shares balance of $9 million to result in a postdeal ordinary shares balance of $24 million.
- Loan stock of $18 million. An amount of $18 million is included in the loan stock line. This amount will be added to the predeal loan stock balance of 0 to result in a postdeal loan stock balance of –$18 million. Note that the negative sign reflects the chosen convention of showing liabilities in the balance sheet as negative numbers.

The resulting postdeal balance sheet is presented on the right-hand side of Figure 9.1. The postdeal balance sheet shows that, as a result of the transaction, the company's cash position has improved substantially, from a negative $2.4 million to a positive $7.6 million. The postdeal balance sheet also shows an increased equity capital base, up by $15 million to reach $24 million. The company's long-term liabilities have also changed to include loan stock of $18 million and also a reduction in the existing debt, which is down by $22 million to reach $5 million.

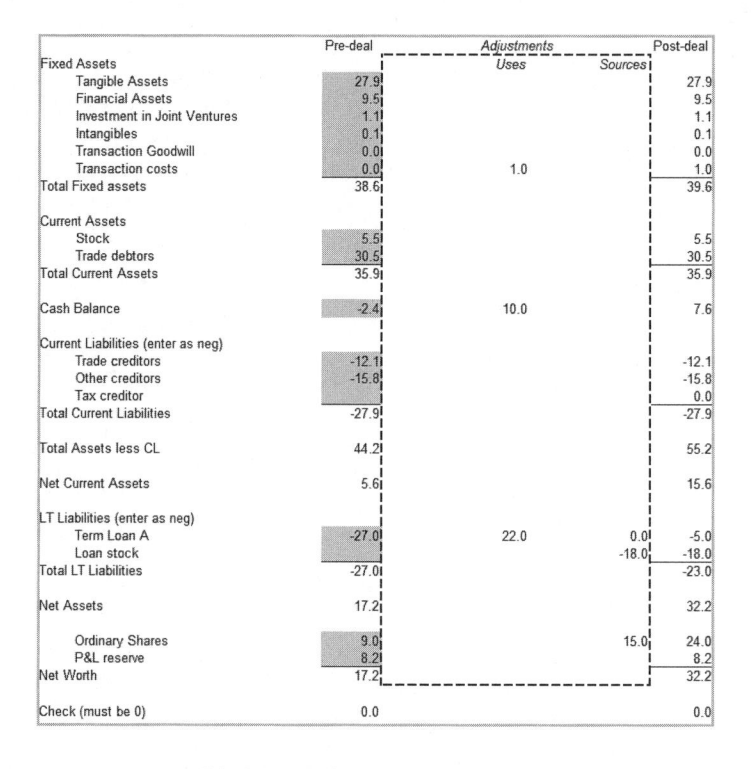

	Pre-deal	Adjustments		Post-deal
		Uses	Sources	
Fixed Assets				
Tangible Assets	27.9			27.9
Financial Assets	9.5			9.5
Investment in Joint Ventures	1.1			1.1
Intangibles	0.1			0.1
Transaction Goodwill	0.0			0.0
Transaction costs	0.0	1.0		1.0
Total Fixed assets	38.6			39.6
Current Assets				
Stock	5.5			5.5
Trade debtors	30.5			30.5
Total Current Assets	35.9			35.9
Cash Balance	-2.4	10.0		7.6
Current Liabilities (enter as neg)				
Trade creditors	-12.1			-12.1
Other creditors	-15.8			-15.8
Tax creditor				0.0
Total Current Liabilities	-27.9			-27.9
Total Assets less CL	44.2			55.2
Net Current Assets	5.6			15.6
LT Liabilities (enter as neg)				
Term Loan A	-27.0	22.0	0.0	-5.0
Loan stock			-18.0	-18.0
Total LT Liabilities	-27.0			-23.0
Net Assets	17.2			32.2
Ordinary Shares	9.0		15.0	24.0
P&L reserve	8.2			8.2
Net Worth	17.2			32.2
Check (must be 0)	0.0			0.0

FIGURE 9.1 POSTDEAL BALANCE SHEET

Post-money valuation	$m
Equity invested	15.0
% shares acquired	46%
Implied Equity value / Market Cap	32.4
Plus debt	23.0
Less cash	-7.6
Enterprise Value	47.8
# new shares acquired by investor	51,724
# outstanding shares at closing	60,000
Price per share ($)	290

FIGURE 9.2 POSTMONEY VALUATION

Postmoney Valuation

The proposed equity transaction is based on a share price of $290. As presented in Figure 9.2, this means that the investor would acquire 51,724 shares (that is, 15,000,000 divided by 290). Based on a total number of outstanding shares of 60,000 before the investment, the investor would acquire 46 percent of the company's equity (that is, 51,724 divided by [60,000 plus 51,724]). Acquiring 46 percent of the equity for $15 million means that 100 percent of the equity would be valued at $32.4 million (that is, $15 million divided by 46 percent). With the equity value at $32.4 million, the postdeal debt at $23 million (that is, $18 million loan stock plus $5 million term loan A), and the postdeal cash of $7.6 million, the enterprise value of the company is $47.8 million (that is, $32.4 million plus $23 million minus $7.6 million), giving an enterprise-value-to-EBITDA multiple for Year 0 of 5 times (that is, 47.8 divided by 9.5).

Investor Exit Assumptions

Exit assumptions are provided in Figure 9.3. The proposed investor exit time frame is five years from the date of the transaction. The exit enterprise-value-to-EBITDA multiple is assumed to be 8 times. This is an improvement from the entry enterprise-value-to-EBITDA multiple of 5 times, reflecting the view that the business will command a higher valuation in five years' time.

The transaction includes warrants giving the investor the option to increase its equity stake at the time of exit by purchasing an additional 4,000 shares at $385.7 per share (or a total of $1.5 million). The warrants are effectively a sweetener to the loan stock, enabling the company to reduce the interest it would otherwise be paying on the loan stock.

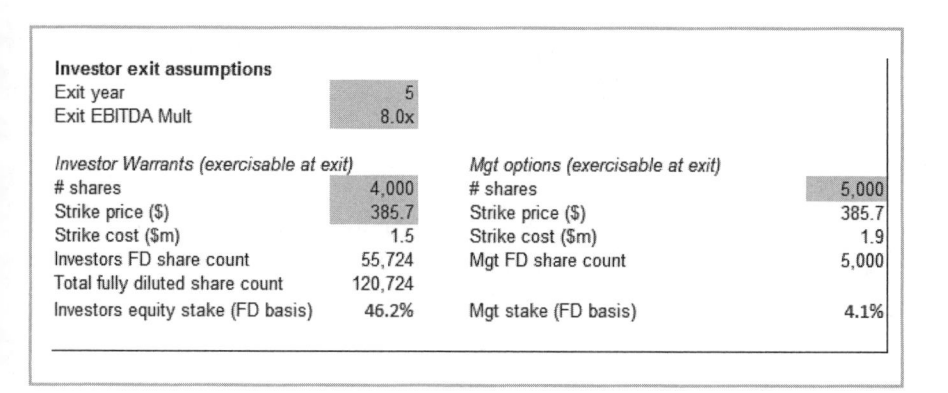

FIGURE 9.3 INVESTOR EXIT ASSUMPTIONS

Furthermore, management has been given an incentive to perform well through management options giving the management team the opportunity to acquire 5,000 shares at $385.7 per share (or a total of $1.9 million) at the time of the investor's exit.

If both the investor warrants and the management options are exercised, the total number of shares will be 120,724 (that is, 60,000 + 51,724 + 4,000 + 5,000) on a fully diluted basis. The investor's stake on a fully diluted basis will be 55,724 shares, or 46.2 percent (that is, 55,724 divided by 120,724).

Debt Assumptions

Term loan A has a five-year maturity and bears an interest rate of 12 percent per annum. Figure 9.4 shows new loans drawn down as part of the deal. For the term loan A there is 0 amount drawn down. In other words, there is no new drawdown of the term loan A. The amortization schedule was provided earlier and is $1 million per annum over five years.

The loan stock is a bullet loan with a nine-year maturity, bearing an interest rate of 20 percent per annum.

Debt assumptions				
Debt	Quantum	tenor		price
TLA	0.0	5		12.0%
Loan stock	18.0	9		20.0%

FIGURE 9.4 DEBT ASSUMPTIONS

Other Assumptions

- Interest is paid in the year in which it is incurred.
- Tax is paid a year after it has been incurred.
- Exit occurs at year-end.

9.1.1 Creating the Operational and Sources and Uses Inputs Sheets

Let's create the Operational Inputs sheet in which we capture these inputs starting from, say, row 7, as illustrated in Figure 9.5. The timeline is also shown on row 1 in Figure 9.5.

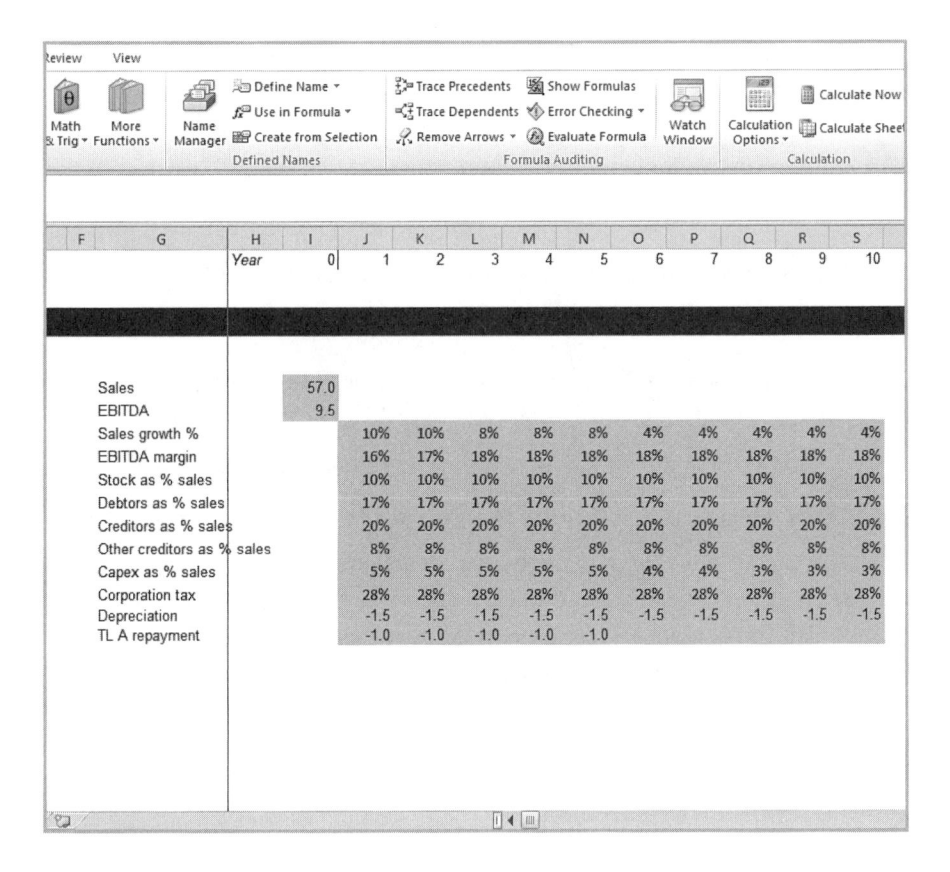

FIGURE 9.5

We can also create the Sources and Uses Inputs sheet, which captures all the key inputs described earlier. An illustration is shown in Figures 9.6 to 9.9.

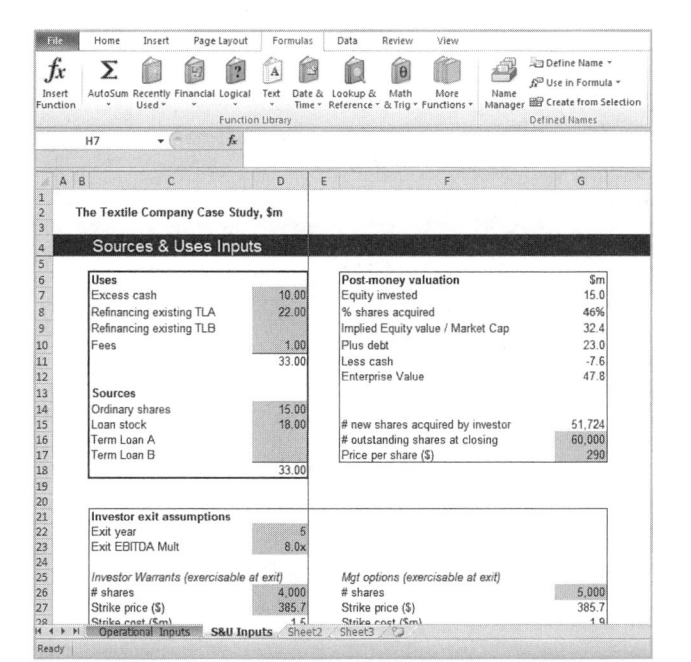

FIGURE 9.6

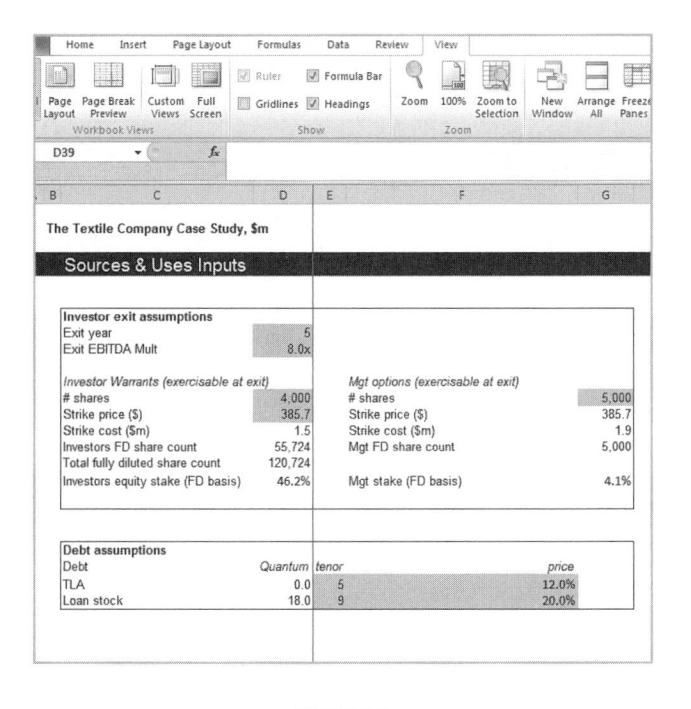

FIGURE 9.7

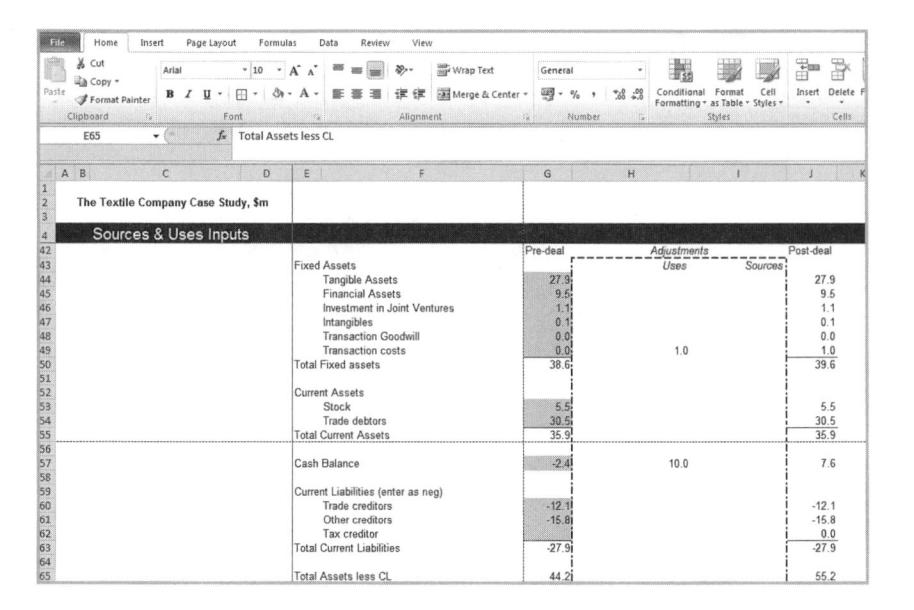

FIGURE 9.8

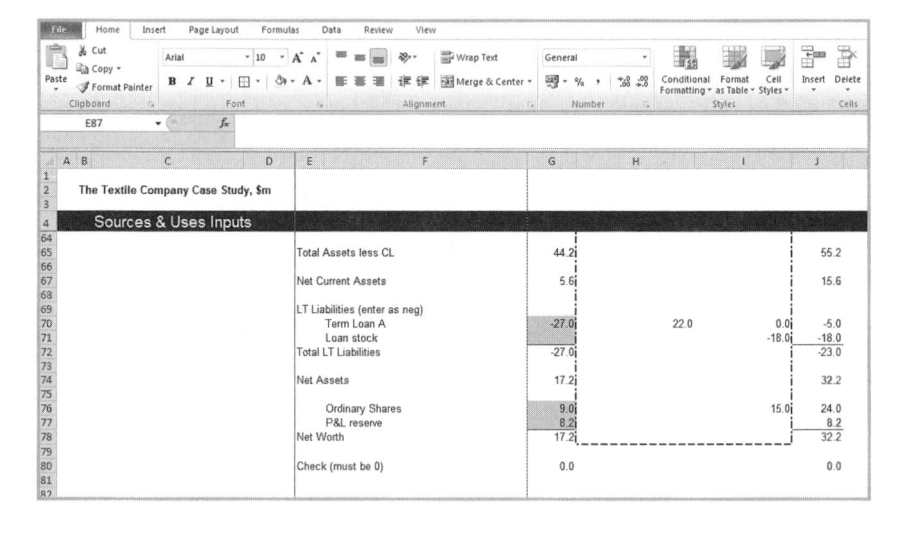

FIGURE 9.9

9.2 WRITING MODEL SPECIFICATIONS

Essentially, here we have two parts: the integrated financial model part (profit and loss statement, balance sheet, and cash flow statement) and the exit schedule. In Chapter 8, we learned to build an integrated financial model, and so for the first part of the model here, we can refer to the previous chapter. Once we have an integrated financial model, we can then build the exit schedule using a combination of the profit and loss statement, the balance sheet, and the cash flow statement.

9.2.1 Building the Integrated Financial Model

Profit and Loss Module
Sales

- Year 1 sales is given.
- Year-over-year sales growth is given.
- For each period of time t, calculate sales_t as sales_t–1 times (1 + sales growth_t).

EBITDA

- For each period of time t, calculate EBITDA_t as EBITDA margin_t times sales_t.

Depreciation

- This is given.

EBIT (Earnings Before Interest and Tax)

- For each period of time t, calculate EBIT_t as EBITDA_t minus Depreciation_t.

Interest

- For each period of time t, the interest charge will be calculated in the Debt module (discussed in the next section).
- Note that we will need to calculate interest for each debt instrument (term loan A and loan stock).

EBT (Earnings Before Tax)

- For each period of time t, calculate EBT_t as EBIT_t minus Interest_t.

Tax

- For each period of time t, calculate tax_t as tax rate times EBT_t if EBT_t is positive. Otherwise, tax_t = 0.

PAT (Profit After Tax)

- For each period of time t, calculate PAT_t as EBT_t minus tax_t.

Retained Profit (Retained Earnings in U.S. Usage)

- This will be calculated using a control account in which retained profit carried forward_t = retained profit brought forward_t plus PAT_t.
- Retained profit brought forward_t = retained profit carried forward_t–1.
- Retained profit brought forward_year 1 = retained profit carried forward in the opening balance sheet.

Debt Module

Since we have two debt instruments (term loan A and loan stock), we need to calculate the debt amounts and interest for each instrument.

The term loan A debt control account will be calculated as follows:

- Term loan A debt opening balance_t = term loan A debt closing balance_t–1, with term loan A debt opening balance_year 1 = term loan A debt balance in postdeal balance sheet.
- Term loan A debt drawdown_t = 0.
- Term loan A debt repayment_t is given in the amortization schedule.
- Term loan A debt closing balance_t = Term loan A debt opening balance_t plus term loan A debt drawdown_t plus term loan A debt repayment_t.

The term loan A interest control account will be calculated as follows:

- Term loan A interest opening balance_t = term loan A interest closing balance_t–1, with term loan A interest opening balance_year 1 = 0.
- Term loan A interest charge_t = term loan A interest rate times (term loan A debt opening balance_t plus term loan A debt drawdown_t).
- Term loan A interest paid_t = – term loan A interest charge_t.
- Term loan A interest closing balance_t = term loan A interest opening balance_t plus term loan A interest charge_t plus term loan A interest paid_t.

The Loan stock debt control account will be calculated as follows:

- Loan stock debt opening balance_t = loan stock debt closing balance_t–1, with loan stock debt opening balance_year 1 = loan stock debt balance in postdeal balance sheet.
- Loan stock debt drawdown_t = 0.
- Loan stock debt repayment_t = 0 if t is between 1 and 8; otherwise, loan stock debt repayment_t = – original loan stock amount drawn down.
- Loan stock debt closing balance_t = loan stock debt opening balance_t plus loan stock debt drawdown_t plus loan stock debt repayment_t.

The loan stock interest control account will be calculated as follows:

- Loan stock interest opening balance_t = loan stock interest closing balance_t–1, with loan stock interest opening balance_year 1 = 0.
- Loan stock interest charge_t = loan stock interest rate times (loan stock debt opening balance_t + loan stock debt drawdown_t).
- Loan stock interest paid_t = – loan stock interest charge_t.
- Loan stock interest closing balance_t = loan stock interest opening balance_t plus loan stock interest charge_t plus loan stock interest paid_t.

Fixed Assets Module

Apart from tangible assets, all long-term assets in the balance sheet are assumed to be unchanged throughout the projection period.

The tangible assets control account will be calculated as follows:

- Tangible assets opening balance_t = tangible asset closing balance_t–1, with tangible assets opening balance_year 1 = tangible assets balance in postdeal balance sheet.
- Capex increases the book value of tangible assets. Capex_t = capex as % of sales_t times sales_t.
- Depreciation decreases the book value of tangible assets. Depreciation_t is already given.
- Tangible assets closing balance_t = tangible assets opening balance_t plus capex_t plus depreciation_t.

Tax Module

According to the tax assumptions given earlier, tax is paid a year after it has been incurred, thus creating a tax creditor on the balance sheet. We can calculate the tax creditor using the control account approach. The tax creditor control account will be calculated as follows:

- Tax creditor opening balance_t = tax creditor closing balance_t–1, with tax creditor opening balance_year 1 = tax creditor balance in postdeal balance sheet.
- A tax charge in the Profit and Loss module increases the tax creditor balance. Tax charge_t = tax_t, taken from the Profit and Loss module.
- Tax paid decreases the tax creditor balance. Tax paid_t = – tax charge_t–1.
- Tax creditor closing balance_t = tax creditor opening balance _t plus tax charge_t plus tax paid_t.

Balance Sheet Module

- Tangible assets closing balance_t is calculated in the Fixed Assets module.
- Financial assets_t = financial assets in postdeal balance sheet.
- Investment in joint ventures_t = investment in joint ventures in postdeal balance sheet.
- Intangibles = intangibles in postdeal balance sheet.
- Transaction goodwill_t = transaction goodwill in postdeal balance sheet.
- Transaction costs_t = transaction costs in postdeal balance sheet.
- Total fixed assets_t = the sum of tangible assets closing balance_t, financial assets_t, investment in joint ventures_t, intangibles_t, transaction goodwill_t, and transaction costs_t.
- Stock_t = stock (inventory) as percent of sales_t times sales_t.
- Trade debtors_t = trade debtors (accounts receivable) as percent of sales_t times sales_t.
- Total current assets_t = stock_t plus debtors_t.
- Closing cash balance_t is calculated in the Cash Flow module (discussed later).
- Trade creditors_t = – trade creditors (accounts payable) as percent of sales_t times sales_t.
- Other creditors_t = – other creditors as percent of sales_t times sales_t.
- Tax creditor_t = – tax creditor closing balance_t.

- Total current liabilities_t = creditors_t plus other creditors_t plus tax creditor_t.
- Working capital_t = stock_t plus trade debtors_t plus trade creditors_t plus other creditors_t.
- Total assets less current liabilities_t = total fixed assets_t plus total current assets_t plus current liabilities_t.
- Net current assets_t = current assets_t plus current liabilities_t plus closing cash balance_t.
- Closing term loan A debt balance_t is calculated in the Debt module (discussed earlier).
- Closing loan stock debt balance_t is calculated in the Debt module (discussed earlier).
- Net assets_t = fixed assets closing balance_t plus net current assets_t plus debt closing balance_t.
- Ordinary shares_t = ordinary shares in postdeal balance sheet.
- Retained profit carried forward_t (also referred to as P&L reserve) is calculated in the Profit and Loss module (discussed earlier).
- Net worth_t = share capital_t plus retained profit carried forward_t.

Since net worth must equal net assets, let us add at the bottom of the balance sheet a balance sheet check that verifies that the balance sheet balances in each period. To this end, we include an additional line as follows:

- Check balance_t = net assets_t minus net worth_t.

Cash Flow Module

- EBITDA_t is calculated in the Profit and Loss module (discussed earlier).
- Movement in stock_t = stock_t–1 minus stock_t, or stock at the start of the year minus stock at the end of the year.
- Movement in trade debtors_t = trade debtors_t–1 minus trade debtors_t, or trade debtors at the start of the year minus trade debtors at the end of the year.
- Movement in trade creditors_t = (trade creditors_t–1 plus other creditors_t–1) minus (trade creditors_t plus other creditors_t), or trade creditors and other creditors at the start of the year minus trade creditors and other creditors at the end of the year.
- Movement in working capital_t = movement in stock_t plus movement in trade debtors_t plus movement in trade creditors_t.

- Operating cash flow_t = EBITDA_t plus movement in working capital_t.
- Capex_t is calculated in the Fixed Assets module (discussed earlier).
- Cash flow before taxation and financing_t = operating cash flow_t minus capex_t.
- Tax_t is calculated in the Tax module (discussed earlier).
- Cash flow available for debt service_t = cash flow before taxation and financing_t minus tax_t.
- Term loan A interest paid_t is calculated in the Debt module (discussed earlier).
- Loan stock interest paid_t is calculated in the Debt module (discussed earlier).
- Term loan A debt repayment_t is calculated in the Debt module (discussed earlier).
- Loan stock debt repayment_t is calculated in the Debt module (discussed earlier).
- Net cash flow_t = cash flow available for debt service_t minus interest paid_t (for term loan A and loan stock) minus debt repayment_t (for term loan A and loan stock).

We also need to include a control account calculating the closing cash balance_t.

- Closing cash balance_t = opening cash balance_t + net cash flow_t.
- Opening cash balance_t = closing cash balance_t–1, with opening cash balance_year 1 given in the postdeal balance sheet.

9.2.2 Building the Exit and Return Schedules

As explained earlier, we have essentially two parts to the calculations: the integrated financial model part (profit and loss statement, balance sheet, and cash flow statement, which was specified in Section 9.2.1) and the exit schedule. The main exit assumption has already been given, namely, the enterprise-value-to-EBITDA multiple. Based on the exit enterprise-value-to-EBITDA multiple, we can calculate the enterprise value. From the enterprise value, we can deduct net debt (that is, debt less cash), and the result is the value of equity. The equity value divided by the number of shares outstanding gives the value of one share. The steps from enterprise value down to equity value are referred to as the exit waterfall.

The exit waterfall can be calculated as follows:

Exit Waterfall

- EBITDA_t is taken from the Profit and Loss module.
- Enterprise-value-to-EBITDA multiple_t is taken from the exit assumptions.
- Enterprise value_t = enterprise-value-to-EBITDA multiple_t times EBITDA_t.
- Term loan A_t is taken from the Balance Sheet module.
- Loan stock_t is taken from the Balance Sheet module.
- Cash_t is taken from the Balance Sheet module.
- Investor warrants proceeds_t = investor warrants strike cost.
- Management options proceeds_t = management options strike cost.
- Equity value_t = sum of (enterprise value_t, term loan A_t, loan stock_t, cash_t, investor warrants proceeds_t, and management options proceeds_t).
- Number of fully diluted shares_t is taken from the exit assumptions.
- Implied share price_t = equity value_t divided by number of fully diluted shares_t.

Notes:

- There are essentially three components that are aggregated in the calculation of equity value. Equity value = enterprise value less debt plus cash.
- The order in which proceeds from the sale of the company are allocated across the different classes of investments is very important, especially when there is not enough proceeds to allocate to all classes of investments. The exit waterfall just discussed results in the same share price whether cash is added to enterprise value before the deduction of debt or not. The reason for this is that the exit proceeds are sufficient to repay all the outstanding debt without the addition of the cash balance, warrants proceeds, and management options proceeds to the enterprise value.

Exit IRR and Money Multiple

The key to calculating the IRR and the money multiple is to make sure that all cash flows to and from the investor, together with the timing of these cash flows, have been captured. A simple table that can help ensure this is given in Table 9.3.

TABLE 9.3

Cash Item	Cash Type (Inflow or Outflow) and Amount	Timing
Loan stock disbursement	Outflow; amount specified in sources of funds	Year 0
Equity disbursement	Outflow; amount specified in sources of funds	Year 0
Fee	Inflow; amount specified in uses of funds	Year 0
Warrant exercise	Outflow; amount specified in exit assumptions	Exit year (Year 5)
Loan stock repayment	Inflow; outstanding loan stock balance in balance sheet	Exit year (Year 5)
Loan stock interest income	Inflow; – loan stock interest paid in Cash Flow module	Year 1 to Year 5
Proceeds from sale of shares	Inflow; equity value times fully diluted investor ownership (or implied share price_t times number of shares held by investor on a fully diluted basis)	Exit year (Year 5)
Proceeds from sale of warrants	Inflow; implied share price_t times number of shares held by investor on a fully diluted basis	Exit year (Year 5)
Net cash flow	Sum of all the above	From Year 0 to exit year

- *IRR.* Based on the net cash flow just given, the IRR can be calculated using the IRR function in Excel.
- *Money multiple.* The money multiple calculates the money returned to the investor as a proportion of the money laid out by the investor.

9.3 CREATING THE CALCULATIONS SHEET

Having gone through *how* the model calculations would work, we can now add the different calculation modules to the Calculations sheet.

9.3.1 Assumptions Module

Let's bring together all the key operational assumptions, debt assumptions, and exit assumptions from the two input sheets.

Operational Assumptions

- Historical sales. In cell I7, we can write the formula "='Operational Inputs'!I7", which picks up the historical sales figure from the Operational Inputs sheet.

Copy cell I7 and paste special its formula into the following cells:

- Historical EBITDA. Paste special the formula into cell I8.
- Sales growth %. Paste special the formula into the block J9:S9.
- EBITDA margin. Paste special the formula into the block J10:S10.
- Stock (inventory) as % of sales. Paste special the formula into the block J11:S11.
- Trade debtors (accounts receivable) as % of sales. Paste special the formula into the block J12:S12.
- Trade creditors (accounts payable) as % of sales. Paste special the formula into the block J13:S13.
- Other creditors as % of sales. Paste special the formula into the block J14:S14.
- Capex as % of sales. Paste special the formula into the block J15:S15.
- Corporation (corporate) tax. Paste special the formula into the block J16:S16.
- Depreciation. Paste special the formula into the block J17:S17.
- TLA repayment. Paste special the formula into the block J18:S18.

Note that a quicker way of completing the operational inputs would be to paste special the formula into the block I8:S18. This would involve only one step instead of eleven steps.

Debt Assumptions

- Term loan A quantum. We can write in cell H21 the formula "='S&U Inputs'!D37".

Copy cell H21 and paste special it into the block H21:J22. This picks up the entire debt assumptions table from the S&U Inputs sheet.

Exit Assumptions

- Exit year. In cell I25, we can write the formula "='S&U Inputs'!D22".

Copy cell I25 and paste special the formula into the following cells:

- # warrant shares. Paste special the formula into cell I26.
- Investors' equity stake (FD basis). Paste special formula into cell I27.

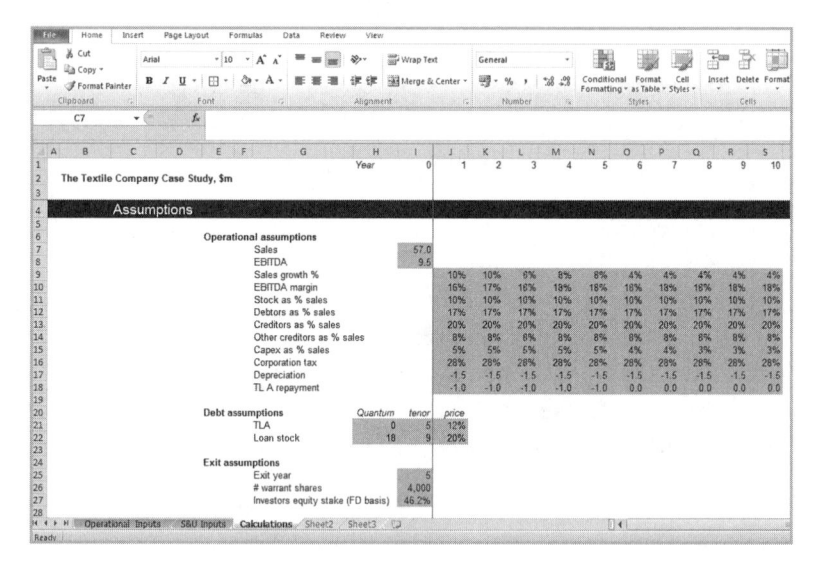

FIGURE 9.10

9.3.2 Profit and Loss Module

Let's create the Profit and Loss module right below the Assumptions module, say on row 31 (see Figure 9.11). We can now add the different lines of the Profit and Loss module following the specifications described earlier.

Sales

- In cell I32, we can write the formula "=IF(I$1=0,I7,H32*(1+I9))", which basically means that if we are in Year 0 (the historical year), then sales = historical sales (which is $57 million); otherwise, sales = sales from the previous year times (1 plus sales growth % for the current year).

EBITDA

- In cell I33, we can write the formula "=IF(I$1=0,I8,I10*I32)", which basically means that if we are in Year 0 (the historical year), then EBITDA = historical EBITDA (which is $9.5 million); otherwise, EBITDA = EBITDA margin times sales.

Copy cells I32:I33 and paste them into the block I32:S33.

Depreciation

- In cell J34, we can write the formula "=J17", which picks up the value of depreciation from row 17.

EBIT

- In cell J35, we can write the formula "=J33+J34", which calculates the profit (or earnings) before interest and tax as EBITDA less depreciation. Note that EBIT is defined as EBITDA less depreciation and amortization. In this case, since there is no amortization, EBIT is simply EBITDA less depreciation.

Term loan A interest

- As indicated in the model specifications, the term loan A interest charge will be calculated in the Debt module. So we skip the interest line for now.

Loan stock interest

- Likewise, the loan stock interest charge will be calculated in the Debt module. So we skip the interest line for now.

EBT

- In cell J41, we can write the formula "=SUM(J39,J35)", which calculates EBT as EBIT less term loan A interest and less loan stock interest (note that interest will be negative, as it counts toward reducing profit; that is, it is a cost to the business).

Taxes

- In cell J42, we can write the formula "= –IF(J41>0,J16*J41,0))", which calculates the taxes as tax rate times EBT if EBT is positive. In other words, taxes are incurred only if the project recorded a profit.

PAT

- In cell J43, we can write the formula "=J42+J41", which calculates PAT as EBT less taxes.

Retained profit b/f

- In cell J45, we can write the formula "=IF(J$1=1,I132,I46)", which means that if we are in Year 1, then the retained profit brought forward equals the retained profit from the postdeal balance sheet. Otherwise, the retained profit brought forward equals the retained profit carried forward at the end of the previous period.

Retained profit c/f

▪ In cell J46, we can write the formula "=J45+J43", which calculates the retained profit carried forward as equal to the retained profit brought forward plus PAT.

Copy cells J32:J46 and paste them into the block I32:S46. The Profit and Loss module is illustrated in Figure 9.11.

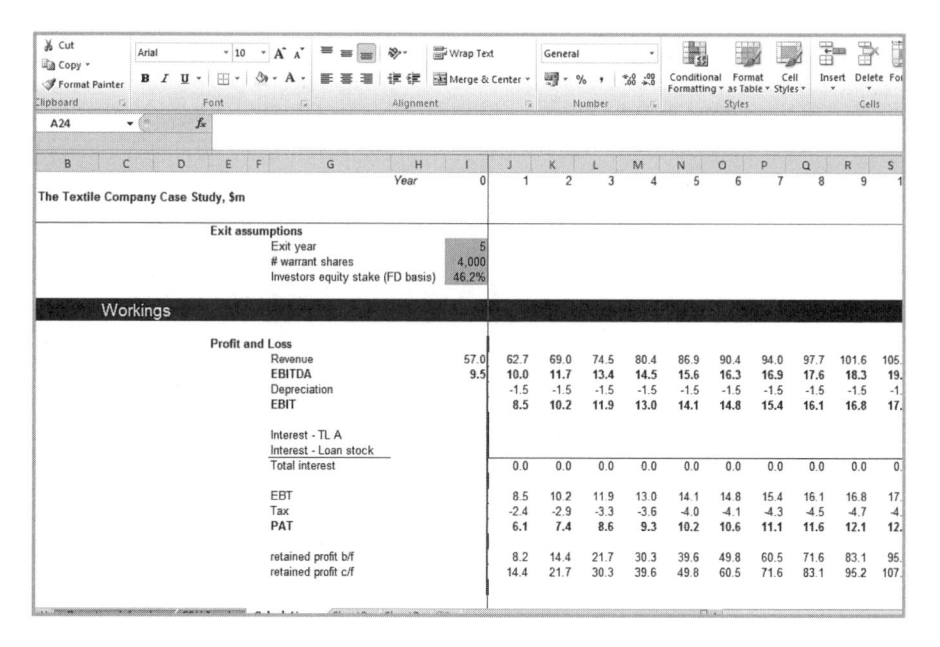

FIGURE 9.11

Note that the Profit and Loss module shown in Figure 9.11 is not yet final, as the term loan A interest and loan stock interest lines have not been completed.

9.3.3 Balance Sheet Module

We will do the balance sheet in two steps. First, we need to bring the postdeal balance sheet from the S&U Inputs sheet into the Calculations sheet. The postdeal balance sheet is the starting balance sheet for our projections and is therefore needed for our calculations.

Then we will return to the balance sheet and complete it once the different components (the Debt module, the Fixed Assets module, and so on) have been calculated.

To bring the postdeal balance sheet from the S&U Inputs sheet into the Calculations sheet, we can do the following:

Fixed Assets

Postdeal tangible assets

- In cell I51, we can write the formula "='S&U Inputs'!J44", which picks up the postdeal tangible assets from the S&U Inputs sheet.

Postdeal financial assets

- In cell I52, we can write the formula "='S&U Inputs'!J45", which picks up the postdeal financial assets from the S&U Inputs sheet.

Postdeal investment in joint ventures

- In cell I53, we can write the formula "='S&U Inputs'!J46", which picks up the postdeal investment in joint ventures from the S&U Inputs sheet.

Postdeal intangibles

- In cell I54, we can write the formula "='S&U Inputs'!J47", which picks up the postdeal intangibles from the S&U Inputs sheet.

Postdeal transaction goodwill

- In cell I55, we can write the formula "='S&U Inputs'!J48", which picks up the postdeal transaction goodwill from the S&U Inputs sheet.

Postdeal transaction costs

- In cell I56, we can write the formula "='S&U Inputs'!J49", which picks up the postdeal transaction costs from the S&U Inputs sheet.

Total fixed assets

- In cell I57, we can write the formula "=SUM(I51:I56)", which aggregates all the components of fixed assets. Copy cell I57 and paste special the formula into the block I57:S57.

Current Assets

Postdeal stock (inventory in U.S. usage)

- In cell I60, we can write the formula "='S&U Inputs'!J53", which picks up the postdeal stock from the S&U Inputs sheet.

Postdeal trade debtors (accounts receivable)

- In cell I61, we can write the formula "='S&U Inputs'!J54", which picks up the postdeal trade debtors from the S&U Inputs sheet.

Total current assets

- In cell I62, we can write the formula "=SUM(I60:I61)", which aggregates all the components of current assets.

Postdeal cash balance

- In cell I64, we can write the formula "='S&U Inputs'!J57", which picks up the postdeal cash balance from the S&U Inputs sheet.

Current Liabilities

Postdeal trade creditors (accounts payable in U.S. usage)

- In cell I67, we can write the formula "='S&U Inputs'!J60", which picks up the postdeal trade creditors from the S&U Inputs sheet.

Postdeal other creditors

- In cell I68, we can write the formula "='S&U Inputs'!J61", which picks up the postdeal other creditors from the S&U Inputs sheet.

Postdeal tax creditor

- In cell I69, we can write the formula "='S&U Inputs'!J62", which picks up the postdeal tax creditor from the S&U Inputs sheet.

Total current liabilities

- In cell I70, we can write the formula "=SUM(I67:I69)", which aggregates all the components of current liabilities. Copy cell I70 and paste special the formula into the block I70:S70.

Total assets less CL

- In cell I72, we can write the formula "=I57+I62+I70", which aggregates fixed assets, total current assets, and total current liabilities. Copy cell I72 and paste special the formula into the block I72:S72.

Net current assets

- In cell I74, we can write the formula "=I62+I64+I70", which aggregates total current assets, total current liabilities, and cash balance. Copy cell I74 and paste special the formula into the block I74:S74.

Long-Term Liabilities

Postdeal term loan A

- In cell I77, we can write the formula "='S&U Inputs'!J70", which picks up the postdeal term loan A from the S&U Inputs sheet.

Postdeal loan stock

- In cell I78, we can write the formula "='S&U Inputs'!J71", which picks up the postdeal loan stock from the S&U Inputs sheet.

Total long-term liabilities

- In cell I79, we can write the formula "=SUM(I77:I78)", which aggregates all the components of long-term liabilities. Copy cell I79 and paste special the formula into the block I79:S79.

Net assets

- In cell I81, we can write the formula "=I57+I74+I79", which aggregates total fixed assets, net current assets, and long-term liabilities. Copy cell I81 and paste special the formula into the block I81:S81.

Postdeal ordinary shares

- In cell I83, we can write the formula "='S&U Inputs'!J76", which picks up the postdeal ordinary shares from the S&U Inputs sheet.

Postdeal P&L reserve

- In cell I84, we can write the formula "='S&U Inputs'!J77", which picks up the postdeal P&L reserve from the S&U Inputs sheet.

Net worth

- In cell I85, we can write the formula "=SUM(I83:I84)", which aggregates all the components of net worth. Copy cell I85 and paste special the formula into the block I85:S85.

Balance sheet check

- In cell I86, we can write the formula "=abs(I81–I85)"; this calculates the difference between net Assets and net worth, which should be 0. Copy cell I86 and paste special the formula into the block I86:S86.

Overall balance sheet check

- In cell C3, we also write the formula "=IF(SUM($I$87:$S$87) <=0.1,"OK","Error")", which gives an overall balance sheet error check. A conditional formatting is applied to cell C3 such that if the value is OK, then the cell background color is green; and if the value is Error, then the cell background color is red.

The postdeal balance sheet is illustrated in Figures 9.12 and 9.13.

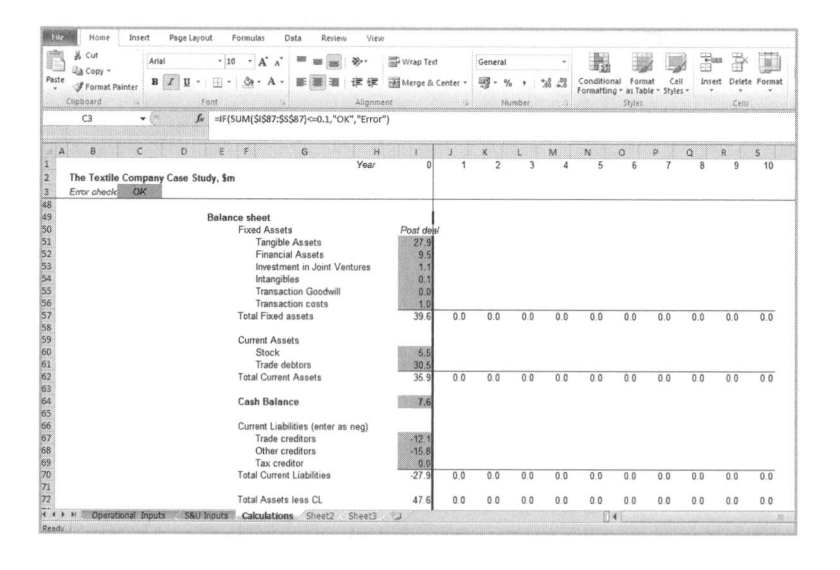

FIGURE 9.12

Having completed the postdeal balance sheet, we will now focus on calculating the projected balance sheet. To this end, we need to calculate the individual components (fixed assets, debt, and so on), after which we will revisit the balance sheet to incorporate the projected figures.

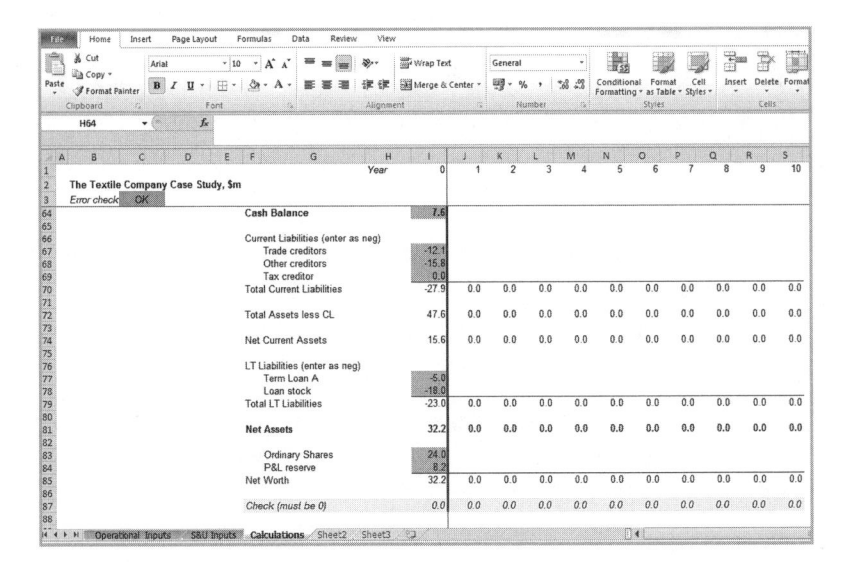

FIGURE 9.13

9.3.4 Debt Module

Let's create the Debt module right below the Balance Sheet module, say on row 90. We can now run a control account for the principal and a control account for the interest for each of term loan A and loan stock in line with the specifications described earlier.

Term Loan A Debt Control Account

Principal balance b/f

- In cell J93, we can write the formula "=IF(J$1=1,–I77,I96)", which basically means that if we are in Year 1, then the principal brought forward equals the principal amount in the postdeal balance sheet (which is in cell I77). Otherwise, the principal brought forward equals the principal carried forward from the previous year.

Principal drawdown

- We can leave this row empty, as there is no planned drawdown after Year 0.

Principal Repayment

- In cell J95, we can write the formula "=J18", which basically picks up row 18 (debt repaid).

Principal balance c/f

- In cell J96, we can write the formula "=SUM(J93:J95)", which basically calculates the principal carried forward as equal to principal brought forward plus principal drawdown less principal repaid.

Copy cells J93:J96 and paste them into the block J93:S96.

Term Loan A Interest Control Account

Interest b/f

- In cell J99, we can write the formula "=I102", which basically means that the interest brought forward equals the interest carried forward from the previous year.

Interest charge

- In cell I100, we can write the formula "=SUM(J93:J94)*$J$21", which calculates the interest charge as being equal to the sum of the (debt balance brought forward plus debt drawdown) times the annual interest rate (which is in cell J21).

Interest paid

- In cell J101, we can write the formula "= –J100", which reflects our assumption that interest charged (or incurred) is paid the same year.

Interest c/f

- In cell J102, we can write the formula "=SUM(J99:J101)", which basically calculates interest carried forward as equal to interest brought forward plus interest charge less interest paid.

Copy cells J99:J102 and paste them into the block J99:S102.

Loan Stock Principal Control Account

Principal balance b/f

- In cell J107, we can write the formula "=IF(J$1=1,–I78,I110)", which basically means that if we are in Year 1, then the principal brought forward equals the principal amount in the postdeal balance sheet (which is in cell I78). Otherwise, the principal brought forward equals the principal carried forward from the previous year.

Principal drawdown

- We can leave this row empty, as there is no planned drawdown after Year 0.

Principal Repayment

- In cell J109, we can write the formula "=IF(J$1=$I$22,–J107,0)", which means that debt repayment is 0 unless we are in Year 9 (which is the value in cell I22).

Principal balance c/f

- In cell J110, we can write the formula "=SUM(J107:J109)", which basically calculates the principal carried forward as equal to the principal brought forward plus principal drawdown less principal repaid.

Copy cells J107:J110 and paste them into the block J107:S110.

Loan Stock Interest Control Account

Interest b/f

- In cell J113, we can write the formula "=I116", which basically means that interest brought forward equals the interest carried forward from the previous year.

Interest charge

- In cell J114, we can write the formula "=SUM(J107:J108)*$J$22", which calculates the interest charge as being equal to the sum of the (principal balance brought forward plus principal drawdown) times the annual interest rate (which is in cell J22).

Interest paid

- In cell J115, we can write the formula "= –J114", which reflects our assumption that interest charged (or incurred) is paid in the same year.

Interest c/f

- In cell J116, we can write the formula "=SUM(J113:J115)", which basically calculates the interest carried forward as equal to the interest brought forward plus interest charge less interest paid.

Copy cells J113:J116 and paste them into the block J113:S116.

The Debt module is illustrated in Figures 9.14 and 9.15.

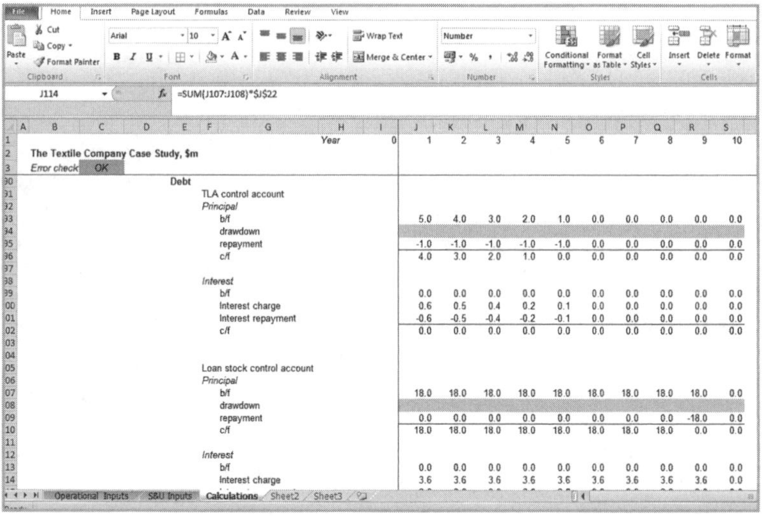

FIGURE 9.14

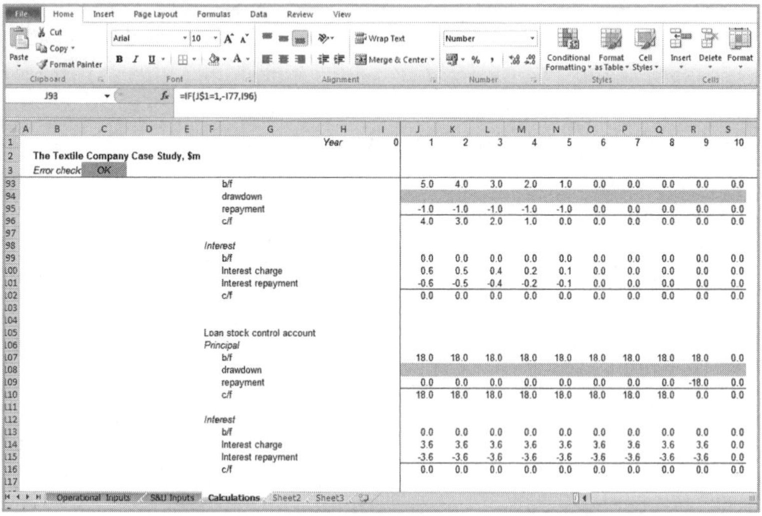

FIGURE 9.15

9.3.5 Fixed Assets Module

Let's create the Fixed Assets module right below the Debt module, say on row 119. We can now run a control account for the tangible assets in line with the specifications described earlier.

Fixed Assets Control Account

Tangible fixed assets balance b/f

- In cell J121, we can write the formula "=IF(J$1=1,I51,I124)", which basically means that if we are in Year 1, then tangible fixed assets brought forward are equal to the tangible fixed assets amount in the postdeal balance sheet (which is in cell I51). Otherwise, tangible fixed assets brought forward are equal to tangible fixed assets carried forward from the previous year.

Capex

- In cell J122, we can write the formula "=J15*J32", which basically calculates capex as capex as % of sales times the sales figure.

Depreciation

- In cell J123, we can write the formula "J17", which basically picks up the depreciation amount from the Profit and Loss module.

Tangible fixed assets balance c/f

- In cell J124, we can write the formula "=SUM(J121:J123)", which basically calculates tangible fixed assets carried forward as equal to tangible fixed assets brought forward plus capex less depreciation.

Copy cells J121:J124 and paste them into the block J121:S124. The Fixed Assets module is illustrated in Figure 9.16.

9.3.6 Tax Module

Let's create the Tax module right below the Fixed Assets module, say on row 127. We can run a control account for the tax creditor in line with the specifications described earlier.

Tax Creditor Control Account

Tax creditor balance b/f

- In cell J129, we can write the formula "=IF(J$1=1,–I69,I132)", which basically means that if we are in Year 1, then the tax creditor balance brought forward is equal to the tax creditor balance in the postdeal balance sheet (which is in cell I69). Otherwise, the tax creditor balance brought forward is equal to the tax creditor balance carried forward from the previous year.

Tax charge

- In cell J130, we can write the formula "= –J42", which basically picks up the tax charge from the Profit and Loss module.

Tax paid

- In cell J131, we can write the formulae "= –I130", which basically calculates the tax paid as being the tax charge from the previous period.

Tax creditor balance c/f

- In cell J132, we can write the formula "=SUM(J129:J131)", which basically calculates the tax creditor balance carried forward as equal to the tax creditor balance b/f plus tax charge less tax paid.

Copy cells J129:J132 and paste them into the block J129:S132. The tax creditor module is also illustrated in Figure 9.16.

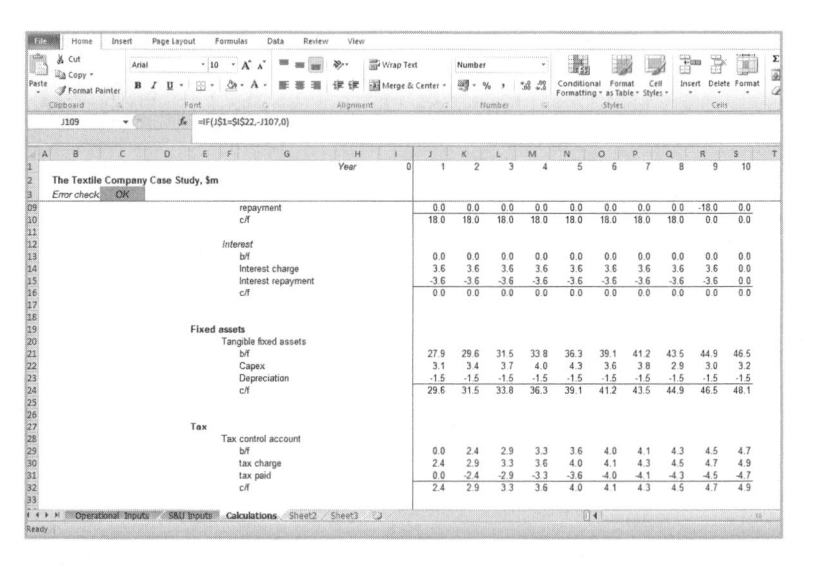

FIGURE 9.16

Note: With the Debt module now completed, we can go back to the Profit and Loss module and complete the interest lines as follows:

Term loan A interest

- In cell I37, we can write the formula "= – J100", which picks up the interest charge for term loan A from the Debt module.

Loan stock interest

- In cell I38, we can write the formula "= –J114", which picks up the interest charge for the loan stock from the Debt module.

Total interest

- In cell I39, we can write the formula "=SUM(J37:J38)", which aggregates the term loan A and loan stock interest.

Copy cells J37:J39 and paste them into the block J37:S39.
The revised Profit and Loss module is illustrated in Figure 9.17.

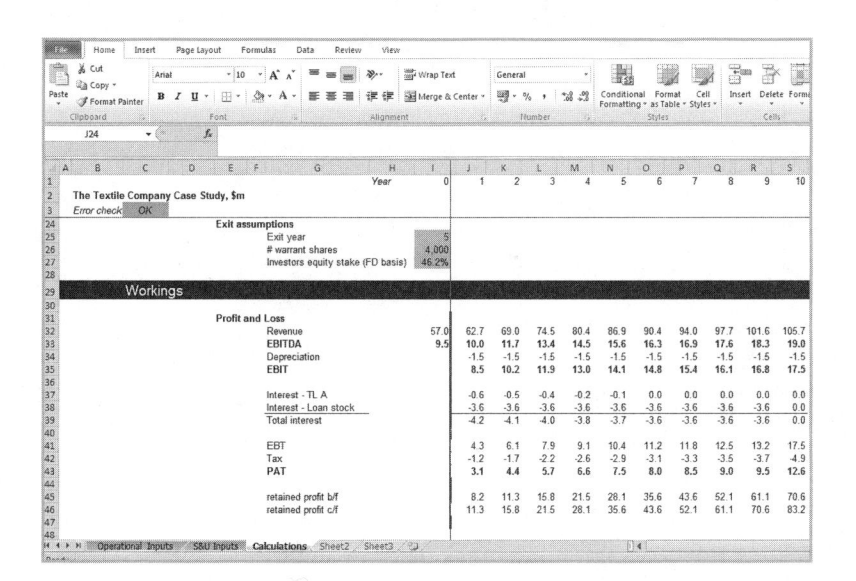

FIGURE 9.17

9.3.7 Revisiting the Balance Sheet Module

We can now revisit the Balance Sheet module and complete it with the projected balance sheet (so far, only the postdeal balance sheet has been completed).

Fixed Assets

Tangible assets

- In cell J51, we can write the formula "=J124", which picks up tangible assets from the Fixed Asset module.

Financial assets

- In cell J52, we can write the formula "=I52", which picks up the financial assets from the previous period.

Investment in joint ventures

- In cell J53, we can write the formula "=I53", which picks up the investment in joint ventures from the previous period.

Intangibles

- In cell J54, we can write the formula "I54", which picks up the intangibles from the previous period.

Transaction goodwill

- In cell J55, we can write the formula "I55", which picks up the transaction goodwill from the previous period.

Transaction costs

- In cell J56, we can write the formula "I56", which picks up the transaction costs from the previous period.

Copy cells J51:J56 and paste special them into the block J51:S56.

Current Assets

Stock (inventory)

- In cell J60, we can write the formula "=J$32*J11", which calculates stock as sales times stock as % of sales.

Trade debtors (accounts receivable)

- In cell J61, we can write the formula "=J$32*J12", which calculates trade debtors as sales times trade debtors as % of sales.

Copy cells J60:J61 and paste special them into the block J60:S61.

Cash Balance

We skip cash for now, as we have yet to complete the Cash Flow module.

Current Liabilities

Trade creditors (accounts payable)

- In cell J67, we can write the formula "=–J$32*J13", which calculates trade creditors as sales times trade creditors as % of sales.

Other creditors

- In cell J68, we can write the formula "=–J$32*J14", which calculates other creditors as sales times other creditors as % of sales.

Tax creditor

- In cell J69, we can write the formula "= –J132", which picks up the tax creditor balance from the Tax module.

Copy cells J67:J69 and paste special the formula into the block J67:S69.

Long-Term Liabilities

Term loan A

- In cell J77, we can write the formula "= –J96", which picks up the term loan A balance from the Debt module.

Loan stock

- In cell J78, we can write the formula "= –J110", which picks up the loan stock balance from the Debt module.

Copy cells J77:J78 and paste special them into the block J77:S78.

Ordinary shares

- In cell J83, we can write the formula "=I83", which picks up the ordinary shares balance from the previous period.

P&L reserve

- In cell J84, we can write the formula "=J46", which picks up the P&L reserve from the Profit and Loss module.

Copy cells J83:J84 and paste special them into block J83:S84. The Balance Sheet module is illustrated in Figures 9.18 and 9.19.

9.3.8 Cash Flow Module

Let's create the Cash Flow module right below the Tax module, say on row 135. We can now add the different lines of the Cash Flow module following the specifications described earlier.

EBITDA

- In cell J136, we can write the formula "=J33", which picks up the EBITDA figure from the Profit and Loss module.

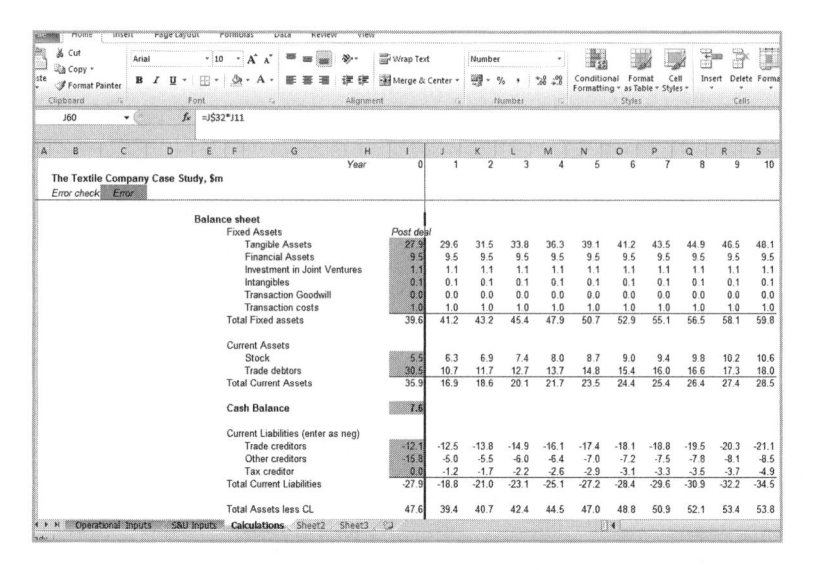

FIGURE 9.18

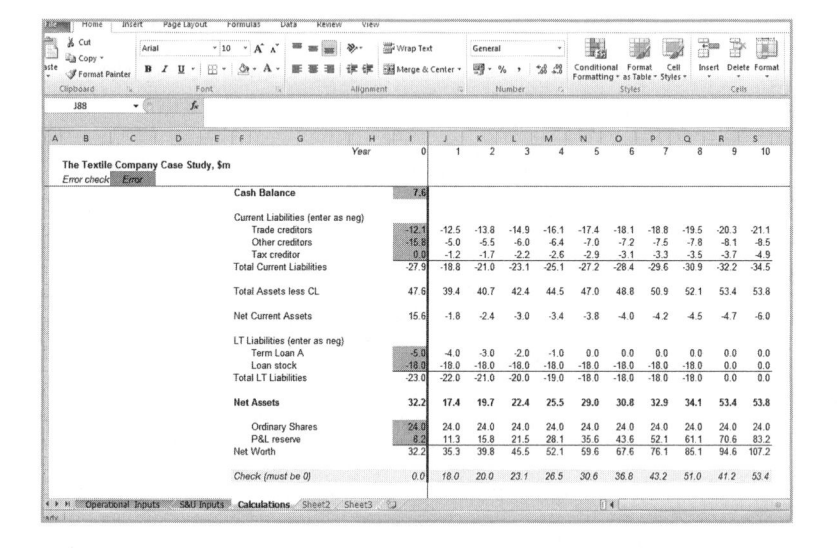

FIGURE 9.19

Note: The balance sheet figures are not yet final, as the cash balance line has yet to be completed.

Movement in stock

- In cell J138, we can write the formula "=I60–J60", which calculates the movement in stock (inventory) as stock at the end of the previous period (I60) minus stock at the end of the current period (J60).

Movement in debtors

- In cell J139, we can write the formula "=I61–J61", which calculates the movement in debtors (accounts receivable) as debtors at the end of the previous period less debtors at the end of the current period.

Movement in creditors

- In cell J140, we can write the formula "=SUM(I67:I68)–SUM(J67:J68)", which calculates the movement in creditors as the sum of trade and other creditors at the end of the previous period less the sum of trade and other creditors at the end of the current period.

Total movement in working capital

- In cell J141, we can write the formula "=SUM(J138:J140)", which calculates the total movement in working capital as the aggregate of movement in stock, movement in debtors, and movement in creditors.

Operating cash flow

- In cell J143, we can write the formula "=J136+J141", which calculates the operating cash flow as EBITDA (J136) plus movement in the sum of stock, debtors, and creditors (J141).

Cash conversion ratio %

- In cell J144, we can write the formula "=J143/J136", which calculates the cash conversion ratio as operating cash flow divided by EBITDA.

Capex

- In cell J146, we can write the formula "= –J122", which picks up capex from the Fixed Assets module.

Cash flow before tax and financing

- In cell J147, we can write the formula "=SUM(J143,J146)", which calculates cash flow before tax and financing as operating cash flow plus capex.

Tax

- In cell J148, we can write the formula "=J131", which picks up tax from the Tax module.

Debt drawdown

- In cell J149, we can write the formula "=SUM(J94,J108)", which calculates Debt drawdown as the sum of the amounts drawn down from the term loan A and the loan stock.

Cash flow available for debt service

- In cell J150, we can write the formula "=SUM(J147:J149)", which calculates cash flow available for debt service as the sum of cash flow before tax and financing, Tax, and Debt drawdown.

Term loan A interest

- In cell J152, we can write the formulae "=J101", which picks up interest for term loan A from the Debt module.

Loan stock interest

- In cell J153, we can write the formula "=J115", which picks up interest for the loan stock from the Debt module.

Total interest

- In cell J154, we can write the formula "=SUM(J152:J153)", which aggregates the term loan interest and the loan stock interest.

Term loan A debt repayment

- In cell J157, we can write the formula "=J95", which picks up the term loan A amount repaid from the Debt module.

Loan stock debt repayment

- In cell J158, we can write the formula "=J109", which picks up the loan stock amount repaid from the Debt module.

Total repayment

- In cell J159, we can write the formula "=SUM(J157:J158)", which aggregates the term loan A and loan stock debt amounts repaid.

Net cash flow

- In cell J161, we can write the formula "=J150+J154+J159", which calculates net cash flow as cash flow available for debt service less interest less repayments on the principal.

Cash balance b/f

- In cell J162, we can write the formula "=IF(J$1=1,$I$64,I163)", which calculates cash balance brought forward as the cash balance in the postdeal balance sheet (I64) if we are in Year 1. Otherwise, the cash balance brought forward is equal to the cash balance carried forward in the previous period.

Cash balance c/f

- In cell J163, we can write the formula "=J162+J161", which calculates the cash balance carried forward as the cash balance brought forward plus net cash flow.

Copy cells J136:J163 and paste them into the block J136:S163. The cash flow module is illustrated in Figures 9.20 and 9.21.

	Year	0	1	2	3	4	5	6	7	8	9	10
The Textile Company Case Study, $m												
Error check	Error											
Cash flow												
EBITDA			10.0	11.7	13.4	14.5	15.6	16.3	16.9	17.6	18.3	19.0
Mvt in stock			-0.8	-0.6	-0.6	-0.6	-0.6	-0.3	-0.4	-0.4	-0.4	-0.4
Mvt in debtors			19.8	-1.1	-0.9	-1.0	-1.1	-0.6	-0.6	-0.6	-0.7	-0.7
Mvt in creditors			-10.3	1.8	1.5	1.7	1.8	1.0	1.0	1.1	1.1	1.1
Total mvt in wc			8.7	0.1	0.1	0.1	0.1	0.1	0.0	0.0	0.0	0.0
OCF			18.7	11.8	13.5	14.5	15.7	16.3	17.0	17.6	18.3	19.1
Cash conversion ratio %			187%	101%	100%	100%	100%	100%	100%	100%	100%	100%
Capex			-3.1	-3.4	-3.7	-4.0	-4.3	-3.6	-3.8	-2.9	-3.0	-3.2
Cash flow before tax and financing			15.6	8.3	9.7	10.5	11.4	12.7	13.2	14.7	15.3	15.9
Tax			0.0	-1.2	-1.7	-2.2	-2.6	-2.9	-3.1	-3.3	-3.5	-3.7
Debt drawdown			0.0	0.0	0.0	0.0	0.0	0.0	0.0	0.0	0.0	0.0
Cash flow available for debt service			15.6	7.1	8.0	8.3	8.8	9.8	10.1	11.4	11.8	12.2
Interest												
TLA			-0.6	-0.5	-0.4	-0.2	-0.1	0.0	0.0	0.0	0.0	0.0
Loan stock			-3.6	-3.6	-3.6	-3.6	-3.6	-3.6	-3.6	-3.6	-3.6	0.0
Total interest			-4.2	-4.1	-4.0	-3.8	-3.7	-3.6	-3.6	-3.6	-3.6	0.0
Repayments												
TLA			-1.0	-1.0	-1.0	-1.0	-1.0	0.0	0.0	0.0	0.0	0.0
Loan stock			0.0	0.0	0.0	0.0	0.0	0.0	0.0	0.0	-18.0	0.0
Total repayments			-1.0	-1.0	-1.0	-1.0	-1.0	0.0	0.0	0.0	-18.0	0.0

FIGURE 9.20

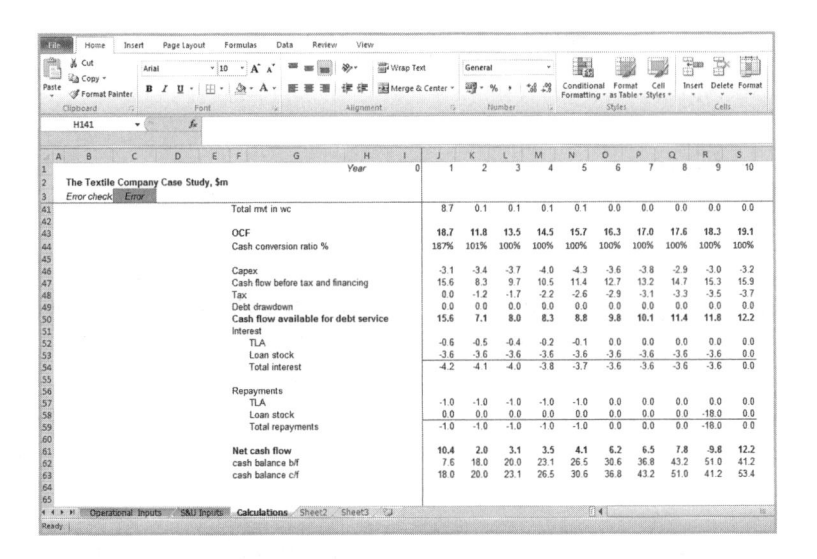

FIGURE 9.21

Note: With the Cash Flow module now completed, we can go back to the Balance Sheet module and complete the cash line as follows:

Cash

- In cell J64, we can write the formula "=J163", which picks up the cash balance carried forward from the Cash Flow module.

Copy cell J163 and paste it into the block J163:S163.

Overall balance sheet check

- Note that after including the cash balance in the balance sheet, the balance sheet check shows a green OK remark.

The revised Balance Sheet module is shown in Figure 9.22.

9.3.9 Exit Schedule Module

Let's create the Exit Schedule module right below the Cash Flow module, say on row 166.

Exit Waterfall

EBITDA

- In cell J167, we can write the formula "=J136", which picks up EBITDA from the Cash Flow module.

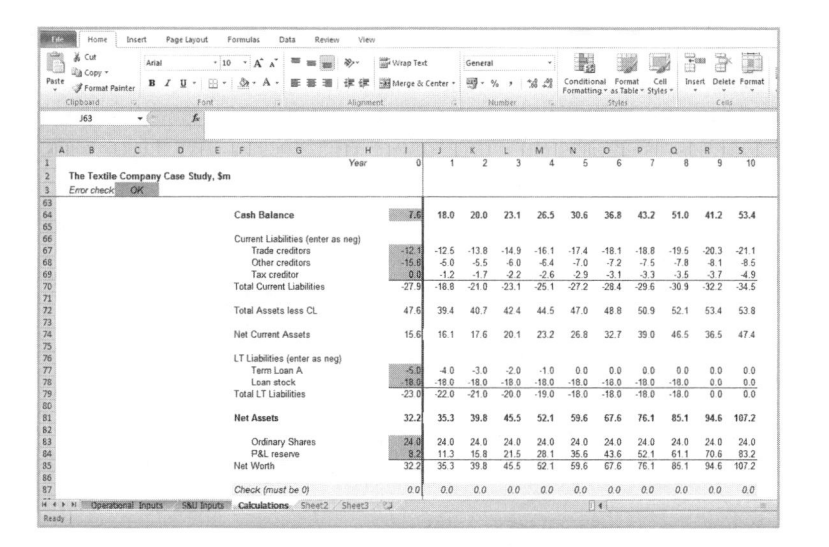

FIGURE 9.22

EV/EBITDA multiple

- In cell J168, we can write the formula "='S&U Inputs'!$D$23", which picks up the exit enterprise-value-to-EBITDA multiple from the S&U Inputs sheet.

Enterprise value

- In cell J169, we can write the formula "=J168*J167", which calculates enterprise value as the enterprise-value-to-EBITDA multiple times EBITDA.

Less

Term loan A

- In cell J171, we can write the formula "= –MIN(J169,–J77)", which calculates the proceeds from exit attributable to term loan A as the lower of enterprise value and the outstanding balance on term loan A as given in the balance sheet.

Loan stock

- In cell J172, we can write the formula "= –MIN(J169+J171,–J78)", which calculates the proceeds from exit attributable to loan stock as the lower of (1) enterprise value less term loan A and (2) the outstanding balance on loan stock as given in the balance sheet.

Plus

Cash

- In cell J174, we can write the formula "=J64", which picks up the cash balance from the balance sheet.

Investor warrants proceeds

- In cell J175, we can write the formula "='S&U Inputs'!$D$28", which picks up the proceeds from the investor warrants from the S&U Inputs sheet.

Management options proceeds

- In cell J176, we can write the formula "='S&U Inputs'!$G$28", which picks up the proceeds from the management options from the S&U Inputs sheet.

Equity value

- In cell J178, we can write the formula "=SUM(J169:J176)", which calculates the equity value as the enterprise value less term loan A and the loan stock, plus cash plus proceeds from investor warrants plus proceeds from management options.

Adjusted fully diluted share count (000s)

- In cell J179, we can write the formula "='S&U Inputs'!$D$30/ 1000", which picks up the adjusted number of shares on a fully diluted basis (000s) from the S&U Inputs sheet.

Implied share price ($ per share)

- In cell J180 we can write the formula "=(J178/ (J179*1000))*1000000", which calculates the implied share price as equity value (in cell J178) divided by the adjusted number of shares on a fully diluted basis (calculated in cell J179).

Copy cells J167:J180 and paste them into the block J167:S180. The Exit Schedule module is illustrated in Figure 9.23.

9.3.10 Investor Blended IRR and Money Multiple

As discussed earlier, the key to calculating the IRR and the money multiple is to ensure that all cash flows to and from the investor have been captured, along with the corresponding timing of these cash flows. The

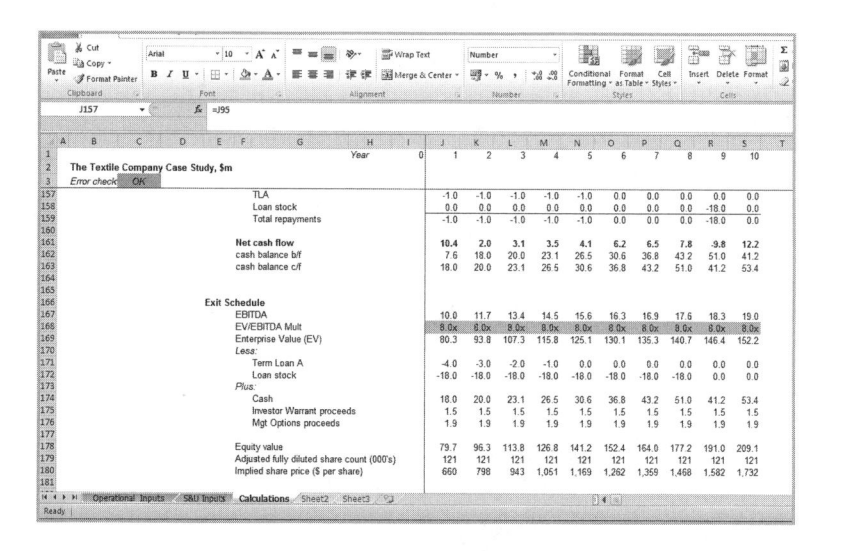

FIGURE 9.23

cash flows, together with the corresponding timing, were determined in Section 9.2.2. We can create the investor IRR and Money Multiple module, say on row 183.

Purchase of equity

- In cell I184, we can write the formula "= –'S&U Inputs'!D14", which picks up the investor's cash outlay for the purchase of equity in the textile project.

Purchase of loan stock

- In cell I185, we can write the formula "= –'S&U Inputs'!D15", which picks up the investor's cash outlay for the purchase of a loan stock in the textile project.

Transaction fee

- In cell I186, we can write the formula "= –'S&U Inputs'!D10", which picks up the investor's cash receipt in relation to the transaction fee.

Warrant exercise

- In cell J187, we can write the formula "= –IF(J$1=$I$25,J175,0)", which calculates warrant exercise cost as the opposite of the warrant proceeds to the company (in cell J175) if this is during the exit year; otherwise, warrant exercise cost is 0.

Loan stock repayment

- In cell J188, we can write the formula "=IF(J$1=$I$25,–J78,0)", which calculates loan stock repayment as the opposite of the loan stock balance in the balance sheet if this is during the exit year; otherwise, loan stock repayment is 0. Note that the formula works as long as the exit year is before the maturity of the loan stock repayment, which is the case here (the loan stock is a bullet loan payable at the end of nine years, whereas the exit year is Year 5).

Loan stock interest

- In cell J189, we can write the formula "=IF(J$1<=$I$25,–J153,0)", which calculates the loan stock interest as the opposite of the loan stock interest in the Cash Flow module if this is before the exit year; otherwise, loan stock interest is 0. Note that just as in the calculation of the loan stock repayment, the formula works as long as the exit year is before the maturity of the loan stock repayment, which is the case here (the loan stock is a bullet loan payable at the end of nine years, whereas the exit year is Year 5).

Sale of ordinary shares

- In cell J190, we can write the formula "=IF(J$1=$I$25,J178*$I$27,0)", which calculates the proceeds from the sale of ordinary shares as equal to the equity value (in cell J178) times the investor's equity stake on a fully diluted basis (in cell I27); otherwise, the proceeds from the sale of ordinary shares is 0.

Sale of warrant shares

- In cell J191, we can write the formula "=IF(J$1=$I$25,J180 *$I$26/1000000,0)", which calculates the proceeds from the sale of warrant shares as equal to the implied share price (in cell J180) times the number of warrant shares (in cell I26); otherwise, proceeds from the sale of warrant shares is 0.

Net cash flows

- In cell J192, we can write the formula "=SUM(I184:I191)", which aggregates the net cash flows to and from the investor as the sum of rows 184 to 191.

IRR

- In cell J194, we can write the formula "=IRR($I192:J192,0.1)", which calculates the internal rate of return (IRR) of the cash flows in row 192. Note the presence of the $ symbol on column I, which ensures that as we copy the formula in cell J194 into future years, the starting point for the cash flows remains unchanged at Year 0.

Money multiple

- In cell J195, we can write the formula "= –SUM($J188:J191)/ $I$192", which calculates the money multiple as equal to all cash inflows [in the block SUM($J188:J191)] divided by all cash outflows (in cell I192). Note here, too, the presence of the $ symbol on column J, which ensures that as we copy the formula in cell J195 into future years, the starting point for the cash flow remains unchanged at Year 1.

Copy cells J187:J191 and paste them into the block J187:S191. Copy cell J192 and paste it into the block J192:S192. Copy cells J194:J195 and paste them into the block J194:S195.

The IRR and Money Multiple module is illustrated in Figure 9.24.

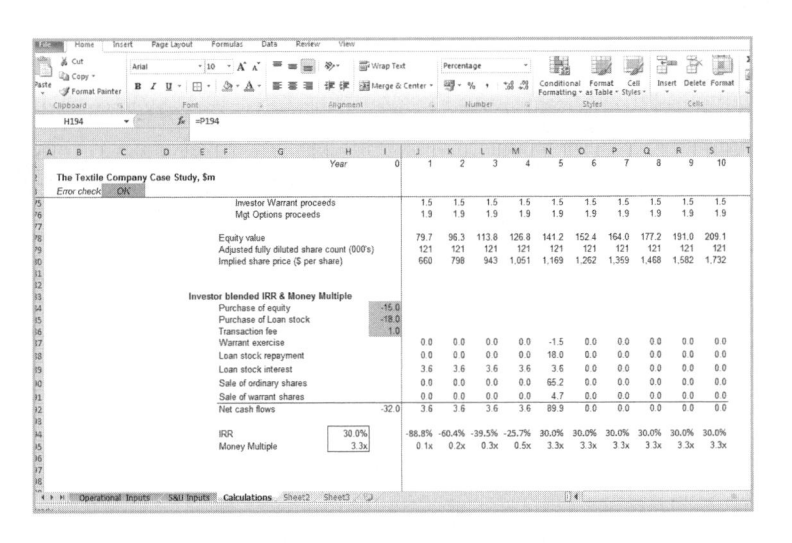

FIGURE 9.24

Note: In cells H194 and H195, we are showing an IRR and money multiple. These are for Year 7, and the content of cell H194 is "=P194" and that of cell H195 is "=P195". The following section explains the purpose of these two cells.

9.3.11 Exit Sensitivity Analysis

When looking at investor returns (for example, in terms of the IRR or the money multiple), it is customary to conduct a sensitivity analysis that analyzes the extent to which a change in the value of the drivers of exit returns will have an impact on the magnitude of the return itself.

Here we have two measures of return: the IRR and the money multiple. We also have two key drivers of return: exit year and exit enterprise-value-to-EBITDA multiple. The year of exit is clearly a driver, as the financial performance of the company (in terms of EBITDA) will be different depending on the year in which we exit the company. Also, the exit enterprise-value-to-EBITDA multiple is another obvious driver of return, as it is the multiple that is applied to the EBITDA for the year of exit.

Our sensitivity analysis will focus on changing the value of these two drivers, exit year and exit multiple, and observing the impact of each on the IRR and the money multiple. The process of changing the values of the drivers can be done manually, but Microsoft Excel has a built-in tool, a data table, for running these sensitivities automatically.

A data table can be regarded in the same way as any other function in Microsoft Excel, and therefore it produces a result based on inputs that the user needs to specify. A data table's inputs are (1) the drivers of the measure and (2) the measure itself. Once the user specifies the values for the drivers in (1) and the formula for the measure in (2), then the function will return a table of values for the measure corresponding to the values of the drivers.

We will create data tables for the IRR and for the money multiple.

IRR Data Table

- Drivers: exit year and exit multiple
- Measure: IRR
- Data table inputs:
    1. Values for exit year: Years 5, 6, and 7; values for exit enterprise-value-to-EBITDA multiple: 7, 8, and 9 times. In other words, we are looking to allow the exit year to vary among 5, 6, and 7. We are also looking to allow the exit enterprise-value-to-EBITDA multiple to vary among 7, 8, and 9 times.
    2. Measure: IRR in Year 7. Based on the data table inputs just given, Year 7 is the latest year in which we are looking to exit the textile company. The cash flow to the investor after exiting the company is 0, and so if we exit in Year 5, the IRR in Year 7 will be the same as the IRR in Year 5. Likewise, if we exit in Year 6, the IRR in Year 7 will be the same as the

IRR in Year 6. Finally, the IRR in Year 7 will apply if we exit in year 7. Cell H194 (shown in Figure 9.24) contains our measure for the purpose of the data table.

We will build the data table in the S&U Inputs sheet using the following steps (refer to Microsoft Excel's Help for further information on creating data tables). The data table we will build is known as a two-variable data table (it has two drivers: exit year and exit multiple). We will have one variable along the row (say, exit Year 5, 6, and 7) and the other variable down the column (say exit multiple 7, 8, and 9 times).

- Select the S&U Inputs sheet.
- Enter the measure (Year 7 IRR) in any given cell, say I24. The formula in cell I24 reads "=Calculations!H194".
- Along row 24 (the same row as the measure, but to the right-hand side of the measure), enter the values for the exit year driver. Thus, in cells J24, K24, and L24, type 5, 6, and 7, respectively.
- Down column I (the same column as the measure, but below the measure), enter the values for the exit enterprise-value-to-EBITDA multiple. And so in cells I25, I26, and I27, type 7x, 8x, and 9x, respectively.
- Select the block of cells that contains the measure (I24) and the values of the two drivers. Thus, this selection will involve the block I24:L27.
- On the Data tab, in the Data Tools group, click on What-If Analysis, and then click on Data Table. This is illustrated in Figure 9.25.

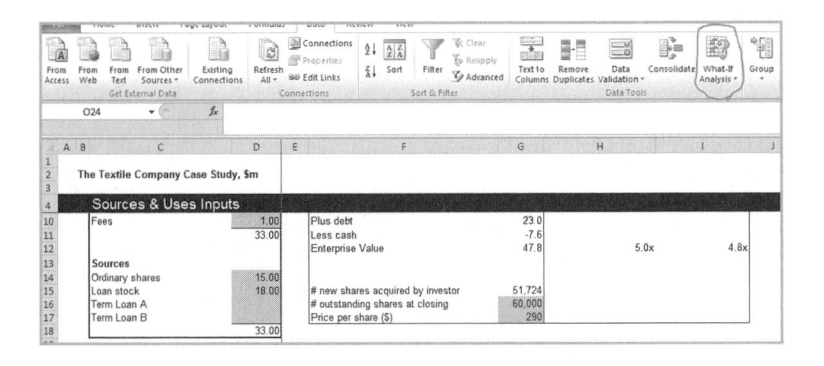

FIGURE 9.25

- After clicking on Data Table, the Data Table dialogue box appears.

- In the Row input cell box, enter the reference to the input cell for the input values in the row, which is the exit year driver and is specified in cell D22. And so we enter D22 in the Row input cell box. Alternatively, click on cell D22 (note that Microsoft Excel automatically writes cell $D$22 in the Row input cell box).
- In the Column input cell box, enter the reference to the input cell for the input values in the column, which is exit enterprise-value-to-EBITDA multiple and is specified in cell D23. And so we enter D23 in the Column input cell box. Alternatively, click on cell D23 (note that Microsoft Excel automatically writes cell $D$23 in the Column input cell box). This is illustrated in Figure 9.26.

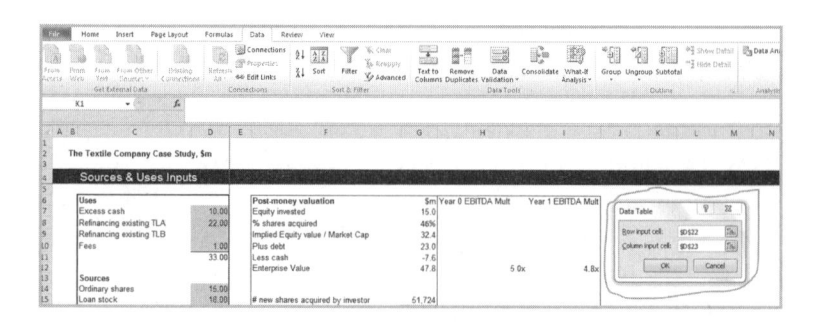

FIGURE 9.26

- Click OK and press F9 to recalculate (recalculating ensures that Microsoft Excel will calculate the data table, in case the Microsoft Excel calculations options were not set to calculate data tables automatically).
- The resulting IRR data table is illustrated in Figure 9.27.

Notes

- For aesthetic reasons, we have formatted the font in cell I24 to a white color (that is, the same color as the cell's background color) so that the cell containing the measure is not visible.
- According to the best practice principles discussed in Chapter 2, the data table is a calculation and therefore should be included in the Calculations sheet. However, Microsoft Excel requires input drivers to be located in the same sheet as the data table itself. Thus, the only reason why we have created the data table in the S&U Inputs sheet instead of the Calculations sheet

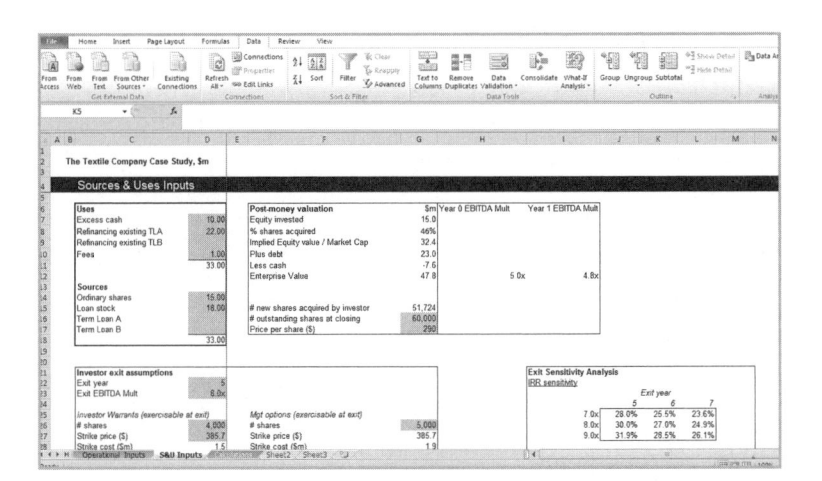

FIGURE 9.27

is Excel's own limitations. Note that there are ways of creating off-sheet data tables in Microsoft Excel (that is, data tables where the input drivers are not necessarily located in the same sheet as the data table itself), but we will not go into these techniques in this book.

Money Multiple Data Table

- Drivers: exit year and exit multiple
- Measure: money multiple
- Data table inputs:
  1. Values for exit year: years 5, 6, and 7; values for exit enterprise-value-to-EBITDA multiple: 7, 8, and 9 times. In other words, we are looking to allow the exit year to vary among 5, 6, and 7. We are also looking to allow the exit enterprise-value-to-EBITDA multiple to vary between 7, 8, and 9 times.
  2. Measure: money multiple in Year 7. Based on the data table inputs just given, Year 7 is the latest year in which we are looking to exit the textile company. The cash flow to the investor after exiting the company is 0, and so if we exit in Year 5, the money multiple in Year 7 is the same as the money multiple in Year 5. Likewise, if we exit in Year 6, the money multiple in Year 7 will be the same as the money multiple in Year 6. Finally, the money multiple in Year 7 will apply if we exit in Year 7. Cell H195 (shown in Figure 9.24) contains our measure for the purpose of the data table.

We will build the money multiple data table in the S&U Inputs sheet just below the IRR data table.

- Select the S&U Inputs sheet.
- Enter the measure (Year 7 Money Multiple), in, say, I31. The formula in cell I31 reads "=Calculations!H195".
- Along row 31 (the same row as the measure, but to the right-hand side of the measure), enter the values for the exit year driver. And so in cells J31, K31, and L31, type 5, 6, and 7, respectively.
- Down column I (the same column as the measure, but below the measure), enter the values for the exit enterprise-value-to-EBITDA multiple. And so in cells I32, I33, and I34, type 7x, 8x, and 9x, respectively.
- Select the block of cells that contains the measure (I31) and the values of the two drivers. Thus this selection will involve the block I31:L34.
- On the Data tab, in the Data Tools group, click on What-If Analysis, and then click on Data Table.
- After clicking on Data Table, the Data Table dialogue box appears.
- As in the IRR data table, enter D22 in the Row input cell box.
- As in the IRR data table, enter D23 in the Column input cell box.
- Click OK and press F9 to recalculate.
- The resulting money multiple data table is illustrated in Figure 9.28.

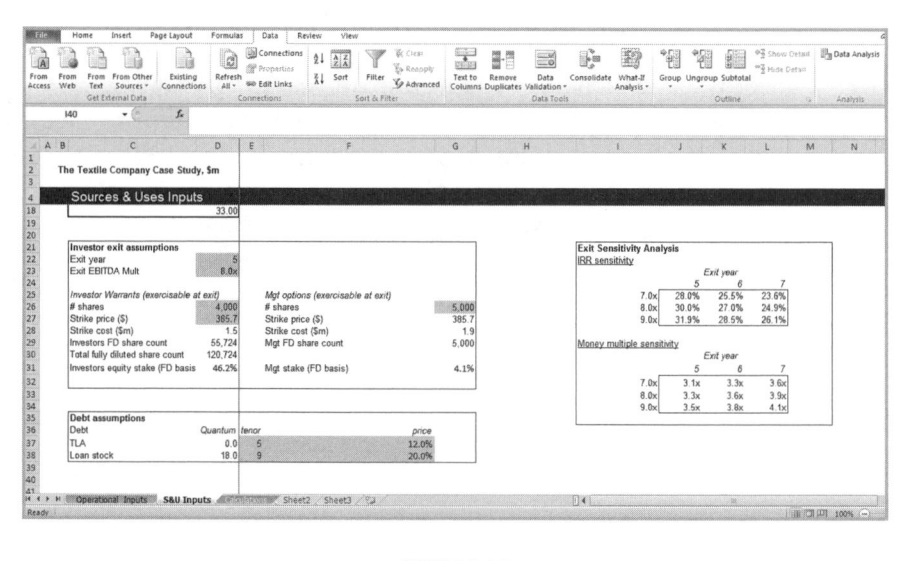

FIGURE 9.28

Note: As in the IRR data table, for aesthetic reasons, we have formatted the font in cell I31 to a white color (that is, the same color as the cell's background color) so that the cell containing the measure is not visible.

Analysis of Data Table Sensitivity

- The data table shows that as the exit enterprise-value-to-EBITDA multiple increases from 7 to 9 times, both the IRR and the money multiple increase, which is to be expected. Indeed, increasing the exit enterprise-value-to-EBITDA multiple will increase the enterprise value, which (given the fixed term loan A and loan stock) will result in an increased equity value.
- As the exit year is delayed, the IRR decreases, which is to be expected. This result reflects the time value of money.
- However, as the exit year is delayed, the money multiple increases. In our projections, EBITDA increases over time, and so delaying the exit means achieving a higher EBITDA figure at exit, which results in a higher enterprise value and consequently a higher equity value.
- The previous point has important implications for the investor. The results of some investment funds are measured by IRR, in which case, all other things being equal, these funds would prefer realizing an earlier exit from their investments. On the other hand, the results of some funds are measured by money multiple as long as the exit is achieved within a certain time frame (for example, five to seven years). In this case, the fund would have a preference for delaying the exit by a couple of years in order to achieve a higher money multiple.

9.4 CREATING THE OUTPUTS SHEET

Now that we have completed all the necessary calculations, we are ready to bring together the key results from our calculations into the Output sheet.

The key outputs are the Profit and Loss, Balance Sheet, Cash Flow, Exit Schedule, Exit IRR & Money Multiple, and Exit Sensitivity Analysis modules.

- Copy the Calculations sheet, rename it Outputs, and color it green. This way, the Outputs sheet initially has the same content as the Calculations sheet. We will then delete the elements of the Calculations sheet that are not going to be included in the Outputs sheet.

- Since the main outputs are the Profit and Loss, Balance Sheet, Cash Flow, Exit Schedule, Exit IRR & Money Multiple, and Exit Sensitivity Analysis modules, we will:
  1. Link the Profit and Loss, Balance Sheet, Cash Flow, Exit Schedule, and Exit IRR & Money Multiple modules in the Outputs sheet to the corresponding Profit and Loss, Balance Sheet, Cash Flow, Exit Schedule, and Exit IRR & Money Multiple modules in the Calculations sheet.
  2. Link the Exit Sensitivity Analysis module in the Outputs sheet to the corresponding Exit Sensitivity Analysis module in the S&U Inputs sheet.
- In Chapter 8, we learned how to link one sheet (the Outputs sheet) to another (the Inputs & Workings Sheet). We can use the same technique to complete steps 1 and 2 here. The result is an Outputs sheet that is exactly the same as the Calculations sheet contentwise except that the Outputs sheet takes its values from the Calculations sheet.
- Select rows 4 to 28 (the Assumptions block) and delete the entire block. This brings the Profit and Loss module right to the top at row 4.
- Delete the Debt, Fixed Assets and Tax modules. This brings the Cash Flow module to immediately below the balance sheet, from row 67.

Let us make a few minor adjustments to make the Outputs sheet more user-friendly.

- We rename the "Workings" blue bar on row 4 as "Outputs."
- We also include a sales growth line and an EBITDA margin line in the Profit and Loss section of the Outputs sheet. Both the sales growth and EBITDA margin lines in the Outputs sheet can be linked to the corresponding line in the Calculations.
- For sales growth, we write in cell J8 the formula "=Calculations !J9".
- Similarly, for EBITDA margin, we write in cell J10 the formula "=Calculations!J10".
- Copy cell J8 and paste it into the block J8:S8.

- Copy cell J10 and paste it into the block J10:S10.
- Remove the gray color from any cell shown as gray.

Also, to create a copy of the Exit Sensitivity Analysis in the Outputs sheet, do as follows:

- Copy block I21:M35 in the S&U Inputs sheet and paste it into K133 in the Outputs sheet.
- To link the IRR and money multiple data tables in the Outputs sheet to the S&U Inputs sheet:
  - Write in cell K136 the formula "='S&U Inputs'!I24".
  - Copy cell K136 and paste special the formula into the block K136:N139.
  - Paste special the formula into the block K143:N146.

The resulting Outputs sheet is shown in the following figures. First we show the Profit and Loss module in Figure 9.29.

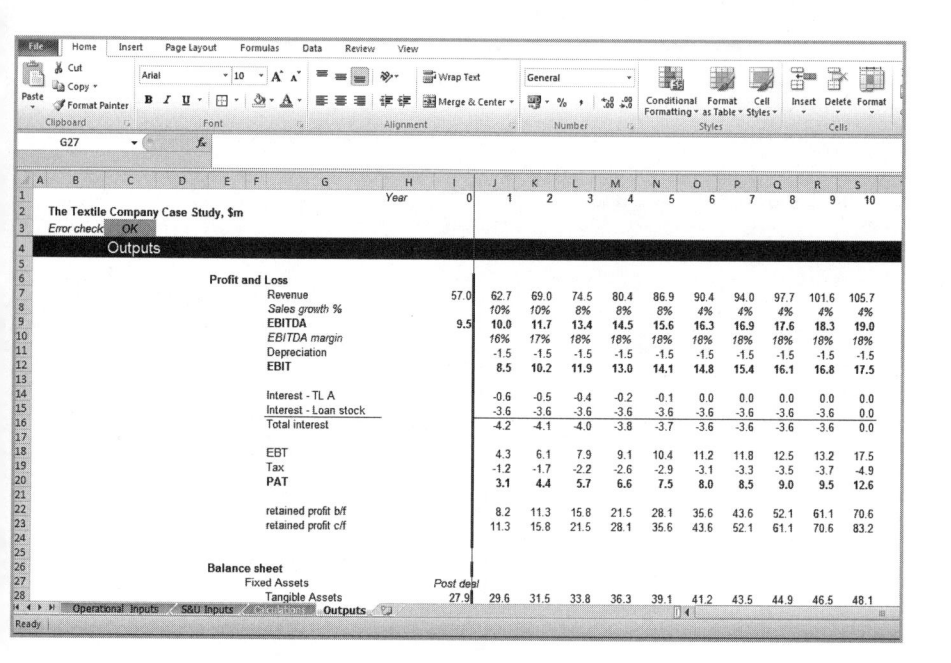

FIGURE 9.29

Next, we show the Balance Sheet module in Figures 9.30 and 9.31.

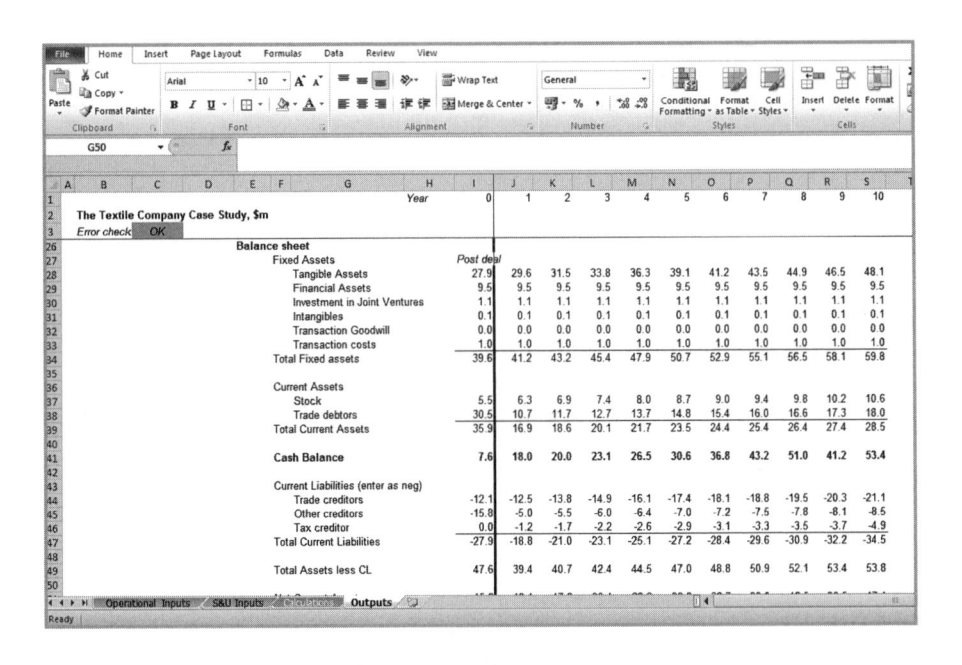

FIGURE 9.30

FIGURE 9.31

Then we show the Cash Flow module in Figure 9.32.

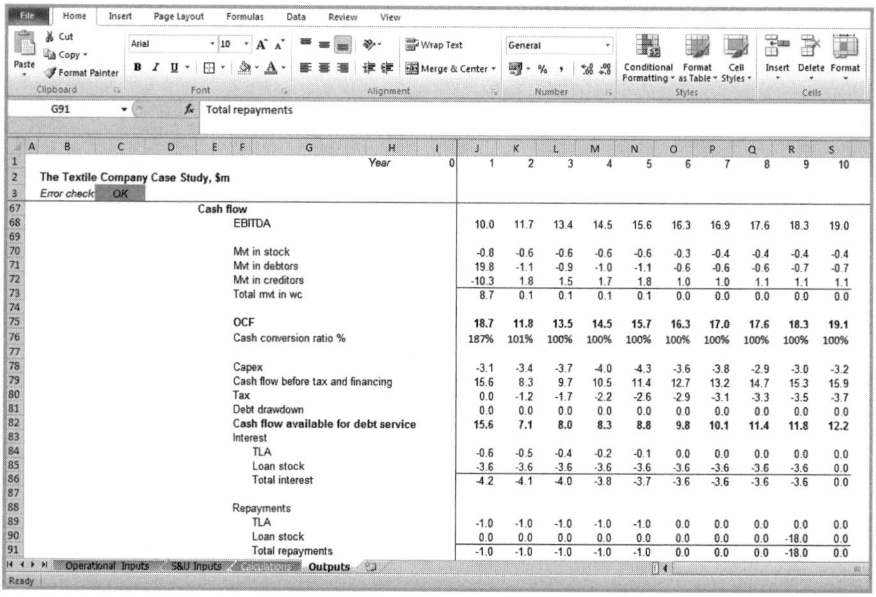

	Year	0	1	2	3	4	5	6	7	8	9	10
The Textile Company Case Study, $m												
Error check OK												
Cash flow												
EBITDA			10.0	11.7	13.4	14.5	15.6	16.3	16.9	17.6	18.3	19.0
Mvt in stock			-0.8	-0.6	-0.6	-0.6	-0.6	-0.3	-0.4	-0.4	-0.4	-0.4
Mvt in debtors			19.8	-1.1	-0.9	-1.0	-1.1	-0.6	-0.6	-0.6	-0.7	-0.7
Mvt in creditors			-10.3	1.8	1.5	1.7	1.8	1.0	1.0	1.1	1.1	1.1
Total mvt in wc			8.7	0.1	0.1	0.1	0.1	0.0	0.0	0.0	0.0	0.0
OCF			18.7	11.8	13.5	14.5	15.7	16.3	17.0	17.6	18.3	19.1
Cash conversion ratio %			187%	101%	100%	100%	100%	100%	100%	100%	100%	100%
Capex			-3.1	-3.4	-3.7	-4.0	-4.3	-3.6	-3.8	-2.9	-3.0	-3.2
Cash flow before tax and financing			15.6	8.3	9.7	10.5	11.4	12.7	13.2	14.7	15.3	15.9
Tax			0.0	-1.2	-1.7	-2.2	-2.6	-2.9	-3.1	-3.3	-3.5	-3.7
Debt drawdown			0.0	0.0	0.0	0.0	0.0	0.0	0.0	0.0	0.0	0.0
Cash flow available for debt service			15.6	7.1	8.0	8.3	8.8	9.8	10.1	11.4	11.8	12.2
Interest												
TLA			-0.6	-0.5	-0.4	-0.2	-0.1	0.0	0.0	0.0	0.0	0.0
Loan stock			-3.6	-3.6	-3.6	-3.6	-3.6	-3.6	-3.6	-3.6	-3.6	0.0
Total interest			-4.2	-4.1	-4.0	-3.8	-3.7	-3.6	-3.6	-3.6	-3.6	0.0
Repayments												
TLA			-1.0	-1.0	-1.0	-1.0	-1.0	0.0	0.0	0.0	0.0	0.0
Loan stock			0.0	0.0	0.0	0.0	0.0	0.0	0.0	0.0	-18.0	0.0
Total repayments			-1.0	-1.0	-1.0	-1.0	-1.0	0.0	0.0	0.0	-18.0	0.0

FIGURE 9.32

Then we show the exit waterfall in Figure 9.33.

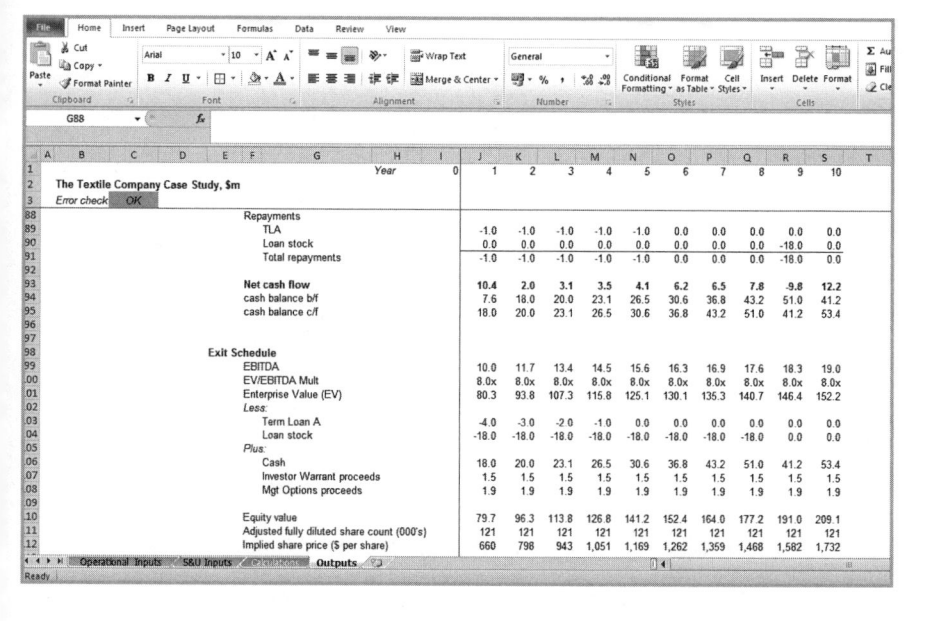

	Year	0	1	2	3	4	5	6	7	8	9	10
The Textile Company Case Study, $m												
Error check OK												
Repayments												
TLA			-1.0	-1.0	-1.0	-1.0	-1.0	0.0	0.0	0.0	0.0	0.0
Loan stock			0.0	0.0	0.0	0.0	0.0	0.0	0.0	0.0	-18.0	0.0
Total repayments			-1.0	-1.0	-1.0	-1.0	-1.0	0.0	0.0	0.0	-18.0	0.0
Net cash flow			10.4	2.0	3.1	3.5	4.1	6.2	6.5	7.8	-9.8	12.2
cash balance b/f			7.6	18.0	20.0	23.1	26.5	30.6	36.8	43.2	51.0	41.2
cash balance c/f			18.0	20.0	23.1	26.5	30.6	36.8	43.2	51.0	41.2	53.4
Exit Schedule												
EBITDA			10.0	11.7	13.4	14.5	15.6	16.3	16.9	17.6	18.3	19.0
EV/EBITDA Mult			8.0x	8.0x	8.0x	8.0x	8.0x	8.0x	8.0x	8.0x	8.0x	8.0x
Enterprise Value (EV)			80.3	93.8	107.3	115.8	125.1	130.1	135.3	140.7	146.4	152.2
Less:												
Term Loan A			-4.0	-3.0	-2.0	-1.0	0.0	0.0	0.0	0.0	0.0	0.0
Loan stock			-18.0	-18.0	-18.0	-18.0	-18.0	-18.0	-18.0	0.0	0.0	0.0
Plus:												
Cash			18.0	20.0	23.1	26.5	30.6	36.8	43.2	51.0	41.2	53.4
Investor Warrant proceeds			1.5	1.5	1.5	1.5	1.5	1.5	1.5	1.5	1.5	1.5
Mgt Options proceeds			1.9	1.9	1.9	1.9	1.9	1.9	1.9	1.9	1.9	1.9
Equity value			79.7	96.3	113.8	126.8	141.2	152.4	164.0	177.2	191.0	209.1
Adjusted fully diluted share count (000's)			121	121	121	121	121	121	121	121	121	121
Implied share price ($ per share)			660	798	943	1,051	1,169	1,262	1,359	1,468	1,582	1,732

FIGURE 9.33

This is followed by the Exit IRR & Money Multiple module in Figure 9.34.

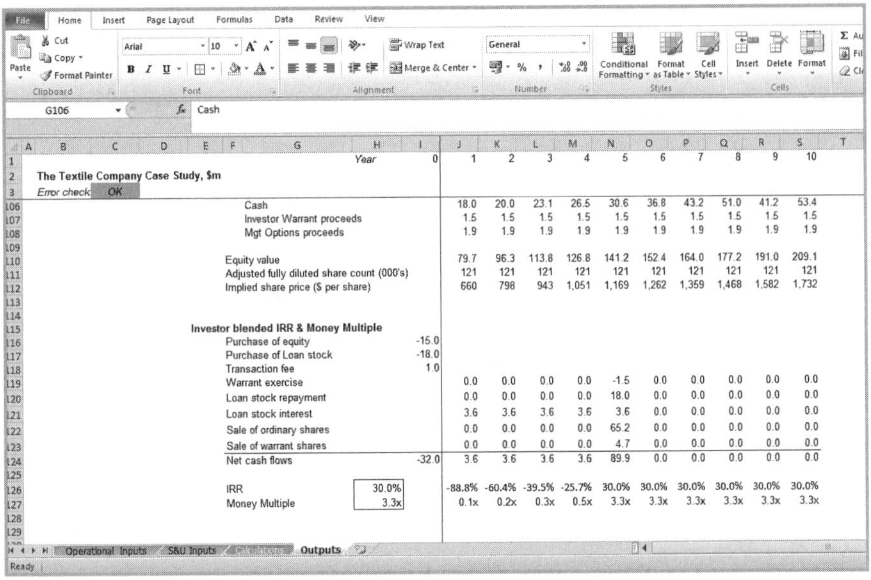

FIGURE 9.34

Finally, we show the Exit Sensitivity Analysis module in Figure 9.35.

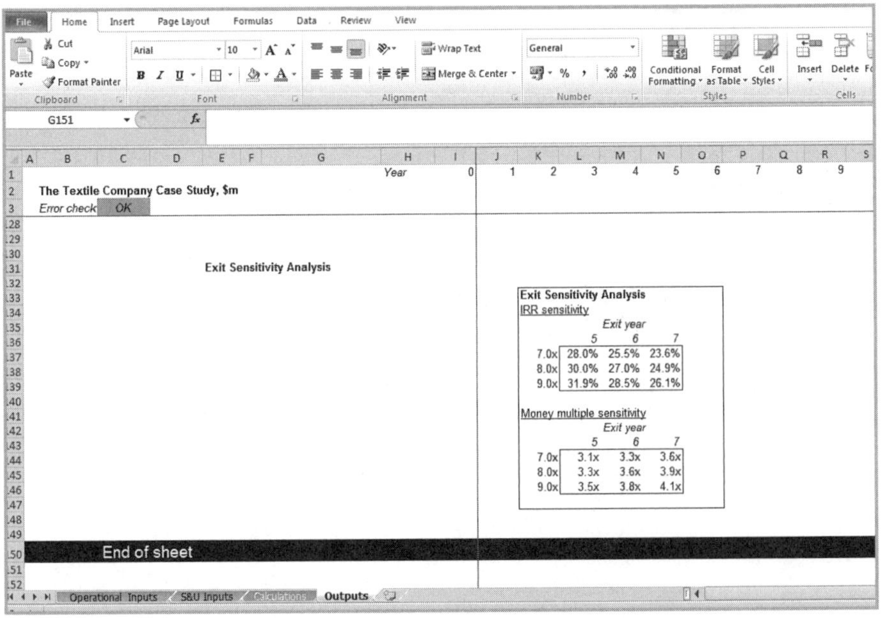

FIGURE 9.35

CHAPTER TEN

CASE STUDY 5:

Leveraged Buyout

The fifth case study features a leveraged buyout (LBO) transaction, the acquisition of a company by a private equity fund. The main feature of an LBO transaction is the use of a high level of debt to finance the acquisition of the target company. In an LBO transaction, the buyer (typically a private equity fund, but it can be a company as well) uses a combination of debt and equity to fund the purchase of the target company. Equity money is provided by the buyer. Debt money is provided by a lender, typically an investment bank. After the acquisition, the buyer of the target company will use the cash generated by the target company to repay the acquisition debt over time.

Here the target company is a business in the hospitality sector called the Travel and Leisure Group (TLG). As its name suggests, TLG is both a travel specialist and an operator of leisure activity centers. The company operates as two divisions: TravelCo (travel) and LeisureCo (leisure). LeisureCo offers residential leisure activities, while TravelCo specializes in offering tours.

TLG's products are marketed through a variety of highly recognizable brands. The company benefits from a high revenue visibility because of its forward booking nature, which is attractive to lenders.

TravelCo Overview

The TravelCo Division has two broad product offerings: tours and mountain bike rides. Its tours offerings include a variety of tours to worldwide destinations, including safaris in Africa and ski trips in Europe. These trips have a mix of educational and leisure elements and are sold under different brands, thus providing the division with a number two or number one market position in various market segments (for example, corporate events and functions, student holiday markets, family holidays, and weddings).

LeisureCo Overview

The LeisureCo Division operates a chain of 50 three-star hotels around the globe. These hotels are used for two purposes: residential activity courses for students and groups (for example, climbing, go-karts, and Quad biking) and accommodation for customers of TravelCo who choose to stay at a TLG-owned hotel rather than a third-party hotel.

In this case study, you are leading negotiations, on behalf of your private equity firm, to acquire TLG by way of a leveraged buyout. The owner of TLG (that is, the vendor) has provided key inputs concerning the operational assumptions (revenue, EBITDA, working capital, and capital expenditures). Key terms of your proposed investment have been agreed upon with the vendor. The inputs are summarized in Table 10.1, and you will need to build a 10-year integrated financial model that includes the profit and loss statement, the balance sheet, and the cash flow statement. You'll need to model the debt package (provided by a bank to fund the acquisition of TLG), including credit statistics. You'll also need to calculate the initial financial returns on your proposed investment to see whether the project makes financial sense for your firm.

10.1 KEY INPUTS

Operational inputs are given in Table 10.1.

TABLE 10.1 OPERATIONAL INPUTS

Revenue

Year	2010A	2011A	2012 (F:9+3)	3 months 2012	2013P	2014P	2015P	2016P	2017P	2018P	2019P	2020P
TravelCo	50.0	52.0	55.0	13.8	63.3	75.9	87.3	94.3	101.8	110.0	117.7	125.9
LeisureCo	20.0	21.6	24.2	6.0	26.6	33.3	38.3	42.1	45.4	48.6	52.0	55.7

EBITDA Margin

Year	2010A	2011A	2012 (F:9+3)	3 months 2012	2013P	2014P	2015P	2016P	2017P	2018P	2019P
TravelCo	15%	15%	15%	15%	15%	15%	15%	15%	15%	15%	15%
LeisureCo	28%	28%	28%	28%	28%	28%	28%	28%	28%	28%	28%

Capex

Year	3 months 2012	2013P	2014P	2015P	2016P	2017P	2018P	2019P
Maintenance capex	0.5	2.0	1.5	1.5	1.5	1.5	1.5	1.5
Growth capex	0.0	2.5	8.5	3.0	0.0	0.0	0.0	0.0
Stock (inventory in U.S. usage) as % of sales	0.1%	0.1%	0.1%	0.1%	0.1%	0.1%	0.1%	0.1%
Trade debtors (accounts receivable) as % of sales	0.1%	0.1%	0.1%	0.1%	0.1%	0.1%	0.1%	0.1%
Trade creditors (accounts payable) as % of sales	7%	7%	7%	7%	7%	7%	7%	7%
Customer deposits	8.0	8.5	9.0	9.0	9.0	9.0	9.0	9.0
Corporation (corporate) tax	28%	28%	28%	28%	28%	28%	28%	28%
Depreciation	1.0	4.0	4.0	5.0	5.0	1.5	1.5	1.5
TLA repayment		25/6	25/6	25/6	25/6	25/6	25/6	
Capex facility drawdown			10.0					
Capex facility repayment				2.0	2.0	2.0	2.0	2.0

- *Timeline.* The company's fiscal year ends on December 31. We are in October 2012.
- *Revenue.* Historical revenue is provided for the last two years, 2010 and 2011. Projected revenues are provided for 2013 to 2020. Since we are in October 2012, the company's fiscal year 2012 has not yet been completed. At this stage, actual results are available through September 30, 2012, or for the first nine months of 2012. Revenue for the remaining three months of 2012 is provided on a forecast basis. This three-month period in 2012 is often referred to as the stub period, or the "portion" of the annual period needed to complete fiscal year 2012. Separate revenue figures are provided for TravelCo and LeisureCo.
- *EBITDA %.* EBITDA margin is projected at 15 percent and 28 percent for TravelCo and LeisureCo, respectively.
- *Capex.* Capex for maintenance and expansion purposes is provided separately. Maintenance capex is projected at between $1.5 and $2 million per year. Growth capex is required in 2013, 2014, and 2015 to fund the expansion of the business.

- *Stock.* The company requires little stock, which is projected to be 0.1 percent of sales.
- *Trade debtors.* The company has limited trade debtor balances, which are projected to be 0.1 percent of sales.
- *Trade creditors.* Trade creditors are projected to be 7 percent of sales.
- *Customer deposits.* The group holds a sizable amount of customer deposits, or money paid in advance by customers to confirm bookings. Customer deposits are projected at between $8 and $9 million at the end of each fiscal year.
- *Corporation tax.* This is projected at 28 percent of profit before tax.
- *Depreciation.* Figures for this are provided in Table 10.1.
- *Term loan.* A term loan is provided as part of the financing of the acquisition of TLG. The repayment profile is provided in Table 10.1.
- *Capex facility.* TLG is set to expand substantially during 2013, 2014, and 2015, and this growth will be partly financed using a capex facility. The capex facility will be drawn down in 2014 and will be repaid over five years.

The sources and uses inputs are given in Table 10.2.

TABLE 10.2 SOURCES AND USES INPUTS

Uses	
Refinancing existing TLA	23.50
Purchase of equity	96.50
Deal costs	7.00
Total	**127.00**
Sources	
Term loan A	25.00
Term loan B	24.00
Mezzanine	13.00
Subordinated loan	64.00
Ordinary equity	1.00
Total	**127.00**

Other Committed Bank Facilities—Undrawn at Closing	
Capex facility	10.00

- *Uses of funds.* The proposed investment is estimated at $127 million and would be used to:
  - Refinance (that is, repay) an existing term loan of $23.5 million.
  - Purchase 100 percent of TLG's equity for $96.5 million.
  - Cover transaction costs totaling $7 million.
- *Sources of funds.* The proposed investment would come from the following sources of funds:
  - An ordinary equity investment of $1 million.
  - A subordinated loan totaling $64 million. Both the ordinary equity and the subordinated loan are provided by your private equity fund.
  - Term loan A totaling $25 million.
  - Term loan B totaling $24 million.
  - A mezzanine loan totaling $13 million. Term loan A, term loan B, and the mezzanine loan are provided by a bank (see the later discussion of the terms of these instruments).

Predeal and Postdeal Balance Sheet

As in the previous case study, we can calculate the postdeal balance sheet based on the predeal balance sheet shown in Figure 10.1 and the sources and uses of funds given in Table 10.2.

Using the approach employed in the previous case study, we will apply the sources and uses of funds to the predeal balance sheet in order to obtain the postdeal balance sheet.

The predeal balance sheet is given on the left-hand side of Figure 10.1. Manual adjustments to the predeal balance sheet are made to reflect the sources and uses of funds in the middle part of the table.

Then the postdeal balance sheet is calculated for each line of the predeal balance sheet by adding the corresponding adjustments to the predeal balance sheet number. These adjustments are made as follows:

- *Uses of funds.* The proposed investment amounts to $127 million, to be used as follows:
  - Refinance (that is, repay) an existing term loan of $23.5 million. An amount of $23.5 million is included in the term loan A line. This amount of $23.5 million comes from the new term loan A of $25 million and will be deducted from the predeal term loan A balance of –$23.5 million, to result in a postdeal term loan A balance of $0 million. In other words, the existing term loan A of $23.5 million is fully repaid using $23.5 million from the new term loan A of $25 million.

- Purchase 100 percent of TLG's equity for $96.5 million. An amount of $96.5 million is included in the goodwill line. This amount is added to the predeal balance sheet. By definition, (positive) goodwill is the premium paid for the shares of TLG over and beyond the net asset value. The predeal value of the net assets is $15.8 million, and this amount is deducted from the predeal goodwill. Taking the predeal goodwill, adding the purchase price of $96.5 million to it, and deducting $15.8 million of net assets from it gives the postdeal goodwill.
- Pay transaction costs totaling $7 million. The transaction fees are capitalized, or added to the long-term assets of the company. An amount of $7 million is included in the transaction costs line. This amount will be added to the predeal transaction costs balance of 0 to result in a postdeal transaction costs balance of $7 million.
- *Sources of funds.* The proposed investment would come from the following sources of funds:
  - An ordinary equity investment of $1 million. An amount of $1 million is included in the ordinary shares line. Since the entire equity of TLG is changing hands, we take out (that is, deduct) non-third-party capital (ordinary shares, P&L reserves [or retained profit or retained earnings], and so on).
  - A subordinated loan of $64 million. An amount of $64 million is included in the subordinated loan line. Since the subordinated loan is a liability, the adjustment amount shown on the subordinated loan line is –$64 million. This amount will be added to the predeal subordinated loan balance of 0 to result in a postdeal subordinated loan balance of –$64 million. Note that the negative sign reflects the convention chosen to show liabilities in the balance sheet as negative numbers.
  - Term loan A totaling $25 million. An amount of $25 million is included in the term loan A line (this is the new term loan A). Since this loan is a liability, the adjustment amount shown on the term loan A line is –$25 million.
  - Term loan B totaling $24 million. An amount of $24 million is included in the term loan B line. Since term loan B is a liability, the adjustment amount shown on the term loan B line is –$24 million.

- Mezzanine financing totaling $13 million. An amount of $13 million is included in the mezzanine line. Since this loan is a liability, the adjustment amount shown on the mezzanine line is –$13 million.

	Pre-deal	Adjustments Uses	Adjustments Sources	Post-deal
Fixed Assets				
Tangible Assets	29.0			29.0
Financial Assets				0.0
Investment in Joint Ventures				0.0
Intangibles				0.0
Transaction Goodwill	24.7	96.5	-15.8	105.5
Transaction costs		7.0		7.0
Total Fixed assets	53.7			141.4
Current Assets				
Stock	0.1			0.1
Trade debtors	0.0			0.0
Total Current Assets	0.1			0.1
Cash Balance	5.1			5.1
Current Liabilities (enter as neg)				
Trade creditors	-2.2			-2.2
Customer deposits	-17.5			-17.5
Tax creditor				0.0
Total Current Liabilities	-19.7			-19.7
Total Assets less CL	39.3			127.0
Net Current Assets	-14.4			-14.4
LT Liabilities (enter as neg)				
Term Loan A	-23.5	23.5	-25.0	-25.0
Term Loan B			-24.0	-24.0
Capex Facility				
Mezzanine		0.0	-13.0	-13.0
Subordinated Loan			-64.0	-64.0
Total LT Liabilities	-23.5			-126.0
Net Assets	15.8			1.0
Ordinary Shares	0.1	-0.1	1.0	1.0
P&L reserve	15.7	-15.7		0.0
Net Worth	15.8			1.0
Check (must be 0)	0.0			0.0

FIGURE 10.1

The resulting postdeal balance sheet is presented on the right-hand side of Figure 10.1. The postdeal balance sheet is the same as the predeal balance sheet as far as fixed assets (excluding goodwill and transaction costs), current assets, and current liabilities are concerned. However, the postdeal balance sheet differs from the predeal balance sheet in terms of long-term liabilities and equity. In particular, the term loan A, term loan B, mezzanine, and subordinated loan amounts are as given in the sources of funds. The equity amount is also as given in the sources of funds, $1 million of ordinary shares.

Exit Assumptions

Investor exit assumptions		Entry EV	114.9
Exit year	7	Entry EBITDA Multiple:	
Exit EBITDA Mult	9.0x	2012	2013
		7.6x	6.8x

FIGURE 10.2

Exit assumptions are provided in Figure 10.2. The proposed investor exit time frame is seven years from the date of the transaction. The exit enterprise-value-to-EBITDA multiple is assumed to be 9 times. This is an improvement from the entry enterprise-value-to-2012-EBITDA multiple of 7.6 times or the entry enterprise-value-to-2013-EBITDA multiple of 6.8 times, reflecting the view that the business would command a higher valuation in seven years' time.

Debt Assumptions

Debt assumptions	Quantum	tenor	price
Term Loan A	25.0	6	8.0%
Term Loan B	24.0	8	9.0%
Capex Facility	10.0	7	8.0%
Mezzanine	13.0	9	12.0%

FIGURE 10.3

Term loan A has a six-year life and an interest rate of 8 percent per annum. The amortization schedule was provided earlier and is $4.2 million (that is, $25 million divided by 6) per annum over six years. Term loan B has an eight-year life and an interest rate of 9 percent per annum. This is a bullet loan. The capex facility is a seven-year loan with interest of 8 percent per annum. Finally, the mezzanine loan has a maturity of nine years and an interest rate of 12 percent per annum.

Other Assumptions
- Interest is paid in the year in which it is incurred.
- Tax is paid in the year in which it is incurred.
- Exit occurs at year-end.

10.1.1 Creating the Operational Inputs and Sources and Uses Inputs Sheets

Let's create the Operational Inputs sheet, in which we capture these inputs starting at row 8, as illustrated in Figures 10.4 and 10.5. The timeline is also shown on rows 1, 2, and 3 in these figures.

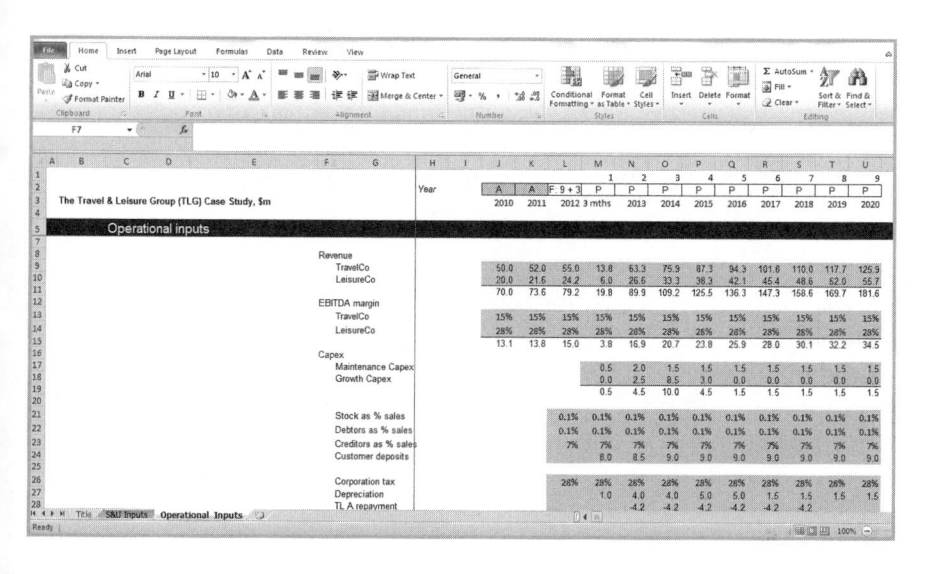

FIGURE 10.4

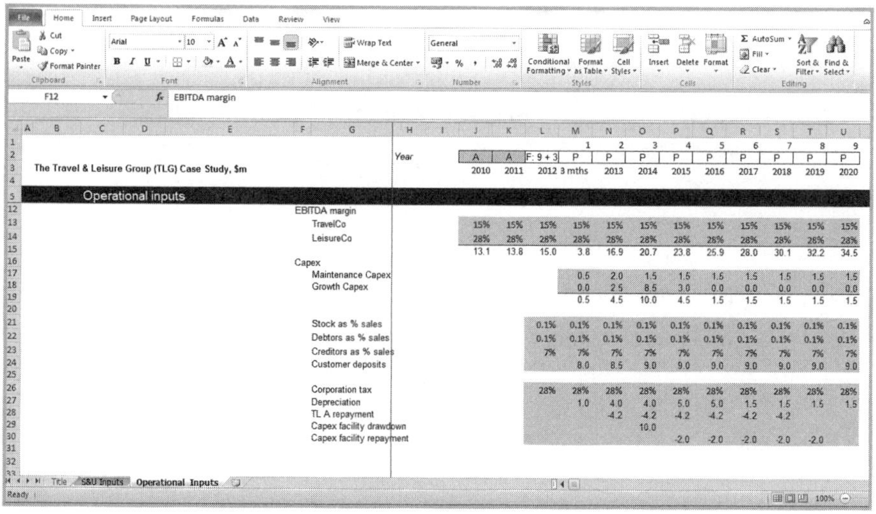

FIGURE 10.5

We can also create the Sources & Uses (S&U) Inputs sheet, which captures all the key inputs described earlier. An illustration is shown in Figures 10.6 to 10.9.

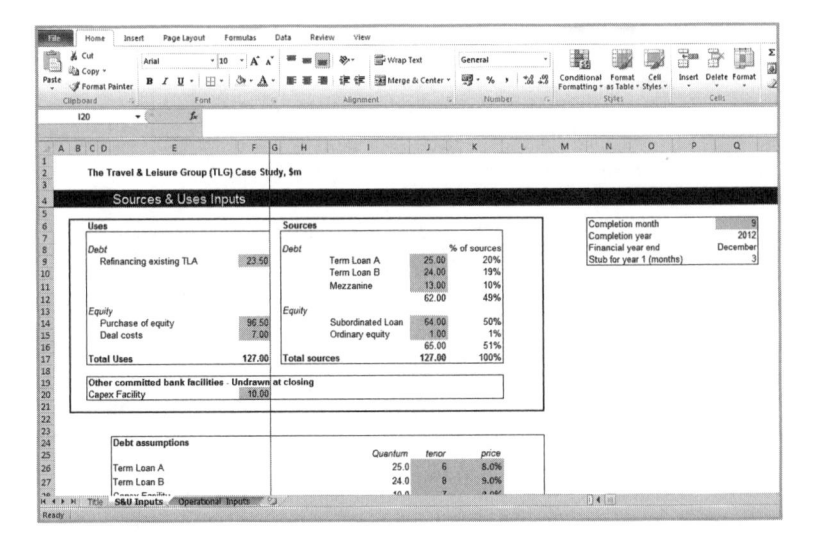

FIGURE 10.6

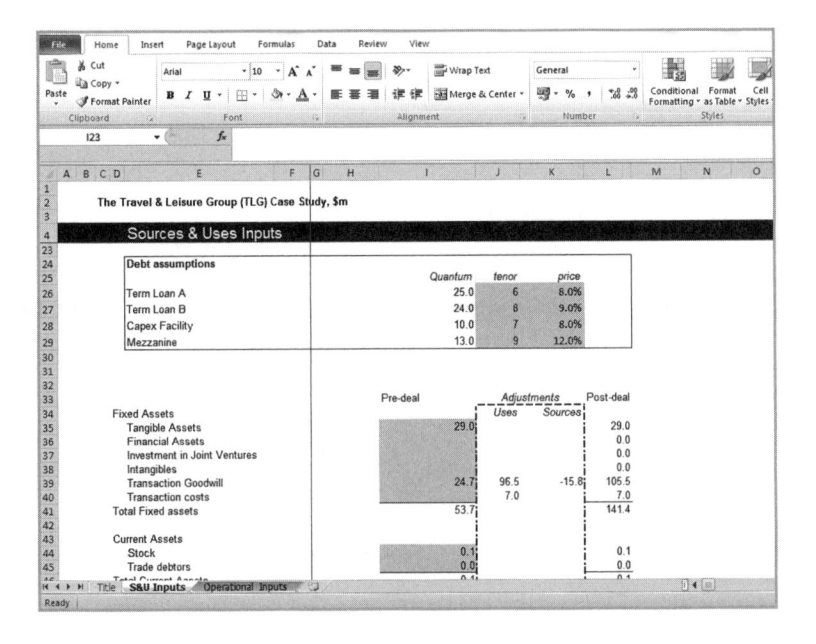

FIGURE 10.7

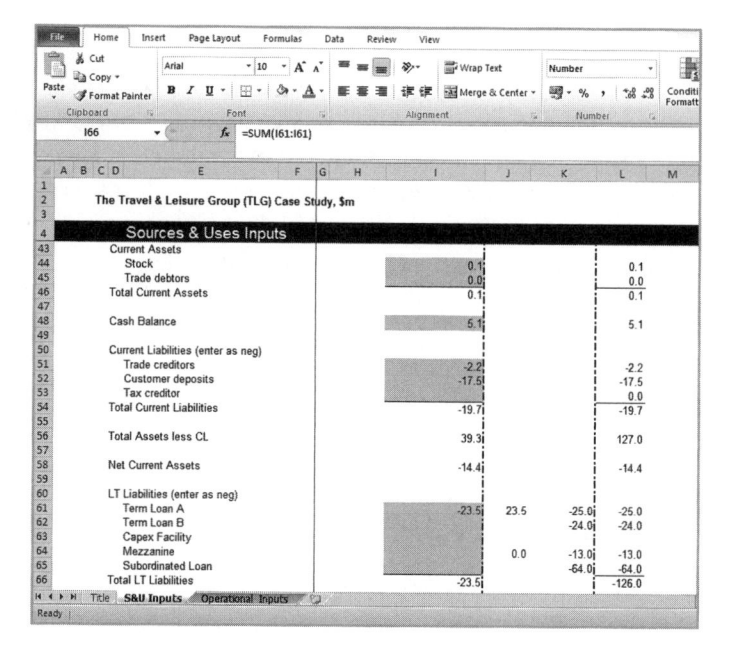

FIGURE 10.8

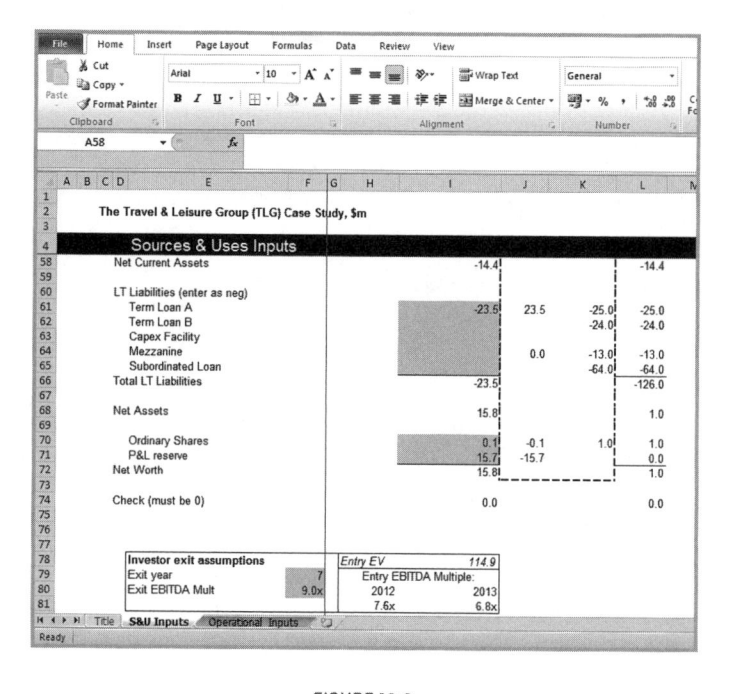

FIGURE 10.9

10.2 WRITING MODEL SPECIFICATIONS

As in the previous chapter, the model has two parts: the integrated financial model part (the profit and loss statement, balance sheet, and cash flow statement) and the other modules, which are built using different components of the integrated financial model: credit statistics and the exit schedule.

10.2.1 Building the Integrated Financial Model

Profit and Loss Module

Sales

- Divisional sales projections are given.
- Total company sales are then obtained by aggregating the divisional sales projections. For each period of time t, calculate company sales_t as TravelCo sales_t plus LeisureCo sales _t.

EBITDA

- For each period of time t, calculate company EBITDA_t as TravelCo EBITDA margin_t times TravelCo sales_t plus LeisureCo EBITDA margin_t times LeisureCo sales_t.

Depreciation

- This is given.

EBIT (Earnings Before Interest and Tax)

- For each period of time t, calculate EBIT_t as EBITDA_t minus depreciation_t.

Interest

- For each period of time t, the interest charge will be calculated in the Debt module (discussed later).
- Note that we will need to calculate interest for each debt instrument (term loan A, term loan B, the capex facility, and the mezzanine financing).
- Total interest is then calculated as the aggregate of the interest on all the different debt instruments.

EBT (Earnings Before Tax)

- For each period of time t, calculate EBT_t as EBIT_t minus total interest_t.

Tax

- For each period of time t, calculate tax_t as tax rate times EBT_t if EBT_t is positive. Otherwise tax_t = 0.

PAT (Profit After Tax)

- For each period of time t, calculate PAT_t as EBT_t minus tax_t.

Retained Profit (Retained Earnings in U.S. Usage)

- This will be calculated using a control account in which retained profit carried forward_t = retained profit brought forward_t plus PAT_t.
- Retained profit brought forward_t = retained profit carried forward_t–1.
- Retained profit brought forward_year 1 = retained profit carried forward in the opening balance sheet.

Debt Module

Since we have four debt instruments (term loan A, term loan B, capex facility, and mezzanine financing), we need to calculate the debt amounts and interest for each instrument.

The term loan A debt control account will be calculated as follows:

- Term loan A debt opening balance_t = term loan A debt closing balance_t–1, with term loan A debt opening balance_year 1 = term loan A debt balance in the postdeal balance sheet.
- Term loan A debt drawdown_t = 0.
- Term loan A debt repayment_t is given in the amortization schedule.
- Term loan A debt closing balance_t = term loan A debt opening balance_t plus term loan A debt drawdown_t plus term loan A debt repayment_t.

The term loan A interest control account will be calculated as follows:

- Term loan A interest opening balance_t = term loan A interest closing balance_t–1, with term loan A interest opening balance_year 1 = 0.
- Term loan A interest charge_t = term loan A interest rate times (term loan A debt opening balance_t plus term loan A debt drawdown_t).
- Term loan A interest paid_t = – term loan A interest charge_t.

- Term loan A interest closing balance_t = term loan A interest opening balance_t plus term loan A interest charg e_t plus term loan A interest paid_t.

The term loan B debt control account will be calculated as follows:

- Term loan B debt opening balance_t = term loan B debt closing balance_t–1, with term loan B debt opening balance_year 1 = term loan B debt balance in the postdeal balance sheet.
- Term loan B debt drawdown_t = 0.
- Term loan B debt repayment_t is given in the amortization schedule.
- Term loan B debt closing balance_t = term loan B debt opening balance_t plus term loan B debt drawdown_t plus term loan B debt repayment_t.

The term loan B interest control account will be calculated as follows:

- Term loan B interest opening balance_t = term loan B interest closing balance_t–1, with term loan B interest opening balance_ year 1 = 0.
- Term loan B interest charge_t = term loan B interest rate times (term loan B debt opening balance_t plus term loan B debt drawdown_t).
- Term loan B interest paid_t = – term loan B interest charge_t.
- Term loan B interest closing balance_t = term loan B interest opening balance_t plus term loan B interest charge_t plus term loan B interest paid_t.

The capex facility debt control account will be calculated as follows:

- Capex facility debt opening balance_t = capex facility debt clos-ing balance_t–1, with capex facility debt opening balance_year 1 = capex facility debt balance in the postdeal balance sheet.
- Capex facility debt drawdown_t = is given in the capex facility drawdown schedule in Table 10.1
- Capex facility debt repayment_t is given in the amortization schedule.
- Capex facility debt closing balance_t = capex facility debt open-ing balance_t plus capex facility debt drawdown_t plus capex facility debt repayment_t.

The capex facility interest control account will be calculated as follows:

- Capex facility interest opening balance_t = capex facility interest closing balance_t–1, with capex facility interest opening balance_year 1 = 0.
- Capex facility interest charge_t = capex facility interest rate times (capex facility debt opening balance_t plus capex facility debt drawdown_t).
- Capex facility interest paid_t = – capex facility interest charge_t.
- Capex facility interest closing balance_t = capex facility interest opening balance_t plus capex facility interest charge_t plus capex facility interest paid_t.

The mezzanine debt control account will be calculated as follows:

- Mezzanine debt opening balance_t = mezzanine debt closing balance_t–1, with mezzanine debt opening balance_year 1 = mezzanine debt balance in the postdeal balance sheet.
- Mezzanine debt drawdown_t = 0.
- Mezzanine debt repayment_t is given in the amortization schedule.
- Mezzanine debt closing balance_t = mezzanine debt opening balance_t plus mezzanine debt drawdown_t plus mezzanine debt repayment_t.

The mezzanine interest control account will be calculated as follows:

- Mezzanine interest opening balance_t = mezzanine interest closing balance_t–1, with mezzanine interest opening balance_year 1 = 0.
- Mezzanine interest charge_t = mezzanine interest rate times (mezzanine debt opening balance_t plus mezzanine debt drawdown_t).
- Mezzanine interest paid_t = – mezzanine interest charge_t.
- Mezzanine interest closing balance_t = mezzanine interest opening balance_t plus mezzanine interest charge_t plus mezzanine interest paid_t.

Fixed Assets Module

Apart from tangible assets, all of the long-term assets in the balance sheet are assumed to be unchanged throughout the projection period.

The tangible fixed assets control account will be calculated as follows:

- Tangible fixed assets opening balance_t = tangible fixed assets closing balance_t–1, with tangible fixed assets opening balance_ year 1 = tangible fixed assets balance in the postdeal balance sheet.
- Capex increases the book value of tangible fixed assets. Capex_t = capex as % of sales_t times sales_t.
- Depreciation decreases the book value of tangible fixed assets. Depreciation_t is already given.
- Tangible fixed assets closing balance_t = tangible fixed assets opening balance_t plus capex_t plus depreciation_t.

Tax Module

According to the tax assumptions, tax is paid in the year in which it has been incurred; hence, there is no tax creditor. Notwithstanding the non-existence of a tax creditor on the balance sheet, we can calculate the tax creditor using the control account approach.

The tax creditor control account will be calculated as follows:

- Tax creditor opening balance_t = tax creditor closing balance_t–1, with tax creditor opening balance_year 1 = tax creditor balance in the postdeal balance sheet.
- A tax charge in the Profit and Loss module increases the tax creditor balance. Tax charge_t = tax_t, taken from the Profit and Loss module.
- Tax paid decreases the tax creditor balance. Tax paid_t = – tax charge_t.
- Tax creditor closing balance_t = tax creditor opening balance_t plus tax charge_t plus tax paid_t.

Balance Sheet Module

- Tangible fixed assets closing balance_t is calculated in the Fixed Assets module (discussed earlier).
- Financial assets_t = financial assets in the postdeal balance sheet.

- Investment in joint ventures_t = investment in joint ventures in the postdeal balance sheet.
- Intangibles = intangibles in the postdeal balance sheet.
- Transaction goodwill_t = transaction goodwill in the postdeal balance sheet.
- Transaction costs_t = transaction costs in the postdeal balance sheet.
- Total fixed assets_t = the sum of (tangible fixed assets closing balance_t, financial assets_t, investment in joint ventures_t, intangibles_t, transaction goodwill_t, and transaction costs_t).
- Stock_t = stock (inventory) as % of sales_t times company sales_t.
- Trade debtors_t = trade debtors (accounts receivable) as % of sales_t times company sales_t.
- Current assets_t = stock_t plus debtors_t.
- Closing cash balance_t is calculated in the Cash Flow module (discussed later).
- Trade creditors_t = – trade creditors (accounts payable) as % of sales_t times company sales_t.
- Customer deposits_t is given in the projected balance sheet.
- Tax creditor_t = – tax creditor closing balance_t.
- Current liabilities_t = creditors_t plus other creditors_t plus tax creditor_t.
- Total assets less CL_t = total fixed assets_t + current assets_t + current liabilities_t.
- Net current assets_t = current assets_t + current liabilities_t + closing cash balance_t.
- Closing term loan A debt balance_t is calculated in the Debt module (discussed earlier).
- Closing term loan B debt balance_t is calculated in the Debt module (discussed earlier).
- Closing capex facility debt balance_t is calculated in the Debt module (discussed earlier).
- Closing mezzanine debt balance_t is calculated in the Debt module (discussed earlier).
- Subordinated loan balance_t = subordinated loan balance in the postdeal balance sheet.
- Net assets_t = fixed assets closing balance_t + net current assets_t + debt closing balance_t.
- Ordinary shares_t = ordinary shares in the postdeal balance sheet.

- Retained profit carried forward_t is calculated in the Profit and Loss module (discussed earlier).
- Net worth_t = ordinary shares_t plus retained profit carried forward_t.

Since net worth must equal net assets, let us add at the bottom of the balance sheet a balance sheet check that verifies that the balance sheet balances in each period. To this end, we include an additional line as follows:

- Check balance_t = net assets_t minus net worth_t.

Cash Flow Module

- EBITDA_t is calculated in the Profit and Loss module (discussed earlier).
- Movement in stock_t = stock_t–1 minus stock_t, or stock at the start of the year minus stock at the end of the year.
- Movement in trade debtors_t = trade debtors_t–1 minus trade debtors_t, or trade debtors at the start of the year minus trade debtors at the end of the year.
- Movement in trade creditors_t = (trade creditors_t–1 plus other creditors_t–1) minus (trade creditors_t plus other creditors_t), or trade creditors and other creditors at the start of the year minus trade creditors and other creditors at the end of the year.
- Movement in working capital_t = movement in stock_t plus movement in trade debtors_t plus movement in trade creditors_t.
- Operating cash flow_t = EBITDA_t + movement in working capital_t.
- Capex_t is calculated in the Fixed Assets module.
- Cash flow before taxation and financing_t = operating cash flow_t minus capex_t.
- Tax_t is calculated in the Tax module.
- Cash flow available for debt service_t = cash flow before taxation and financing_t minus tax_t.
- Term loan A interest paid_t is calculated in the Debt module.
- Term loan B interest paid_t is calculated in the Debt module.
- Capex facility interest paid_t is calculated in the Debt module.
- Mezzanine interest paid_t is calculated in the Debt module.
- Term loan A debt repayment_t is calculated in the Debt module.

- Term loan B debt repayment_t is calculated in the Debt module.
- Capex facility debt repayment_t is calculated in the Debt module.
- Mezzanine debt repayment_t is calculated in the Debt module.
- Net cash flow_t = cash flow available for debt service_t minus aggregate interest paid_t (for term loan A, term loan B, capex facility, and mezzanine debt) minus aggregate debt repayment_t (for term loan A, term loan B, capex facility, and mezzanine debt).

We also need to include a control account calculating the closing cash balance_t.

- Closing cash balance_t = opening cash balance_t plus net cash flow_t.
- Opening cash balance_t = closing cash balance_t–1, with opening cash balance_year 1 given in the postdeal balance sheet.

10.2.2 Credit Statistics

Lenders often use credit statistics or credit ratios to monitor the performance of loans they make to companies. In particular, these ratios are often set as covenants that the borrowing company must adhere to during the life of the loan. A breach of such covenants would result in sanctions or penalties (such as an increased interest rate or penalty fees), and in more serious cases a default. In a default scenario, the lender would be entitled to accelerate the repayment of the outstanding loan, thus leading to a liquidation of the company. In this case study, we will calculate the following credit statistics, which are among the most widely used ratios in leveraged finance.

- *EBITDA : net senior interest.* This is calculated as EBITDA divided by net senior interest, where net senior interest is calculated as the sum of interest income and interest cost incurred on senior loans (in this case, term loan A, term loan B, and the capex facility). Unless otherwise specified, the interest is taken from the profit and loss statement (that is, interest charge) and not from the cash flow statement (that is, not interest paid). EBITDA : net senior interest_t = EBITDA_t divided by the sum of (term loan A interest charge_t, term loan B interest charge_t, and capex facility interest charge _t).

- *EBITDA : net total interest.* This is calculated as EBITDA divided by net total interest, where net total interest is calculated as the sum of interest income and interest cost incurred on all loans (term loan A, term loan B, the capex facility, and mezzanine debt). Unless otherwise specified, the interest is taken from the profit and loss statement (that is, interest charge) and not from the cash flow statement (that is, not interest paid). EBITDA : net total interest_t = EBITDA_t divided by the sum of (term loan A interest charge_t, term loan B interest charge_t, capex facility interest charge _t, and mezzanine interest charge _t).
- *CFADS : senior debt service.* This is calculated as cash flow available for debt service divided by senior debt service. Cash flow available for debt service is taken from the Cash Flow module. Senior debt service is taken from the Cash Flow module and is the aggregate of interest and principal payments on the senior loans (in this case, term loan A, term loan B, and the capex facility). CFADS : senior debt service_t = cash flow available for debt service_t divided by the sum of (term loan A interest paid_t, term loan A debt repayment_t, term loan B interest paid_t, term loan B debt repayment_t, capex facility interest paid_t, and capex facility debt repayment_t).
- *CFADS : total debt service.* This is calculated as cash flow available for debt service divided by total debt service. Cash flow available for debt service is taken from the Cash Flow module. Total debt service is taken from the Cash Flow module and is the aggregate of interest and principal payments across all loans (term loan A, term loan B, the capex facility, and mezzanine debt). CFADS : total debt service_t = cash flow available for debt service_t divided by the sum of (term loan A interest paid_t, term loan A debt repayment_t, term loan B interest paid_t, term loan B debt repayment_t, capex facility interest paid_t, capex facility debt repayment_t, mezzanine interest paid_t, and mezzanine debt repayment_t). CFADS : total debt service_t is often referred to as the debt service cover ratio (DSCR).
- *Net senior debt : EBITDA.* This is calculated as net senior debt outstanding on the balance sheet divided by EBITDA. Net senior debt : EBITDA_t = the sum of (closing cash balance_t, closing term loan A debt balance_t, closing term loan B debt balance_t, and closing capex facility debt balance_t) divided by EBITDA_t.

- *Total net debt: EBITDA.* This is calculated as total debt outstanding on the balance sheet divided by EBITDA. Total net debt : EBITDA_t = the sum of (closing cash balance_t, closing term loan A debt balance_t, closing term loan B debt balance_t, closing capex facility debt balance_t, and closing mezzanine debt balance_t) divided by EBITDA_t.

10.2.3 Building the Exit and Return Schedules

As in the previous chapter, the main exit assumption has already been given, namely, the enterprise-value-to-EBITDA multiple. Based on the exit enterprise-value-to-EBITDA multiple, we can calculate the enterprise value. From the enterprise value, we can deduct net debt (that is, debt less cash), and the result is the value of equity. In this case, your private equity fund is the 100 percent owner of the equity, and so it is not necessary to calculate the value of one share. The exit waterfall can be calculated as follows.

Exit Waterfall

- EBITDA_t is taken from the Profit and Loss module.
- Enterprise-value-to-EBITDA multiple_t is taken from the exit assumptions.
- Enterprise value_t = enterprise-value-to-EBITDA multiple_t times EBITDA_t.
- Total enterprise value_t = enterprise value_t + closing cash balance_t.
- Term loan A_t = the minimum of closing term loan A debt balance_t and total enterprise value_t.
- Term loan B_t = the minimum of closing term loan B debt balance_t and total enterprise value_t less term loan A_t.
- Capex facility_t = the minimum of closing capex facility debt balance_t and total enterprise value_t less term loan A_t less term loan B_t.
- Mezzanine_t = the minimum of closing mezzanine debt balance_t and total enterprise value_t less term loan A_t less term loan B_t less capex facility_t.
- Subordinated loan_t = the minimum of closing subordinated loan debt balance_t and total enterprise value_t less term loan A_t less term loan B_t less capex facility _t less mezzanine_t.

- Equity value_t = total enterprise value_t less term loan A_t less term loan B_t less capex facility _t less mezzanine_t less subordinated loan _t.

Exit IRR and Money Multiple

As in the previous chapter, the key to calculating the IRR and the money multiple is to make sure that all cash flows to and from the investor, together with the timing of these cash flows, have been captured. A simple table can help ensure this, as shown in Table 10.3.

TABLE 10.3

Cash Item	Cash Type (Inflow or Outflow) and Amount	Timing
Purchase of equity	Outflow; amount specified in sources of funds	Year 0
Purchase of subordinated loan	Outflow; amount specified in sources of funds	Year 0
Repayment of subordinated loan	Inflow; amount taken from the balance sheet	Exit year (Year 7)
Proceeds from sale of equity	Inflow; amount taken from the exit waterfall	Exit year (Year 7)
Net cash flow	Sum of all the above	From Year 0 to exit year

- *IRR.* Based on the net cash flow just given, the IRR can be calculated using the IRR function in Excel.
- *Money multiple.* The money multiple calculates money returned to the investor as a proportion of the money laid out by the investor.

10.3 CREATING THE CALCULATIONS SHEET

Having gone through *how* the model calculations would work, we can now add the different calculation modules into the Calculations sheet.

10.3.1 Assumptions Module

Let's bring all the key operational assumptions, debt assumptions, and exit assumptions from the two input sheets (see Figures 10.10 and 10.11).

Operational Assumptions

- Revenue TravelCo. In cell J9, we can write the formula "='Operational Inputs'!J9", which picks up the TravelCo revenue figure from the Operational Inputs sheet.
- Revenue LeisureCo. In cell J10, we can write the formula "='Operational Inputs'!J10", which picks up the LeisureCo revenue figure from the Operational Inputs sheet.
- Consolidated revenue. In cell J11, we can write the formula "=SUM(J9:J10)", which aggregates the TravelCo and LeisureCo revenue figures in the previous rows.

Copy the block J9:J11 and paste special its formula into the block J9:U11.

- EBITDA margins. Copy cell J9 and paste special the formula into the block J13:U14.
- Consolidated EBITDA. In cell J15, we can write the formula "=J13*J9+J14*J10", which multiplies TravelCo EBITDA margin by TravelCo revenue, multiplies LeisureCo EBITDA margin by LeisureCo revenue, and aggregates the TravelCo and LeisureCo figures.
- Maintenance capex. In cell M17, we can write the formula "='Operational Inputs'!M17", which picks up the maintenance capex figure.
- Growth capex. In cell M18, we can write the formula "='Operational Inputs'!M18", which picks up the growth capex figure.
- Total capex. In cell M19, we can write "=SUM(M17:M18)", which aggregates the maintenance capex and the growth capex.
- Stock (inventory) as % of sales. In cell L21, we can write the formula "'Operational Inputs'!L21", which picks up stock (inventory) as a percentage of sales from the Operational Inputs sheet.

Copy cell L21 and paste special its formula into the following cells:

- Debtors (accounts receivable) as % of sales. Paste special the formula into the block L22:U22.
- Creditors (accounts payable) as % of sales. Paste special the formula into the block L23:U23.
- Customer deposits. Paste special the formula into the block L24:U24.

- Corporation tax. Paste special the formula into the block L26:U26.
- Depreciation. Paste special the formula into the block L27:U27.
- TLA repayment. Paste special the formula into the block L28:U28.
- Capex facility drawdown. Paste special the formula into the block L29:U29.
- Capex facility repayment. Paste special the formula into the block L30:U30.

Note that a quicker way of completing the Operational Inputs would be to paste special the formula into the block L22:U24 and the block L26:U30. This would involve only two steps instead of eight steps.

Debt Assumptions

- Term loan A quantum. In cell H33, we can write the formula "='S&U Inputs'!I26".

Copy cell H33 and paste special it into the block H33:J36. This picks up the entire debt assumptions table from the S&U Inputs sheet.

Exit Assumptions

- Exit year. In cell I42, we can write the formula "='S&U Inputs'!F79".

Copy cell I42 and paste special the formula into cell I43.

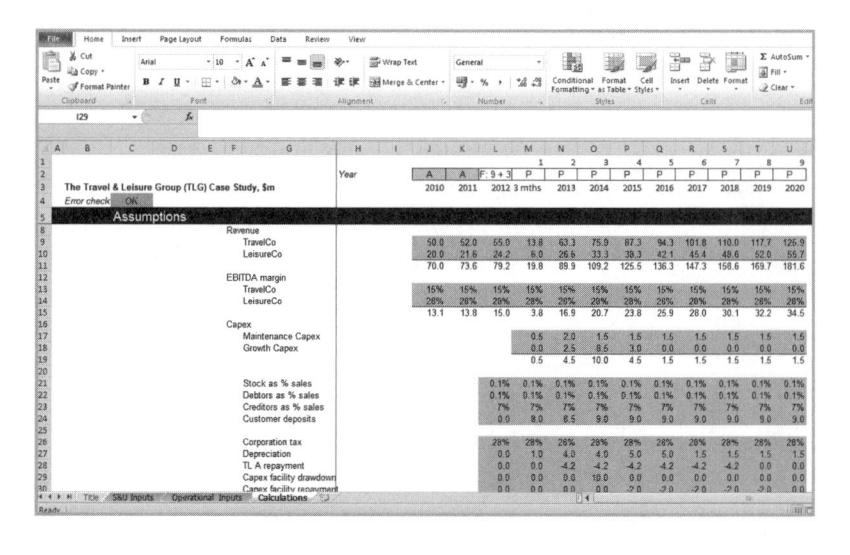

FIGURE 10.10

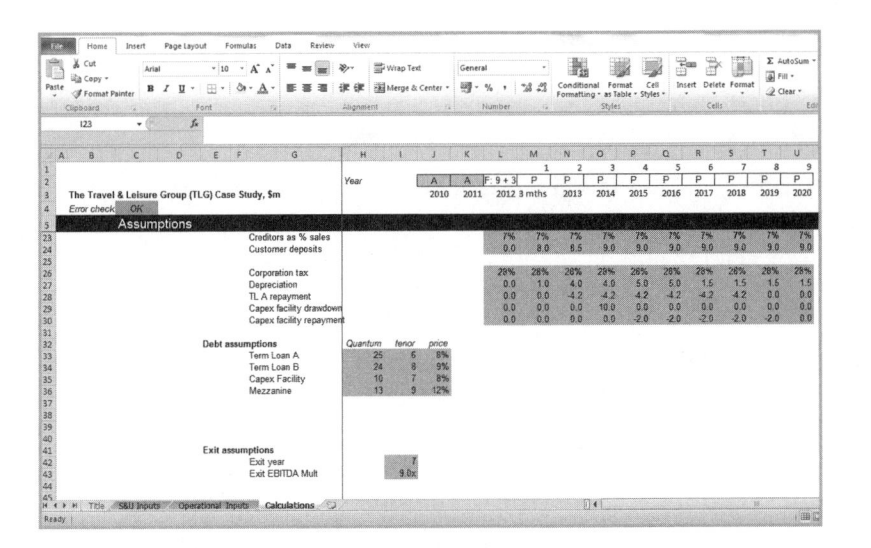

FIGURE 10.11

10.3.2 Profit and Loss Module

Let's create the Profit and Loss module right below the Assumptions module, say on row 48. We can now add the different lines of the Profit and Loss following the specifications described earlier.

Revenue

- In cell J49, we can write the formula "=J11", which basically picks up the revenue figure from row 11 of the Assumptions module.

Copy cell J49 and paste it into the block J49:S49.

Revenue growth

- In cell K50, we can write the formula "=IF(K1=1,"",IF(K1=2,K49/I49–1,K49/J49–1))", which calculates revenue growth as current year revenue divided by previous year revenue less 1.

Copy cell K50 and paste it into the block K50:U50.

EBITDA

- In cell J51, we can write the formula "=J15", which basically picks up the EBITDA figure from row 15 of the Assumptions module.

Copy cell J51 and paste it into the block J51:U51.

EBITDA margin

- In cell J52, we can write the formula "=J51/J49", which calculates EBITDA margin as EBITDA divided by revenue.

Copy cell J52 and paste it into the block J52:U52.

Depreciation

- In cell M53, we can write the formula "= –M27", which picks up the value of depreciation from row 27.

EBIT

- In cell M54, we can write the formula "=M51+M53", which calculates the profit (or earnings) before interest and tax as EBITDA less depreciation. Note that EBIT is defined as EBITDA less depreciation and amortization. Since there is no amortization here, EBIT is simply EBITDA less depreciation.

Term loan A interest

- As illustrated in the model specifications, the term loan A interest charge will be calculated in the Debt module, so we skip the interest line for now.

Term loan B interest

- Likewise, the term loan B interest charge will be calculated in the Debt module, so we skip the interest line for now.

Capex facility interest

- Likewise, the capex facility interest charge will be calculated in the Debt module, so we skip the interest line for now.

Mezzanine interest

- Likewise, the mezzanine interest charge will be calculated in the Debt module, so we skip the interest line for now.

Total interest

- In cell M60, we can write the formula "=SUM(M56:M59)", which aggregates the interest charges for term loan A, term loan B, capex facility, and mezzanine financing. The result of the aggregation is 0 for now, since the interest lines for term loan A, term loan B, capex facility, and mezzanine are empty (or 0).

EBT

- In cell M62, we can write the formula "=SUM(M60,M54)", which calculates EBT as equal to EBIT less total interest (note that interest will be negative, as it counts toward reducing profit; that is, it is a cost to the business).

Tax

- In cell M63, we can write the formula "=–IF(M62>0,M26*M62,0)", which calculates the tax as equal to the tax rate times EBT if EBT is positive. In other words, tax is incurred only if the business records a profit.

PAT

- In cell M64, we can write the formula "=M63+M62", which calculates PAT as EBT less tax.

Retained profit b/f

- In cell M66, we can write the formula "=IF(M$1=1,L108,L67)", which means that if we are in Year 1, then the retained profit brought forward is equal to the retained profit amount in the postdeal balance sheet. Otherwise, retained profit brought forward is equal to retained profit carried forward at the end of the previous period.

Retained profit c/f

- In cell M67, we can write the formula "=M66+M64", which calculates retained profit carried forward as equal to retained profit brought forward plus PAT.

Copy cells M53:M67 and paste them into the block M53:U67. The Profit and Loss module is illustrated in Figure 10.12.

Note that the Profit and Loss module shown in Figure 10.12 is not yet final, as the term loan A, term loan B, capex facility, and mezzanine interest charges have not been completed.

10.3.3 Balance Sheet Module

We will do the balance sheet in two steps. First, we need to bring the postdeal balance sheet from the S&U Inputs sheet into the Calculations sheet. The postdeal balance sheet is the starting balance sheet for our projections and is therefore needed for our calculations.

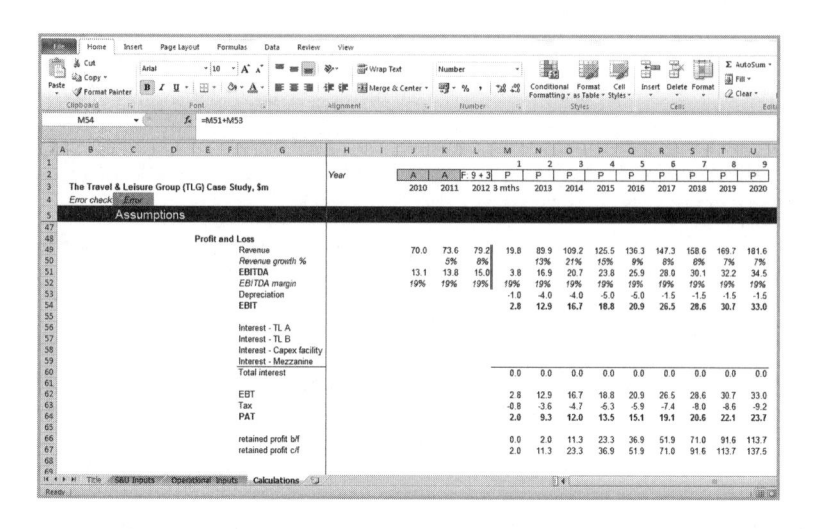

FIGURE 10.12

Then we will return to the balance sheet and complete it once the different components (the Debt module, the Fixed Assets module, and so on) have been completed.

To bring the postdeal balance sheet from the S&U Inputs sheet into the Calculations sheet, we can do as follows.

Fixed Assets

Postdeal tangible assets

- In cell L72, we can write the formula "='S&U Inputs'!L35", which picks up the postdeal tangible assets from the S&U Inputs sheet.

Copy cell L72.

Postdeal financial assets

- Paste special the formula into cell L73.

Postdeal investment in joint ventures

- Paste special the formula into cell L74.

Postdeal intangibles

- Paste special the formula into cell L75.

Postdeal transaction goodwill

- Paste special the formula into cell L76.

Postdeal transaction costs

■ Paste special the formula into cell L77.

Total fixed assets

■ In cell L78, we can write the formula "=SUM(L72:L77)", which aggregates all the components of fixed assets. Copy cell L78 and paste special the formula into the block L78:U78.

Current Assets

Postdeal stock (inventory)

■ In cell L81, we can write the formula "='S&U Inputs'!L44", which picks up the postdeal stock from the S&U Inputs sheet.

Copy cell L81.

Postdeal trade debtors (accounts receivable)

■ Paste special the formula into cell L82.

Total current assets

■ In cell L83, we can write the formula "=SUM(L81:L82)", which aggregates all the components of current assets.

Postdeal cash balance

■ In cell L85, we can write the formula "='S&U Inputs'!L48", which picks up the postdeal cash balance from the S&U Inputs sheet.

Current Liabilities

Postdeal trade creditors (accounts payable)

■ In cell L88, we can write the formula "='S&U Inputs'!L51", which picks up the postdeal trade creditors from the S&U Inputs sheet.

Copy cell L88.

Postdeal customer deposits

■ Paste special the formula into cell L89.

Postdeal tax creditor

■ Paste special the formula into cell L90.

Total current liabilities

- In cell L91, we can write the formula "=SUM(L88:L90)", which aggregates all the components of current liabilities. Copy cell L91 and paste special the formula into the block L91:U91.

Total assets less CL

- In cell L93, we can write the formula "=L78+L83+L91", which aggregates fixed assets, total current assets, and total current liabilities. Copy cell L93 and paste special the formulae into the block L93:U93.

Net current assets

- In cell L95, we can write the formula "=L83+L85+L91", which aggregates total current assets, total current liabilities, and cash balance. Copy cell L95 and paste special the formula into the block L95:U95.

Long-Term Liabilities

Postdeal term loan A

- In cell L98, we can write the formula "='S&U Inputs'!L61", which picks up the postdeal term loan A figure from the S&U Inputs sheet.

Copy cell L98.

Postdeal term loan B

- Paste special the formula into cell L99.

Postdeal capex facility

- Paste special the formula into cell L100.

Postdeal mezzanine

- Paste special the formula into cell L101.

Postdeal subordinated loan

- Paste special the formula into cell L102.

Total long-term liabilities

- In cell L103, we can write the formula "=SUM(L98:L102)", which aggregates all the components of long-term liabilities. Copy cell L103 and paste special the formula into the block L103:U103.

Net assets

- In cell L105, we can write the formula "=L78+L95+L103", which aggregates total fixed assets, net current assets, and long-term liabilities. Copy cell L105 and paste special the formula into the block L105:U105.

Postdeal ordinary shares

- In cell L107, we can write the formula "='S&U Inputs'!L70", which picks up the postdeal ordinary shares from the S&U Inputs sheet.

Copy cell L107.

- Postdeal P&L reserve
- Paste special the formula into cell L108.

Net worth

- In cell L109, we can write the formula "=SUM(L107:L108)", which aggregates all the components of net worth. Copy cell L109 and paste special the formula into the block L109:U109.

Balance sheet check

- In cell L111, we can write the formula "=ABS(L105–L109)", which calculates the difference between net assets and net worth, which should be 0. Copy cell L111 and paste special the formula into the block L111:U111.

Overall balance sheet check

- We've also written in cell C4 the formula "=IF(SUM($J$111:$ V$111)<=0.1,"OK","Error")", which gives an overall balance sheet error check. As in the previous chapter, a conditional formatting is applied to cell C4 such that if the value is OK, then the cell background color is green, and if the value is Error, then the cell background color is red.

The postdeal balance sheet is illustrated in Figures 10.13 and 10.14.

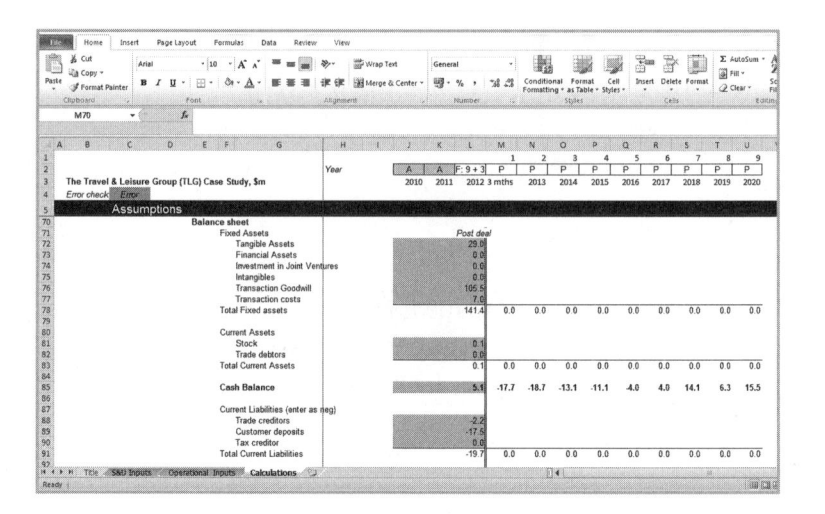

FIGURE 10.13

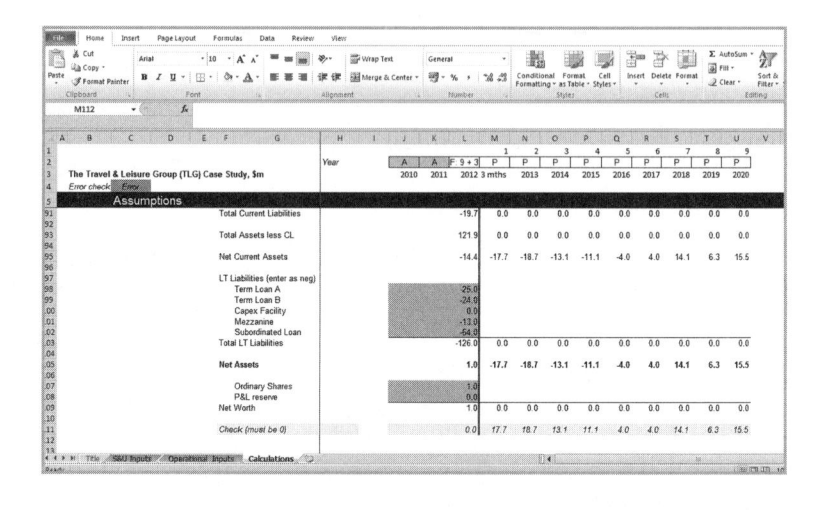

FIGURE 10.14

Having completed the postdeal balance sheet, we will now focus on calculating the projected balance sheet. To this end, we need to calculate the individual components (fixed assets, debt, and so on), after which we will revisit the balance sheet to incorporate the projected figures.

10.3.4 Debt Module

Let's create the Debt module right below the Balance Sheet module, say on row 114. We can now run a control account for the principal and a control account for the interest for each of term loan A, term loan B, the capex facility, and mezzanine in line with the specifications described earlier.

Term Loan A Debt Control Account

Debt balance b/f

- In cell M117, we can write the formula "=IF(M$1=1, –L98,L120)", which basically means that if we are in Year 1, then the term loan A debt brought forward is equal to the term loan A debt amount in the postdeal balance sheet (which is in cell L98). Otherwise, term loan A debt brought forward is equal to the term loan A debt carried forward from the previous year.

Debt drawdown

- We can leave this row empty, as there is no planned drawdown after year 0.

Debt repayment

- In cell M119, we can write the formula "=M28", which basically picks up row 28 (debt repaid).

Debt balance c/f

- In cell M120, we can write the formula "=SUM(M117:M119)", which basically calculates term loan A debt carried forward as being equal to term loan A debt brought forward plus term loan A debt drawdown less term loan A debt repaid.

Copy cells M117:M120 and paste them into the block M117:U120.

Term Loan A Interest Control Account

Interest b/f

- In cell M123, we can write the formula "=L126", which basically means that term loan A interest brought forward is equal to term loan A interest carried forward from the previous year.

Interest charge

- In cell M124, we can write the formula "=SUM(M117:M118)*$J$33", which calculates the term loan

A interest charge as being equal to the sum of the (term loan A debt balance brought forward plus term loan A debt drawdown) times the annual interest rate (which is in cell J33).

Interest paid

- In cell M125, we can write the formula "= –M124", which reflects our assumption that interest charged (or incurred) is paid in the same year.

Interest c/f

- In cell M126, we can write the formula "=SUM(M123:M125)", which basically calculates interest carried forward as being equal to interest brought forward plus interest charge less interest paid.

Copy cells M123:M126 and paste them into the block M123:U126.

Term Loan B Debt Control Account

Debt balance b/f

- In cell M131, we can write the formula "=IF(M$1=1,–L99,L134)", which basically means that if we are in Year 1, then term loan B debt brought forward is equal to the term loan B debt amount in the postdeal balance sheet (which is in cell L99). Otherwise, term loan B debt brought forward is equal to term loan B debt carried forward from the previous year.

Debt drawdown

- We can leave this row empty, as there is no planned drawdown after Year 0.

Debt repayment

- In cell M133, we can write the formula "=IF(M$1=$I$34, –M131,0)", which calculates debt repayment as 0 until term loan B reaches maturity (which is Year 8 or the value of cell I34).

Debt balance c/f

- In cell M134, we can write the formula "=SUM(M131:M133)", which basically calculates term loan B debt carried forward as equal to term loan B debt brought forward plus term loan B debt drawdown less term loan B debt repaid.

Copy cells M131:M134 and paste them into the block M131:U134.

Term Loan B Interest Control Account

Interest b/f

- In cell M137, we can write the formula "=L140", which basically means that term loan B interest brought forward equals term loan B interest carried forward from the previous year.

Interest charge

- In cell M138, we can write the formula "=SUM(M131:M132) *$J$34", which calculates the term loan B interest charge as being equal to the sum of the (term loan B debt balance brought forward plus term loan B debt drawdown) times the annual interest rate (which is in cell J34).

Interest paid

- In cell M139, we can write the formula "=–M138", which reflects our assumption that interest charged (or incurred) is paid in the same year.

Interest c/f

- In cell M140, we can write the formula "=SUM(M137:M139)", which basically calculates interest carried forward as being equal to interest brought forward plus interest charge less interest paid.

Copy cells M137:M140 and paste them into the block M137:U140.

Capex Facility Debt Control Account

Debt balance b/f

- In cell M145, we can write the formula "=IF(M$1=1, –L100,L148)", which basically means that if we are in Year 1, then the capex facility debt brought forward equals the capex facility debt amount in the postdeal balance sheet (which is in cell L100). Otherwise, capex facility debt brought forward is equal to the capex facility debt carried forward from the previous year.

Debt drawdown

- In cell M146, we can write the formula "M29", which picks up the capex facility amount drawdown from row 29.

Debt repayment

- In cell M147, we can write the formula "=M30", which picks up the capex facility amount repaid from row 30.

Debt balance c/f

- In cell M148, we can write the formula "=SUM(M145:M147)", which basically calculates the capex facility debt carried forward as being equal to the capex facility debt brought forward plus the capex facility debt drawdown less the capex facility debt repaid.

Copy cells M145:M148 and paste them into the block M145:U148.

Capex Facility Interest Control Account

Interest b/f

- In cell M151, we can write the formula "=L154", which basically means that the capex facility interest brought forward equals the capex facility interest carried forward from the previous year.

Interest charge

- In cell M152, we can write the formula "=SUM(M145:M146)*$J$35", which calculates the capex facility interest charge as being equal to the sum of the (capex facility debt balance brought forward plus the capex facility debt drawdown) times the annual interest rate (which is in cell J35).

Interest paid

- In cell M153, we can write the formula "= –M152", which reflects our assumption that interest charged (or incurred) is paid in the same year.

Interest c/f

- In cell M154, we can write the formula "=SUM(M151:M153)", which basically calculates interest carried forward as being equal to interest brought forward plus interest charge less interest paid.

Copy cells M151:M154 and paste them into the block M151:U154.

Mezzanine Debt Control Account

Debt balance b/f

- In cell M159, we can write the formula "=IF(M$1=1, –L101,L162)", which basically means if we are in Year 1, then mezzanine debt brought forward equals the mezzanine debt amount in the postdeal balance sheet (which is in cell L101). Otherwise, mezzanine debt brought forward equals mezzanine debt carried forward from the previous year.

Debt drawdown

- We can leave this row empty, as there is no planned drawdown after Year 0.

Debt repayment

- In cell M161, we can write the formula "=IF(M$1=$I$36, –M159,0)", which means that debt repayment is 0 unless we are in Year 9 (which is the value of cell I36).

Debt balance c/f

- In cell M162, we can write the formula "=SUM(M159:M161)", which basically calculates mezzanine debt carried forward as being equal to mezzanine debt brought forward plus mezzanine debt drawdown less mezzanine debt repaid.

Copy cells M159:M162 and paste them into the block M159:U162.

Mezzanine Interest Control Account

Interest b/f

- In cell M165, we can write the formula "=L168", which basically means that mezzanine interest brought forward equals mezzanine interest carried forward from the previous year.

Interest charge

- In cell M166, we can write the formula "=SUM(M159:M160)*$J$36" which calculates the mezzanine interest charge as being equal to the sum of the (mezzanine debt balance brought forward plus mezzanine debt drawdown) times the annual interest rate (which is in cell J36).

Interest paid

- In cell M167, we can write the formula "= –M166", which reflects our assumption that interest charged (or incurred) is paid in the same year.

Interest c/f

- In cell M168, we can write the formula "=SUM(M165:M167)", which basically calculates interest carried forward as being equal to interest brought forward plus interest charge less interest paid.

Copy cells M165:M168 and paste them into the block M165:U168. The debt module is illustrated in Figures 10.15 to 10.18.

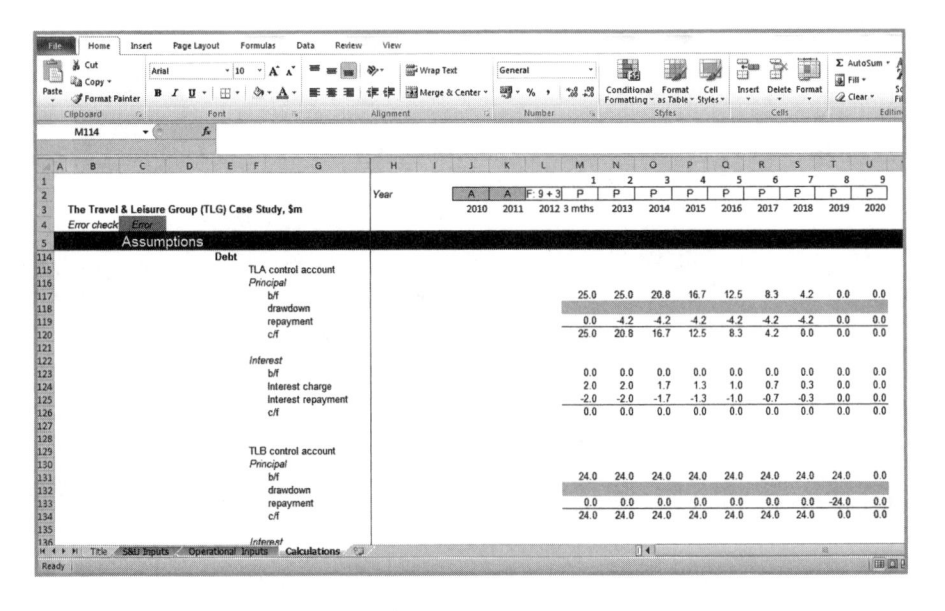

FIGURE 10.15

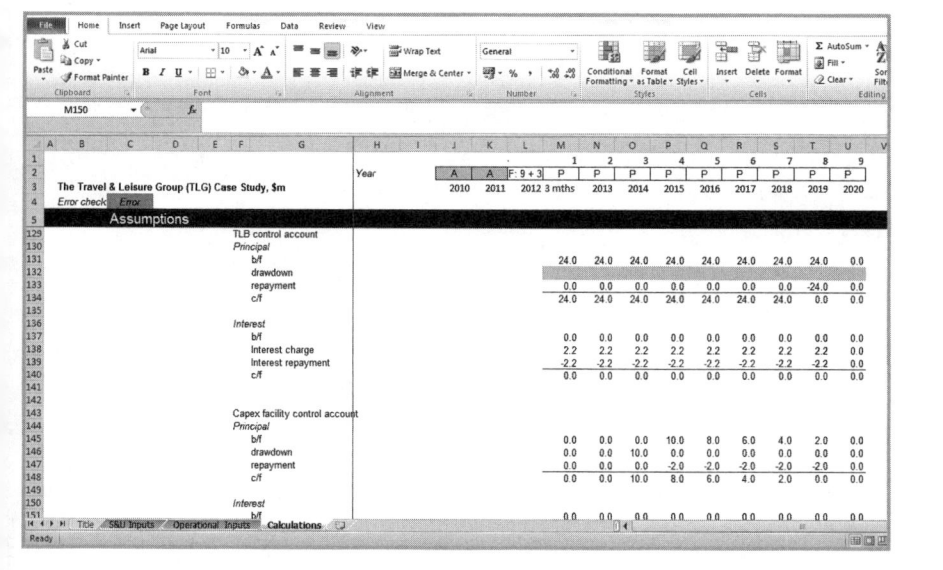

FIGURE 10.16

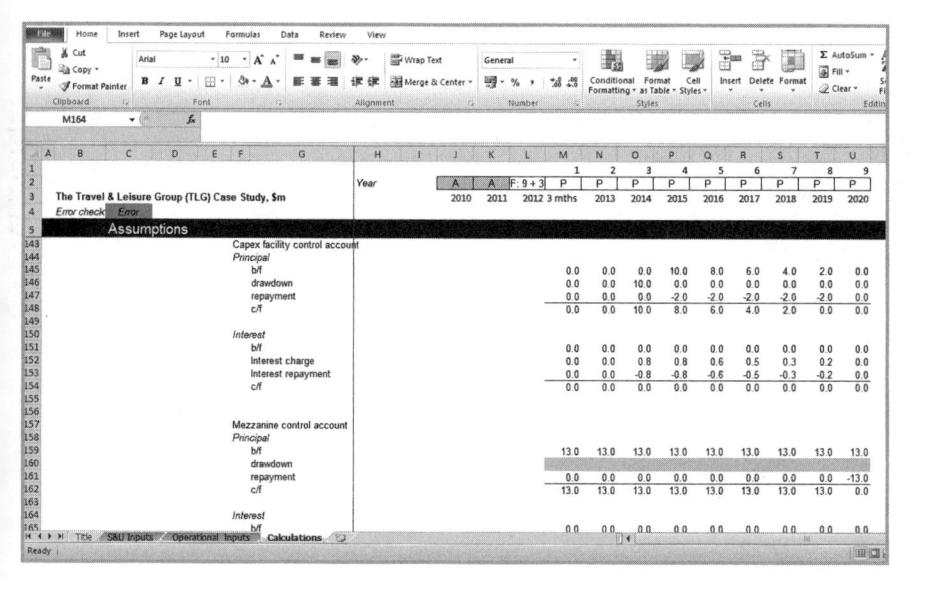

FIGURE 10.17

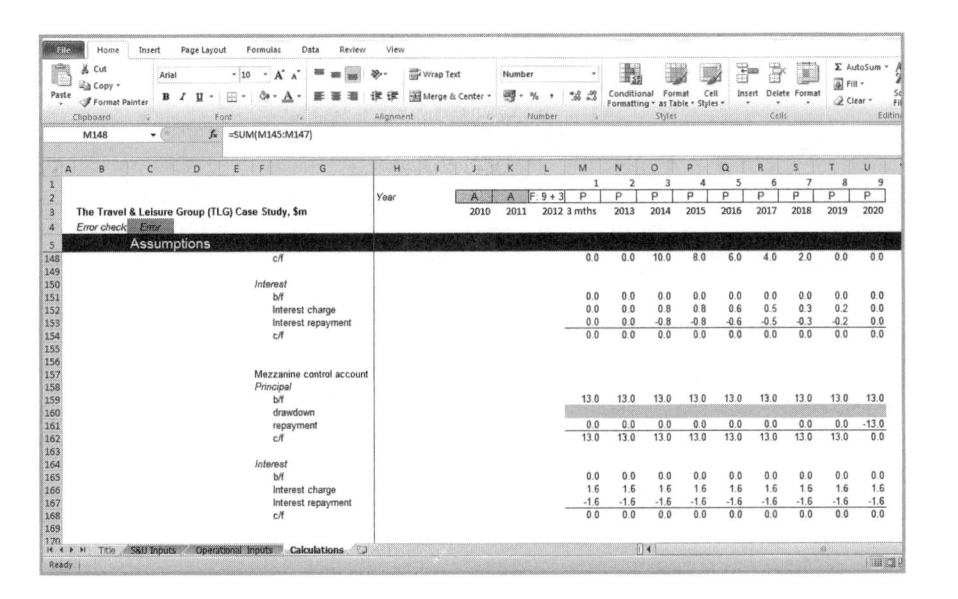

FIGURE 10.18

10.3.5 Fixed Assets Module

Let's create the Fixed Assets module right below the Debt module, say on row 171. We can now run a control account for the tangible assets in line with the specifications described earlier.

Tangible Fixed Assets Control Account

Tangible fixed assets balance b/f

- In cell M173, we can write the formula "=IF(M$1=1,L72,L176)", which basically means that if we are in Year 1, then tangible fixed assets brought forward equals the tangible fixed assets amount in the postdeal balance sheet (which is in cell L72). Otherwise, tangible fixed assets brought forward equals tangible fixed assets carried forward from the previous year.

Capex

- In cell M174, we can write the formula "=M19", which basically picks up the capex amount from row 19 of the Assumptions module.

Depreciation

- In cell M175, we can write the formula "= −M27", which basically picks up the depreciation amount from row 27 of the Profit and Loss module.

Tangible fixed assets balance c/f

- In cell M176, we can write the formula "=SUM(M173:M175)", which basically calculates tangible fixed assets carried forward as being equal to tangible fixed assets brought forward plus capex less depreciation.

Copy cells M173:M176 and paste them into the block M173:U176. The tangible fixed assets module is illustrated in Figure 10.19.

10.3.6 Tax Module

Let's create the Tax module right below the Fixed Assets module, say on row 179. We can run a control account for the tax creditor in line with the specifications described earlier.

Tax Creditor Control Account

Tax creditor balance b/f

- In cell M181, we can write the formula "=IF(M$1=1, −L90,L184)", which basically means that if we are in Year 1, then the tax creditor balance brought forward is equal to the tax creditor balance in the postdeal balance sheet (which is in cell L90). Otherwise, the tax creditor balance brought forward equals the tax creditor balance carried forward from the previous year.

Tax charge

- In cell M182, we can write the formula "= −M63", which basically picks up the tax charge from the Profit and Loss module.

Tax paid

- In cell M183, we can write the formula "= −M182", which basically reflects our assumption that the tax charge is paid in the same year.

Tax creditor balance c/f

- In cell M184, we can write the formula "=SUM(M181:M183)", which basically calculates the tax creditor balance carried forward as being equal to the tax creditor balance b/f plus tax charge less tax paid.

Copy cells M181:M184 and paste them into the block M181:U184. The Tax module is also illustrated in Figure 10.19.

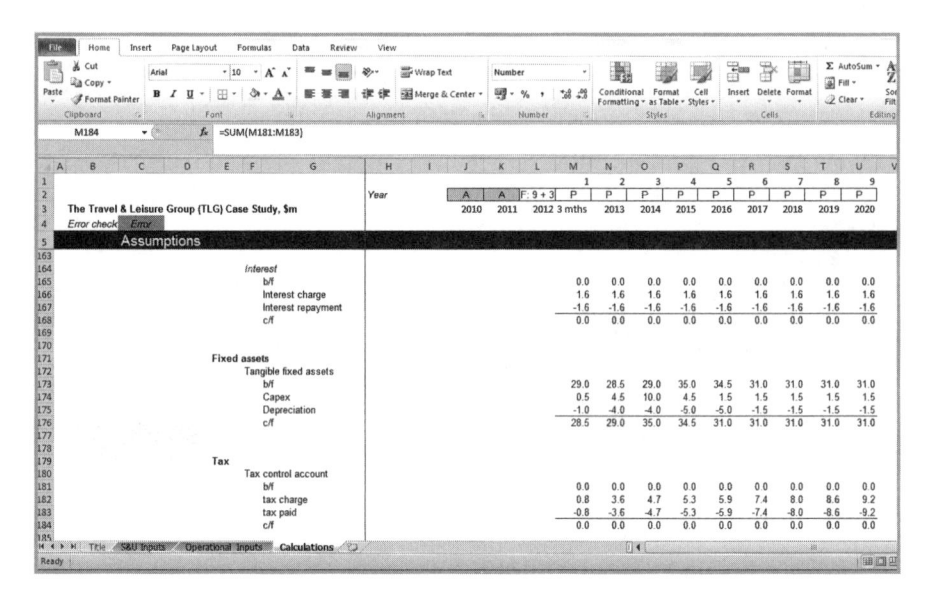

FIGURE 10.19

Note:

With the Debt module now completed, we can go back to the Profit and Loss module and complete the interest lines as follows:

Term loan A interest

- In cell M56, we can write the formula "= –M124", which picks up the interest charge from the term loan A control account in the Debt module.

Term loan B interest

- In cell M57, we can write the formula "= –M138", which picks up the interest charge from the term loan B control account in the Debt module.

Capex facility interest

- In cell M58, we can write the formula "= –M152", which picks up the interest charge from the capex facility control account in the Debt module.

Mezzanine interest

- In cell M59, we can write the formula "= –M166", which picks up the interest charge from the mezzanine control account in the Debt module.

Copy cells M56:M59 and paste them into the block M56:U59. The revised Profit and Loss module is illustrated in Figure 10.20.

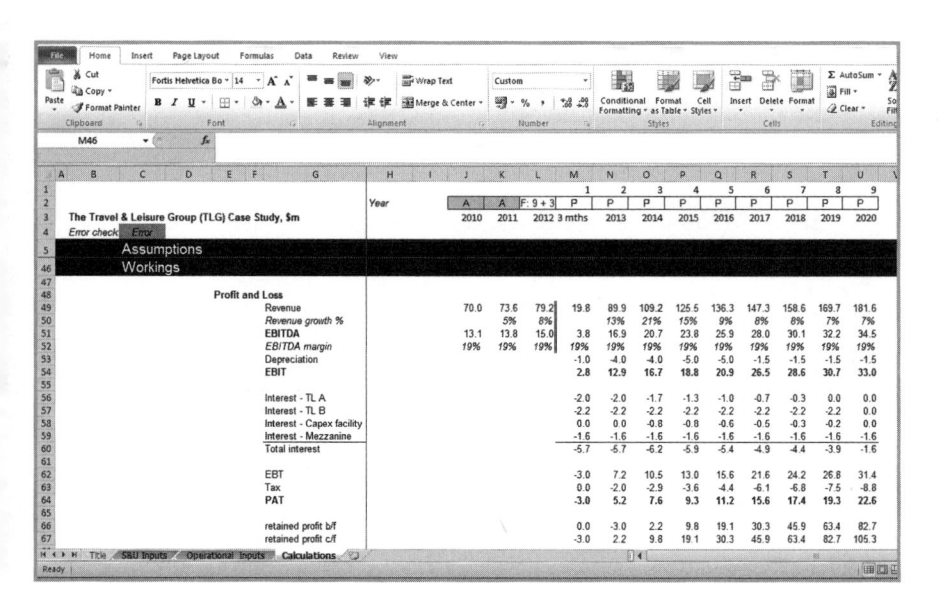

FIGURE 10.20

10.3.7 Revisiting the Balance Sheet Module

We can now revisit the Balance Sheet module and complete it with the projected balance sheet (so far, only the postdeal balance sheet has been completed).

Fixed Assets

Tangible assets

- In cell M72, we can write the formula "=M176", which picks up tangible assets from the Fixed Assets module.

Financial assets

- In cell M73, we can write the formula "=L73", which picks up the financial assets from the previous period.

Investment in joint ventures

- In cell M74, we can write the formula "=L74", which picks up the investment in joint ventures from the previous period.

Intangibles

- In cell M75, we can write the formula "L75", which picks up the intangibles from the previous period.

Transaction goodwill

- In cell M76, we can write the formula "L76", which picks up the transaction goodwill from the previous period.

Transaction costs

- In cell M77, we can write the formula "L77", which picks up the transaction costs from the previous period.

Copy cells M72:M77 and paste special the formulas into the block M72:U77.

Current Assets

Stock (inventory)

- In cell M81, we can write the formula "=M$49*M21", which calculates stock as sales times stock as % of sales.

Trade debtors (accounts receivable)

- In cell M82, we can write the formula "=M$49*M22", which calculates trade debtors as sales times trade debtors as % of sales.

Copy cells M81:M82 and paste special the formulas into the block M82:U82.

Cash balance

- We skip cash for now, as we have yet to complete the Cash Flow module.

Current Liabilities

Trade creditors (accounts payable)

- In cell M88, we can write the formula "= –M$49*M23", which calculates trade creditors as sales times trade creditors as % of sales.

Customer deposits

- In cell M89, we can write the formula "= –M24", which picks up customer deposits from row 24 of the Assumptions module.

Tax creditor

- In cell M90, we can write the formula "= –M184", which picks up the tax creditor balance from the Tax module.

Copy cells M88:M90 and paste special the formulas into the block M88:U90.

Long-Term Liabilities

Term loan A

- In cell M98, we can write the formula "= –M120", which picks up the term loan A balance from the Debt module.

Term loan B

- In cell M99, we can write the formula "= –M134", which picks up the term loan B balance from the Debt module.

Capex facility

- In cell M100, we can write the formula "= –M148", which picks up the capex facility balance from the Debt module.

Mezzanine

- In cell M101, we can write the formula "= –M162", which picks up the mezzanine balance from the Debt module.

Subordinated loan

- In cell M102, we can write the formula "=L102", which picks up the subordinated loan balance from the previous period.

Copy cells M98:M102 and paste special the formulas into the block M98:U102.

Ordinary shares

- In cell M107, we can write the formula "=L107", which picks up the ordinary shares balance from the previous period.

P&L reserve

- In cell M108, we can write the formula "=M67", which picks up the P&L reserve (or retained earnings or retained profit) from the Profit and Loss module.

Copy cells M107:M108 and paste special the formulas into the block M107:U108. The revised Balance Sheet module is illustrated in Figures 10.21 and 10.22.

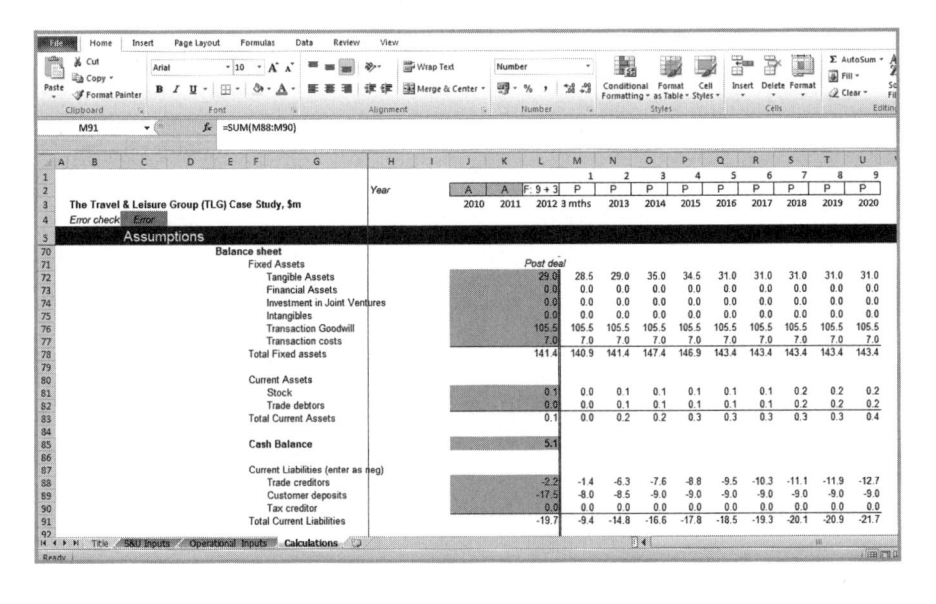

FIGURE 10.21

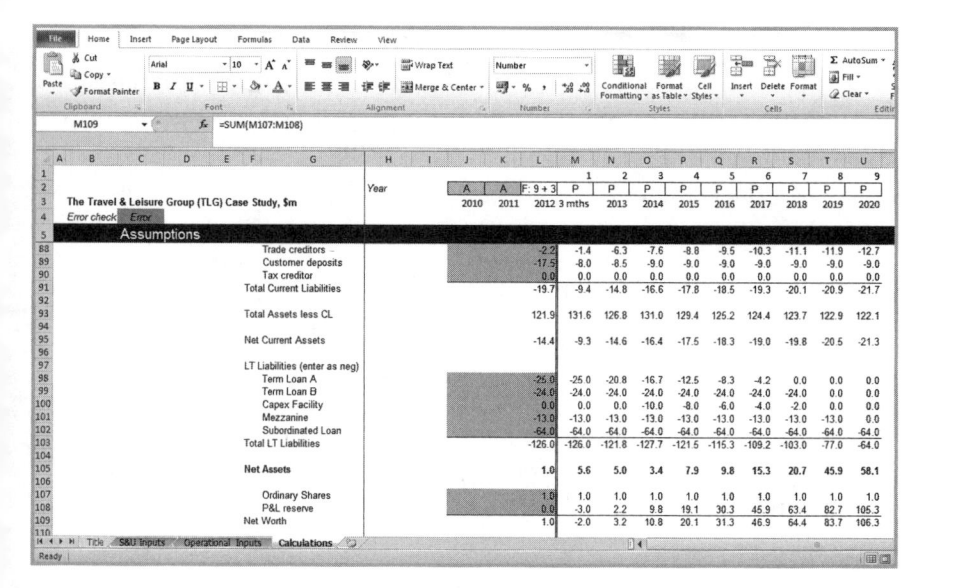

FIGURE 10.22

Note: The balance sheet figures are not yet final, as the cash line has not yet been completed.

10.3.8 Cash Flow Module

Let's create the Cash Flow module right below the Tax module, say on row 187. We can now add the different lines of the Cash Flow module following the specifications described earlier.

EBITDA

- In cell M188, we can write the formula "=M51", which picks up the EBITDA figure from the Profit and Loss module.

Movement in stock (inventory)

- In cell M190, we can write the formula "=L81–M81", which calculates the movement in stock as stock at the end of previous period (L81) less stock at the end of the current period (M81).

Movement in debtors (accounts receivable)

- In cell M191, we can write the formula "=L82–M82", which calculates the movement in debtors as debtors at the end of the previous period less debtors at the end of the current period.

Movement in creditors (accounts payable)

- In cell M192, we can write the formula "=SUM(L88:L89)–SUM (M88:M89)", which calculates the movement in creditors as the sum of trade and other creditors at the end of the previous period less the sum of trade and other creditors at the end of the current period.

Movement in working capital

- In cell M193, we can write the formula "=SUM(M190:M192)", which calculates the movement in working capital as the aggregate of movement in stock, movement in debtors, and movement in creditors.

Operating cash flow

- In cell M195, we can write the formula "=M188+M193", which calculates the operating cash flow as EBITDA (M188) plus movement in the sum of stock, debtors, and creditors (M193).

Cash conversion ratio %

- In cell M196, we can write the formula "=M195/M188" which calculates the cash conversion ratio as operating cash flow divided by EBITDA.

Capex

- In cell M198, we can write the formula "= –M174", which picks up capex from the Fixed Assets module.

Cash flow before tax and financing

- In cell M199, we can write the formula "=SUM(M195,M198)", which calculates cash flow before tax and financing as operating cash flow plus capex.

Tax

- In cell M200, we can write the formula "=M183", which picks up tax from the Tax module.

Debt drawdown

- In cell M201, we can write the formula "=SUM(M118,M146,M160,M132)", which aggregates debt amounts drawn down for term loan A, term loan B, capex facility, and mezzanine from the Debt module.

Cash flow available for debt service

- In cell M202, we can write the formula "=SUM(M199:M201)", which calculates cash flow available for debt service as cash flow before tax and financing plus tax plus debt drawdown.

Term loan A interest

- In cell M204, we can write the formula "=M125", which picks up interest for Term Loan A from the Debt module.

Term loan B interest

- In cell M205, we can write the formula "=M139", which picks up interest for term loan B from the Debt module.

Capex facility interest

- In cell M206, we can write the formula "=M153", which picks up interest for the capex facility from the Debt module.

Mezzanine interest

- In cell M207, we can write the formula "=M167", which picks up interest for the mezzanine debt from the Debt module.

Total interest

- In cell M208, we can write the formula "=SUM(M204:M207)", which aggregates the interest paid on term loan A, term loan B, the capex facility, and mezzanine debt from the Debt module.

Term loan A debt repayment

- In cell M211, we can write the formula "=M119", which picks up the term loan A debt amount repaid from the Debt module.

Term loan B debt repayment

- In cell M212, we can write the formula "=M133", which picks up the term loan B debt amount repaid from the Debt module.

Capex facility debt repayment

- In cell M213, we can write the formula "=M147", which picks up the capex facility debt amount repaid from the Debt module.

Mezzanine debt repayment

- In cell M214, we can write the formula "=M161", which picks up the mezzanine debt amount repaid from the Debt module.

Total repayment

- In cell M215, we can write the formula "=SUM(M211:M214)", which aggregates the debt amounts repaid for term loan A, term loan B, the capex facility, and the mezzanine debt in the Debt module.

Net cash flow

- In cell M217, we can write the formula "=M202+M208+M215", which calculates net cash flow as cash flow available for debt service less interest less repayments on the principal.

Cash balance b/f

- In cell M218, we can write the formula "=IF(M$1=1,$L$85, L219)", which calculates cash balance brought forward as the cash balance in the postdeal balance sheet (L85) if we are in Year 1. Otherwise, cash balance brought forward equals cash balance carried forward in the previous period.

Cash balance c/f

- In cell M219, we can write the formula "=M218+M217", which calculates cash balance carried forward as cash balance brought forward plus net cash flow.

Copy cells M188:M219 and paste them into the block M188:U219. The Cash Flow module is illustrated in Figures 10.23 and 10.24.

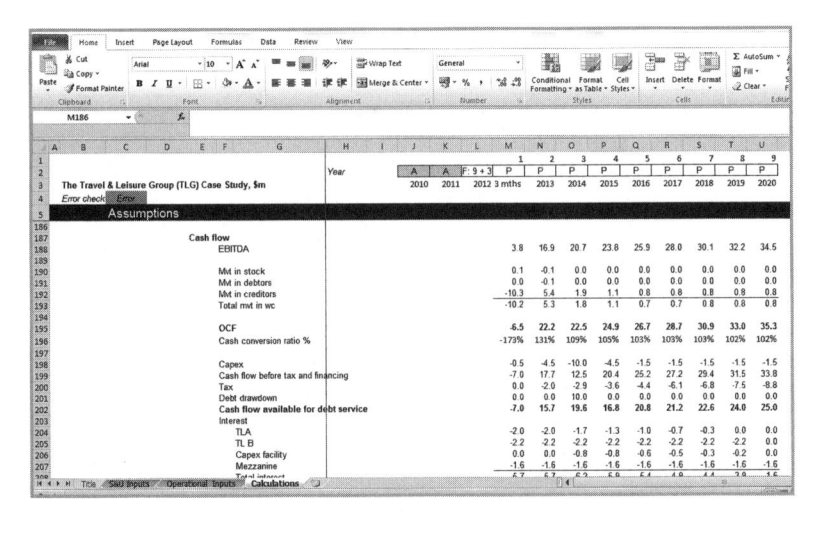

FIGURE 10.23

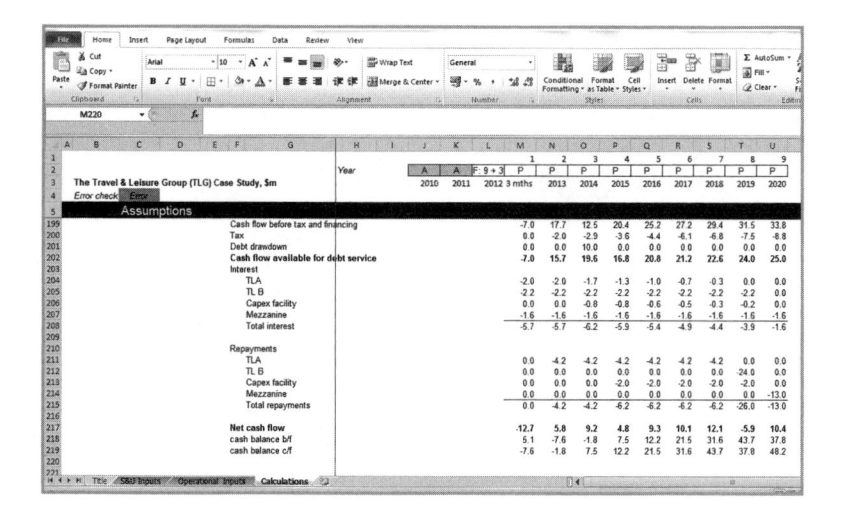

FIGURE 10.24

Note:

With the Cash Flow module now completed, we can go back to the Balance Sheet module and complete the cash line as follows:

Cash

- In cell M85, we can write the formula "=M219", which picks up the cash balance carried forward from the Cash Flow module.

Copy cell M85 and paste it into the block M85:U85.

Overall balance sheet check

- Note that once the cash balance has been included in the balance sheet, the balance sheet check shows a green OK.

The revised Balance Sheet module is shown in Figures 10.25 and 10.26.

10.3.9 Credit Statistics Module

Let's create the Credit Statistics module right below the Cash Flow module, say on row 222. We first bring the key ingredients needed to calculate the different ratios.

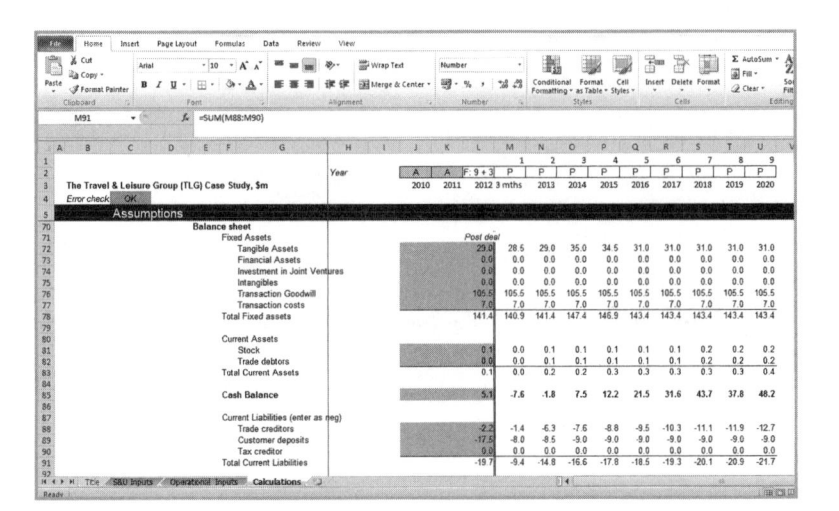

FIGURE 10.25

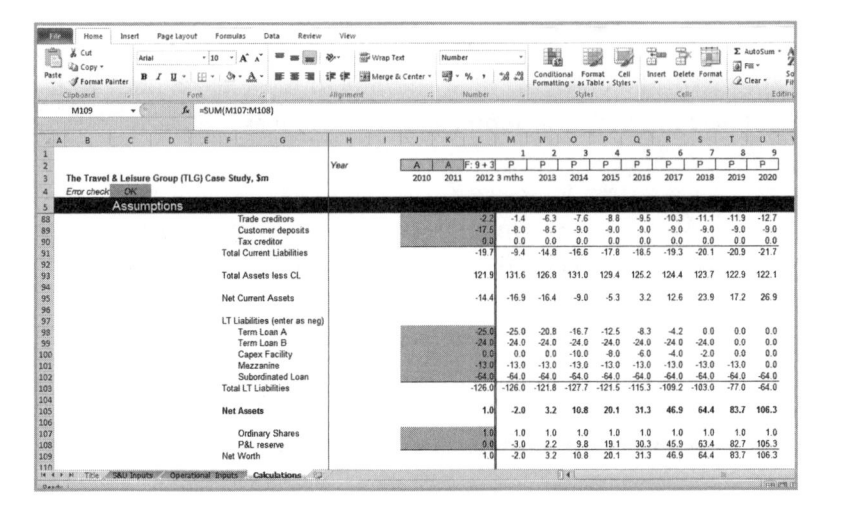

FIGURE 10.26

Senior debt

- In cell M223, we can write the formula "= –SUM(M98:M100)" which picks up the outstanding balances for the senior debt (that is, term loan A, term loan B, and the capex facility) from the Balance Sheet module.

Total debt

- In cell M224, we can write the formula "= –SUM(M98:M101)", which picks up the outstanding balances for the total debt (that is, term loan A, term loan B, the capex facility, and the mezzanine financing) from the Balance Sheet module.

Cash

- In cell M225, we can write the formula "=M85", which picks up the outstanding cash balance from the Balance Sheet module.

Net senior debt

- In cell M226, we can write the formula "=M223–M225", which adds the senior debt (M223) and the cash balance (M225) together.

Net total debt

- In cell M227, we can write the formula "=M224–M225", which adds the total debt (M224) and the cash balance (M225) together.

EBITDA

- In cell M229, we can write the formula "=M51", which picks up EBITDA from the Profit and Loss module.

Net senior interest

- In cell M230, we can write the formula "=–SUM(M56:M58)", which aggregates the interest charge for the senior debt instruments (term loan A, term loan B, and the capex facility) with the interest income. Since in this case there is no interest income, net senior interest is the same as senior interest (that is, the total excluding interest income).

Net total interest

- In cell M231, we can write the formula "=–SUM(M56:M59)", which aggregates the interest charge for all the debt instruments (term loan A, term loan B, the capex facility, and mezzanine financing) with the interest income. Since in this case there is no interest income, net senior interest is the same as senior interest (that is, the total excluding interest income).

CFADS

- In cell M233, we can write the formula "=M202", which picks up the cash available for debt service (CFADS) from the Cash Flow module.

Senior debt service

■ In cell M234, we can write the formula "=–SUM(M204:M206, M211:M213)", which aggregates the interest paid and principal paid for the senior debt instruments (term loan A, term loan B, and the capex facility) from the Cash Flow module.

Total debt service

■ In cell M235, we can write the formula "=–SUM(M204:M207, M211:M214)", which aggregates the interest paid and principal paid for all the debt instruments (term loan A, term loan B, the capex facility, and mezzanine) from the Cash Flow module.

EBITDA: net senior interest

■ In cell M237, we can write the formula "=IF(M230=0,"",M229/M230)", which divides EBITDA (M229) by net senior interest (M230) if the denominator is different from 0. Otherwise. the result is an empty cell.

EBITDA: net total interest

■ In cell M238, we can write the formula "=IF(M231=0,"", M229/M231)", which divides EBITDA (M229) by net total interest (M231) if the denominator is different from 0. Otherwise. the result is an empty cell.

CFADS: senior debt service

■ In cell M239, we can write the formula "=IF(M234=0,"",M233/M234)", which divides CFADS (M233) by senior debt service (M234) if the denominator is different from 0. Otherwise, the result is an empty cell.

CFADS: total debt service

■ In cell M240, we can write the formula "=IF(M235=0,"", M233/M235)", which divides CFADS (M233) by total debt service (M235) if the denominator is different from 0. Otherwise, the result is an empty cell.

Net senior debt to EBITDA

■ In cell M241, we can write the formula "=IF(M229=0,"", M226/M229)", which divides net senior debt (M226) by

EBITDA (M229) if the denominator is different from 0. Otherwise, the result is an empty cell.

Total net debt: EBITDA

- In cell M242, we can write the formula "=IF(M229=0,"", M227/M229)", which divides total net debt (M227) by EBITDA (M229) if the denominator is different from 0. Otherwise, the result is an empty cell.

Copy the block M223:M242 and paste it into the block M223:U242. The Credit Statistics module is illustrated in Figure 10.27.

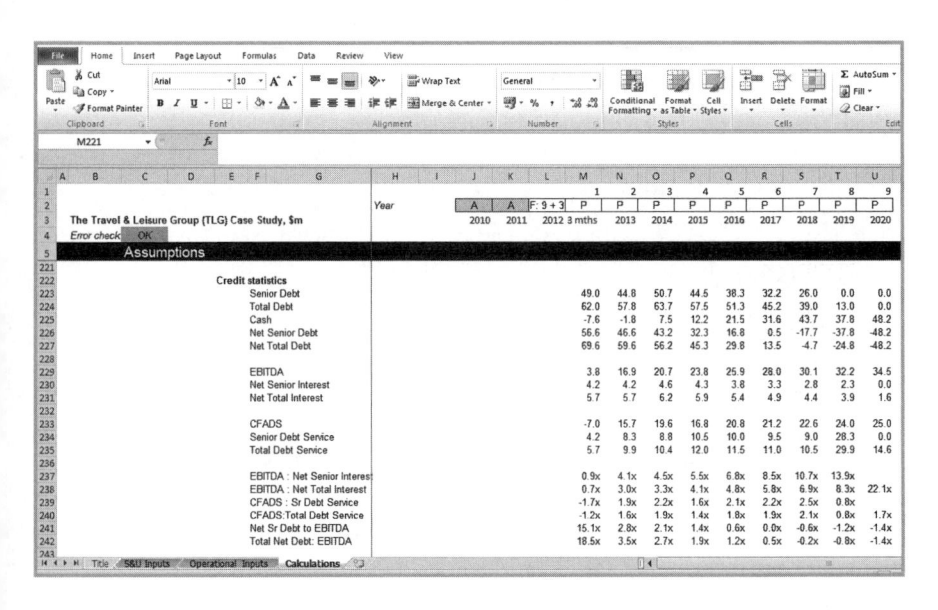

FIGURE 10.27

10.3.10 Exit Module

Let's create the Exit module right below the Credit Statistics module, say on row 245.

Exit Waterfall

EBITDA

- In cell M246, we can write the formula "=M188", which picks up EBITDA from the Cash Flow module.

EV/EBITDA multiple

- In cell M247, we can write the formulae "=$I$43", which picks up the exit enterprise-value-to-EBITDA multiple from the Assumptions module.

Enterprise value

- In cell M248, we can write the formula "=M247*M246", which calculates enterprise value as being equal to the enterprise-value-to-EBITDA multiple times EBITDA.

Plus

Cash

- In cell M250, we can write the formula "=M85", which picks up the cash balance from the Balance Sheet module.

Total enterprise value

- In cell M251, we can write the formula "=SUM(M248,M250)", which adds the cash balance (M250) to the enterprise value (M248).

Less

Term loan A

- In cell M254, we can write the formula "= –MIN(M251, –M98)", which calculates the proceeds from exit attributable to term loan A as the lower of total enterprise value (M251) and the outstanding balance on term loan A (M98) as given in the Balance Sheet module.

Capex facility

- In cell M255, we can write the formula "= –MIN(SUM(M$251: M254),–M100)", which calculates the proceeds from exit attributable to the capex facility as the lower of total enterprise value less the proceeds allocated to term loan A (SUM(M$251:M254)) and the outstanding balance on the capex facility (M100) as given in the Balance Sheet module.

Term loan B

- In cell M256, we can write the formula "= –MIN(SUM(M$251: M255),–M99)", which calculates the proceeds from exit attributable to term loan B as the lower of total enterprise value less the proceeds allocated to term loan A less the proceeds allocated to the capex facility (SUM(M$251:M255)) and the outstanding balance on term loan B (M99) as given in the Balance Sheet module.

Mezzanine

- In cell M257, we can write the formula "= −MIN(SUM(M$251 :M256),−M101)", which calculates the proceeds from exit attributable to the mezzanine financing as the lower of total enterprise value less the proceeds allocated to term loan A less the proceeds allocated to the capex facility less the proceeds allocated to term loan B (SUM(M$251:M256)) and the outstanding balance on the mezzanine financing (M101) as given in the Balance Sheet module.

Subordinated loan

- In cell M258, we can write the formula "= −MIN(SUM(M$251 :M257),−M102)", which calculates the proceeds from exit attributable to the subordinated loan as the lower of total enterprise value less the proceeds allocated to term loan A less the proceeds allocated to the capex facility less the proceeds allocated to term loan B less the proceeds allocated to the mezzanine financing (SUM(M$251:M257)) and the outstanding balance on the subordinated loan (M102) as given in the Balance Sheet module.

Equity value

- In cell M260, we can write the formula "=SUM(M251:M258)", which calculates equity value as total enterprise value less the proceeds allocated to term loan A less the proceeds allocated to the capex facility less the proceeds allocated to term loan B less the proceeds allocated to the mezzanine financing less the proceeds allocated to the subordinated loan.

Copy cells M246:M260 and paste them into the block M246:U260. The Exit schedule is illustrated in Figure 10.28.

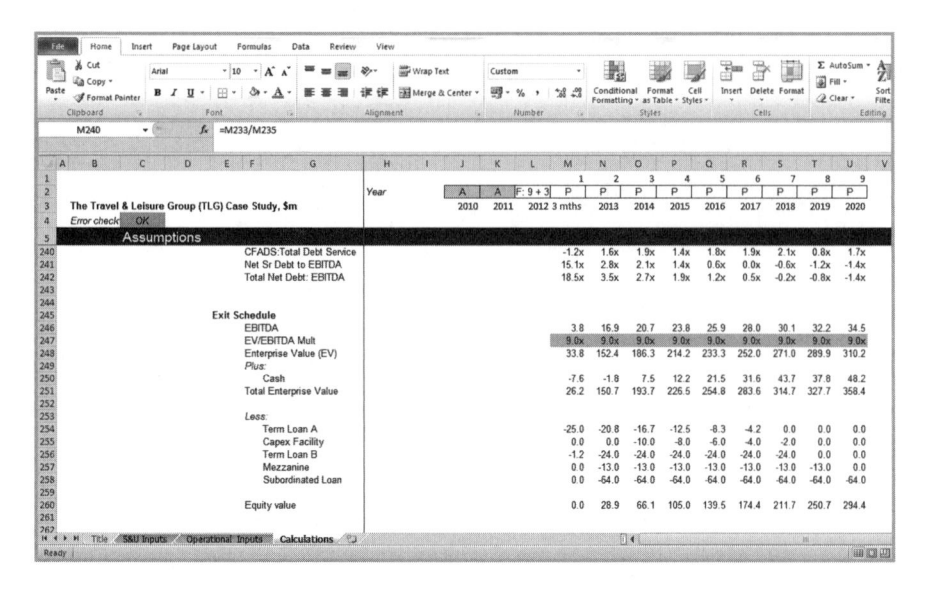

FIGURE 10.28

10.3.11 Investor Blended IRR and Money Multiple

As previously discussed, the key to calculating the IRR and the money multiple is to ensure that all cash flows to and from the investor have been captured, along with the corresponding timing of these cash flows. The cash flows, together with the corresponding timing, were determined in Section 10.2.3. We can create the Investor Blended IRR and Money Multiple module, say on row 263.

Purchase of equity

- In cell L264, we can write the formula "=–'S&U Inputs'!J15", which picks up the investor's cash outlay for the purchase of equity in TLG.

Purchase of subordinated loan

- In cell L265, we can write the formula "=–'S&U Inputs'!J14", which picks up the investor's cash outlay for the purchase of a subordinated loan in TLG.

Proceeds from repayment of subordinated loan

- In cell M266, we can write the formula "=IF(M$1=$I$42, –M258,0)", which calculates repayment of the subordinated loan as equal to the exit proceeds allocated to the subordinated loan if we are in the year of exit (Year 7); otherwise, proceeds from repayment of subordinated loan is 0.

Equity proceeds

- In cell M267, we can write the formula "=IF(M$1=$I$42,M260,0))", which calculates proceeds from the sale of equity as equal to the equity value determined in the exit schedule (in cell M260) if we are in the year of exit (Year 7); otherwise, equity proceeds is 0.

Copy the block M266:M267 and paste special the formulas into the block M266:U267.

Net cash flows

- In cell L268, we can write the formula "=SUM(L264:L267)", which aggregates the net cash flows to and from the investor as the sum of rows 264 to 267.

IRR

- In cell M270, we can write the formula "=IF(ISERROR(IRR($ L268:M268,0.1)),"",IRR($L268:M268,0.1))", which calculates the internal rate of return (IRR) of the cash flows in row 268. Note that if there is an error in calculating IRR, then the formula returns an empty cell.

Money multiple

- In cell M271, we can write the formula "= –SUM($M266 :M267)/$L$268", which calculates the money multiple as equal to all cash inflows (in the block SUM($M266:M267)) divided by all cash outflows (in cell L268).

Copy cells M270:M271 and paste them into the block M270:U271. For the purpose of calculating a data table on the IRR and the money multiple for sensitivity analysis, we also write the Year 9 IRR and money multiple in cells H270 (the formula is "=T270") and H271 (the formula is "=T271"), respectively.

The IRR and Money Multiple module is illustrated in Figure 10.29.

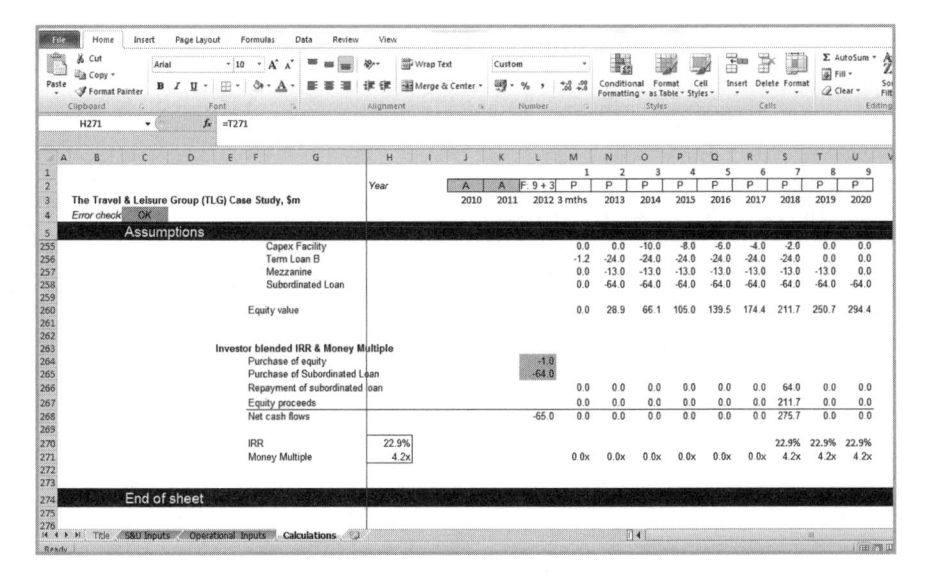

FIGURE 10.29

Exit Sensitivity Analysis

As in the previous case study, we will create a data table to run sensitivities on the IRR and the money multiple. Our measures of returns are IRR and money multiple. We also have two key drivers of return: exit year and exit enterprise-value-to-EBITDA multiple. The sensitivity analysis will focus on changing the exit year and exit multiple and observing the impact on the IRR and the money multiple.

IRR Data Table

- Drivers: exit year and exit multiple
- Measure: IRR
- Data table inputs:
    1. Values for exit year: Years 6, 7, and 8; values for exit enterprise-value-to-EBITDA multiple: 8, 9, and 10 times.
    2. Measure: IRR in Year 8.

We will build the data table in the S&U Inputs sheet using the following steps (refer to Microsoft Excel's Help for further information on creating data tables). The data table we will build is known as a two-variable data table (it has two drivers: exit year and exit multiple). We will have one variable along the row (say, exit Years 6, 7, and 8) and the other variable down the column (say, exit multiple 8, 9, and 10 times).

- Select the S&U Inputs sheet.
- Enter the measure (Year 8 IRR) in any given cell, say K86. The formula in cell K86 reads "=Calculations!H270".
- Along row 86, (that is, the same row as the measure, but to the right-hand side of the measure), enter the values for the exit year driver. Thus, in cells L86, M86, and N86, type 6, 7, and 8, respectively.
- Down column K (that is, the same column as the measure, but below the measure) enter the values for the exit enterprise-value-to-EBITDA multiple. Thus, in cells K87, K88, and K89, type 8x, 9x, and 10x, respectively.
- Select the block of cells that contains the measure (K86) and the values of the two drivers. Thus, this selection will involve the block K86:N89.
- On the Data tab, in the Data Tools group, click on What-If Analysis, and then click on Data Table. After clicking on Data Table, the Data Table dialogue box appears.
- In the Row input cell box, enter the reference to the input cell for the input values in the row, which is the exit year driver and is specified in cell F79. And so we enter F79 in the Row input cell box. Alternatively, click on cell F79 (note that Microsoft Excel automatically writes cell $F$79 in the Row input cell box).
- In the Column input cell box, enter the reference to the input cell for the input values in the column, which is exit enterprise-value-to-EBITDA multiple and is specified in cell F80. And so we enter F80 in the Column input cell box. Alternatively, click on cell F80 (note that Microsoft Excel automatically writes cell $F$80 in the Column input cell box).
- Click OK and press F9 to recalculate (recalculating ensures that Microsoft Excel will calculate the data table, in case the Microsoft Excel calculations options were not set to calculate data tables automatically).
- The resulting IRR data table is illustrated in Figure 10.30.

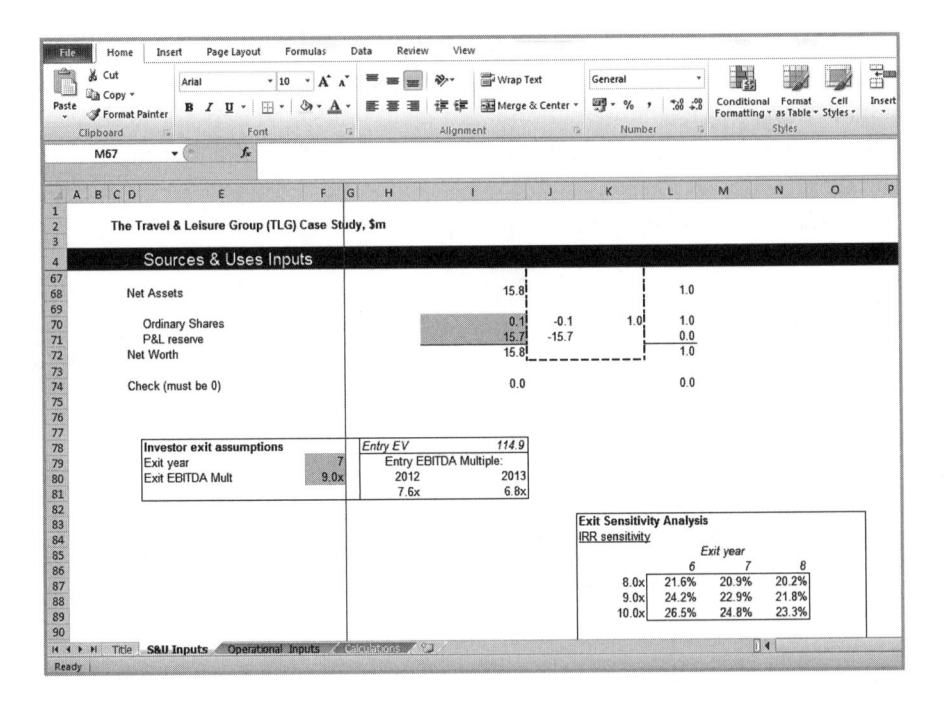

FIGURE 10.30

Note: For aesthetic reasons, we have formatted the font in cell K86 to a white color (that is, the same color as the cell's background color) so that the cell containing the measure is not visible.

Money Multiple Data Table

- Drivers: exit year and exit multiple
- Measure: money multiple
- Data table inputs:
    1. Values for exit year: Years 6, 7, and 8; values for exit enterprise-value-to-EBITDA multiple: 8, 9, and 10 times.
    2. Measure: money multiple in Year 8.

We will build the money multiple data table in the S&U Inputs sheet just below the IRR data table.

- Select the S&U Inputs sheet.
- Enter the measure (Year 8 Money Multiple), in, say, cell K93. The formula in cell K93 reads "=Calculations!H271".

- Along row 93 (that is, the same row as the measure, but to the right-hand side of it), enter the values for the exit year driver. Thus, in cells L93, M93, and N93, type 6, 7, and 8, respectively.
- Down column K (that is, the same column as the measure, but below it), enter the values for the exit enterprise-value-to-EBITDA multiple. Thus, in cells K94, K95, and K96, type 8x, 9x, and 10x, respectively.
- Select the block of cells that contains the measure (K93) and the values of the two drivers. Thus this selection will involve the block K93:O96.
- On the Data tab, in the Data Tools group, click on What-If Analysis, and then click on Data Table.
- After clicking on Data Table, the Data Table dialogue box appears.
- As in the IRR data table, enter F79 in the Row input cell box.
- As in the IRR data table, enter F80 in the Column input cell box.
- Click OK and press F9 to recalculate.
- The resulting money multiple data table is illustrated in Figure 10.31.

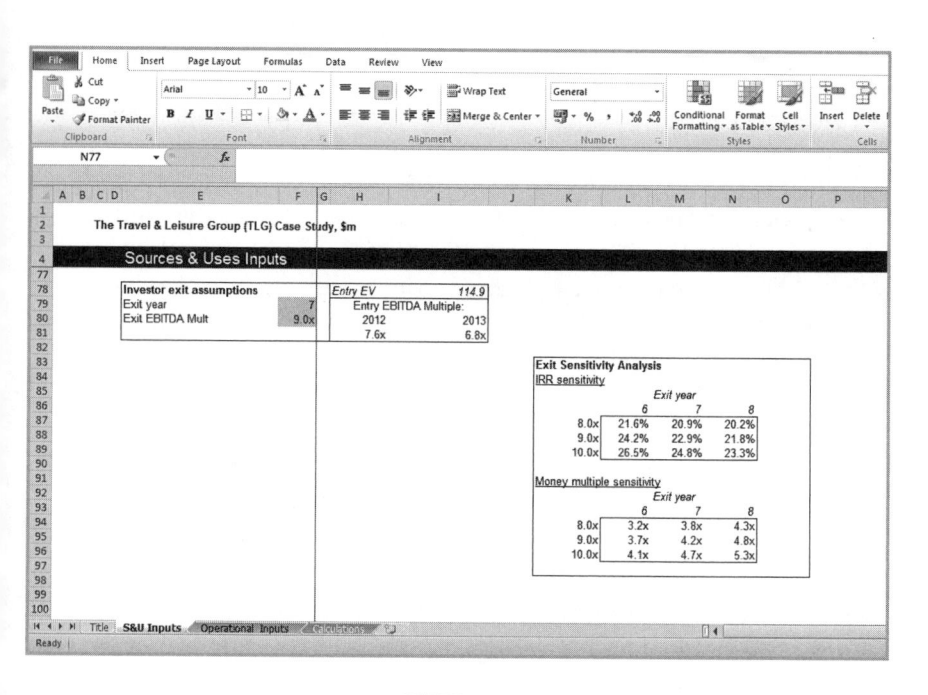

FIGURE 10.31

Note: As in the IRR data table, for aesthetic reasons, we have formatted the font in cell K93 to a white color (that is, the same color as the cell's background color) so that the cell containing the measure is not visible.

Analysis of Data Table Sensitivity

- The data table shows that as the exit enterprise-value-to-EBITDA multiple increases from 8 times to 10 times, both the IRR and the money multiple increase, which is to be expected. Indeed, increasing the exit enterprise-value-to-EBITDA multiple will increase the enterprise value, which (given the fixed term loan A, term loan B, capex facility, and mezzanine financing) will result in an increased equity value.
- As the exit year is delayed, the IRR decreases, which is to be expected. This result reflects the time value of money.
- However, as the exit year is delayed, the money multiple increases. In our projections, EBITDA increases over time, and so delaying the exit means achieving a higher EBITDA figure at exit, which results in a higher enterprise value and consequently a higher equity value.

10.4 CREATING THE OUTPUTS SHEET

Now that we have completed all the necessary calculations, we are ready to bring together the key results from our calculations into the Outputs sheet.

The key outputs to summarize are the Profit and Loss, Balance Sheet, Cash Flow, Credit Statistics, Exit Schedule, Investor Blended IRR & Money Multiple, and Exit Sensitivity Analysis modules.

- Copy the Calculations sheet, rename it Outputs, and color it green. This way, the Outputs sheet initially has the same content as the Calculations sheet. We will then delete the elements of the Calculations sheet that are not going to be included in the Outputs sheet.
- Since the main outputs are the Profit and Loss, Balance Sheet, Cash Flow, Credit Statistics, Exit Schedule, Investor Blended IRR & Money Multiple, and Exit Sensitivity Analysis modules, we will:

1. Link the Profit and Loss, Balance Sheet, Cash Flow, Credit Statistics, Exit Schedule, and Investor Blended IRR & Money Multiple modules in the Outputs sheet to the corresponding Profit and Loss, Balance Sheet, Cash Flow, Credit Statistics, Exit Schedule, and Investor Blended IRR & Money Multiple modules in the Calculations sheet.

2. Link the Exit Sensitivity Analysis module in the Outputs sheet to the corresponding Exit Sensitivity Analysis module in the S&U Inputs sheet.

- In Chapters 8 and 9, we learned how to link one sheet (here the Outputs sheet) to another (here the Calculations sheet). We can use the same technique to complete steps 1 and 2. The result is an Outputs sheet that is exactly the same as the Calculations sheet contentwise except that the Outputs sheet takes its values from the Calculations sheet.

- Select rows 5 to 45 (the Assumptions block) and delete the entire block. This now brings the Profit and Loss module right to the top at row 5.

- Delete the Debt, Fixed Assets, and Tax modules. This now brings the Cash Flow module immediately below the balance sheet, beginning on row 73.

Let us make a few minor adjustments to make the Outputs sheet more user-friendly.

- Rename the "Workings" blue bar on row 5 as "Outputs."
- In the Credit Statistics module, we delete the workings and retain the actual credit statistics, that is, the last six rows of the module.

Also, to create a copy of the Exit Sensitivity Analysis in the Outputs sheet, do as follows:

- Copy the block K83:O97 in the S&U Inputs sheet and paste it into M147 in the Outputs sheet.
- To link the IRR and money multiple data tables in the Outputs sheet to the S&U Inputs sheet:
  - In cell M150, write the formula "='S&U Inputs'!K86".
  - Copy cell M150 and paste special the formula into the block M150:P153.
  - Paste special the formula into the block M157:P160.

The resulting Outputs sheet is shown in the following figures. First we show the Profit and Loss module in Figure 10.32.

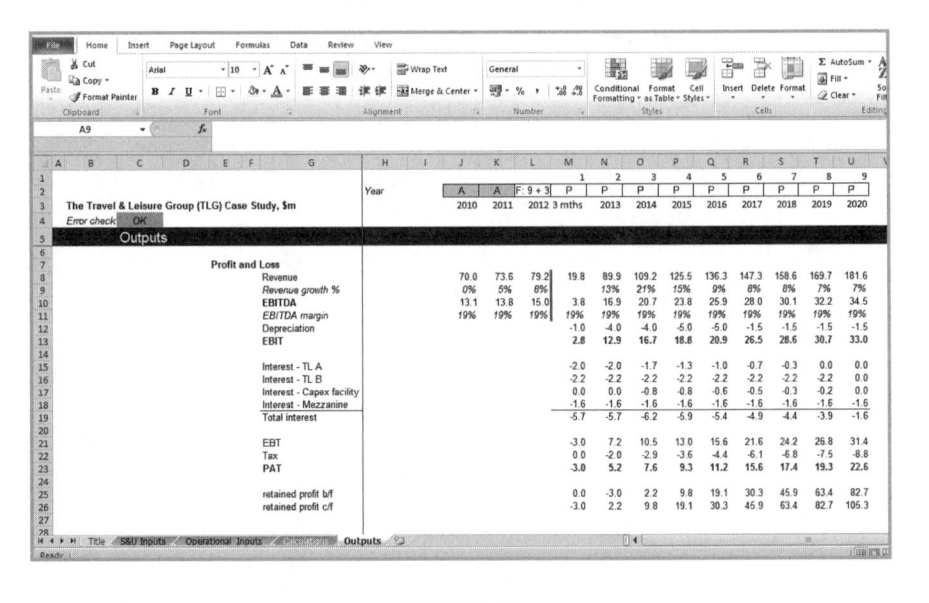

FIGURE 10.32

Next, we show the Balance Sheet module in Figures 10.33 and 10.34.

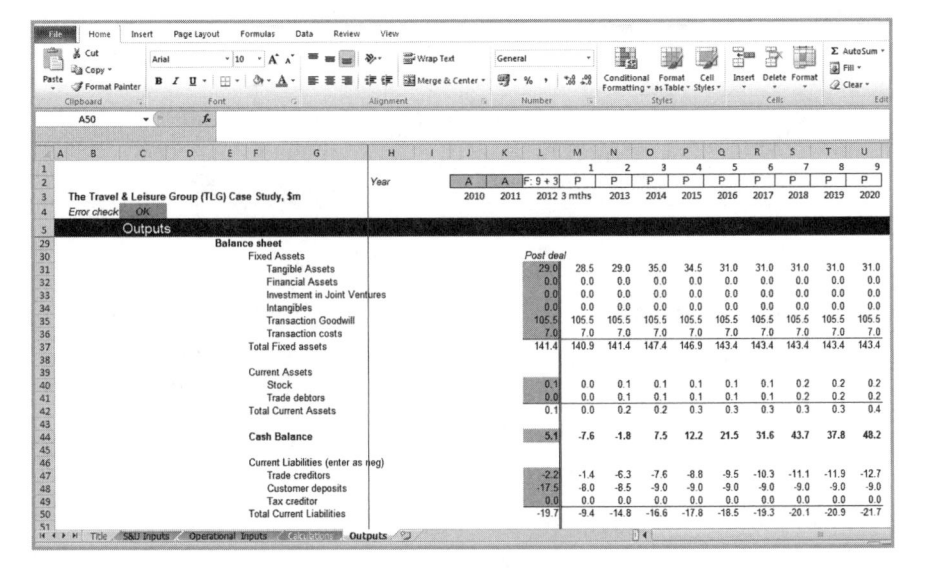

FIGURE 10.33

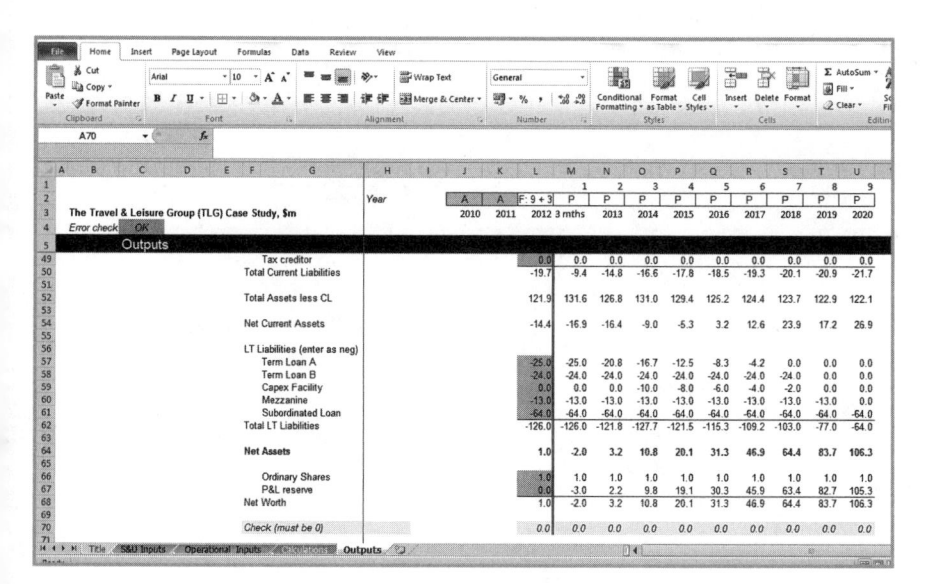

FIGURE 10.34

Then we show the Cash Flow and Credit Statistics modules in Figures 10.35 and 10.36.

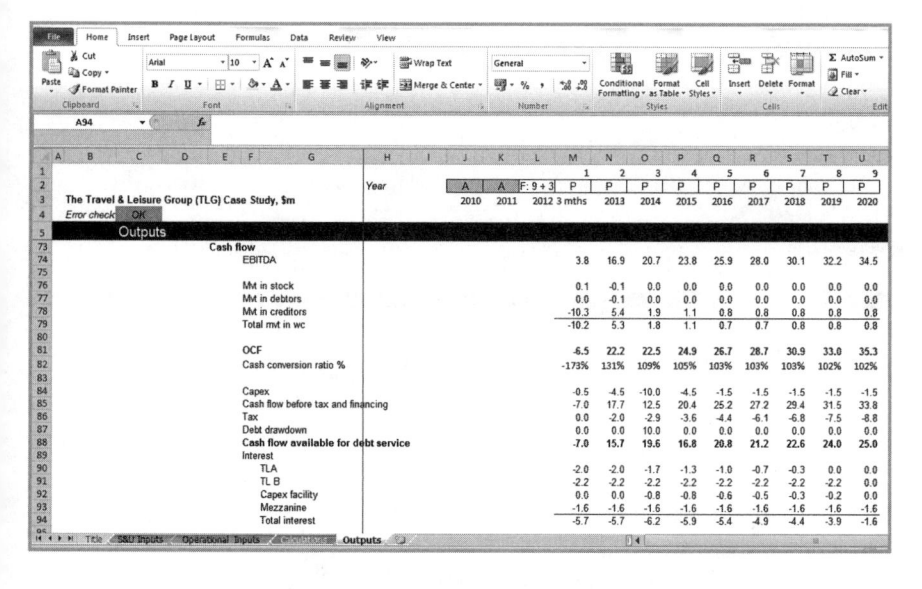

FIGURE 10.35

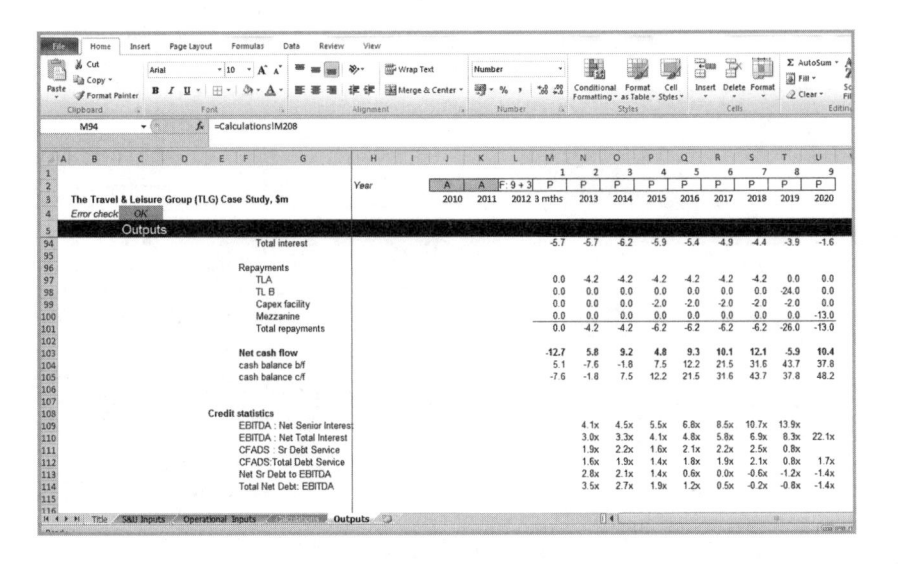

FIGURE 10.36

Note that the credit statistics for the stub year have not been shown, as the stub year is not a full year and so the credit statistics are not necessarily giving a meaningful representation of TLG's credit performance (for example, senior debt to EBITDA during the stub year is 15 times as a result of the denominator's being a fraction of annual EBITDA results).

Then we show the exit waterfall in Figure 10.37.

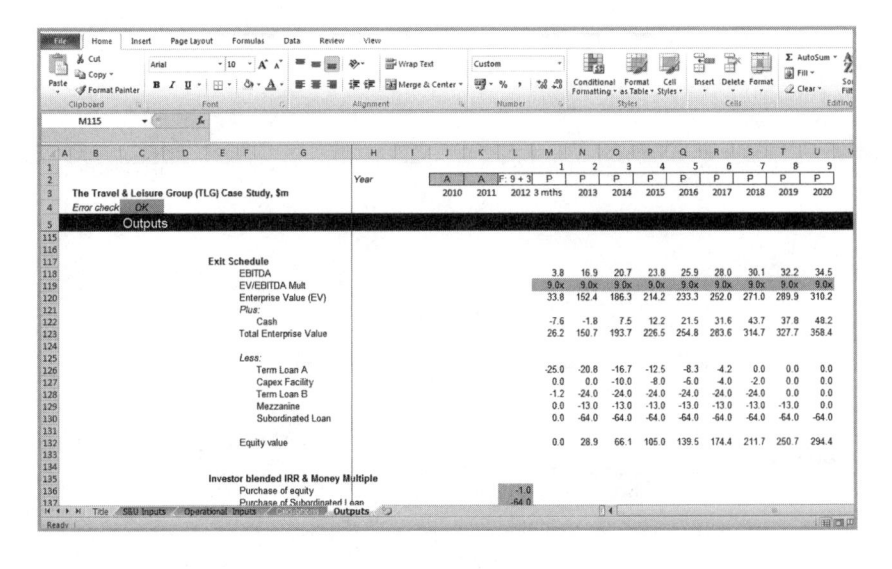

FIGURE 10.37

This is followed by the Investor Blended IRR & Money Multiple in Figure 10.38.

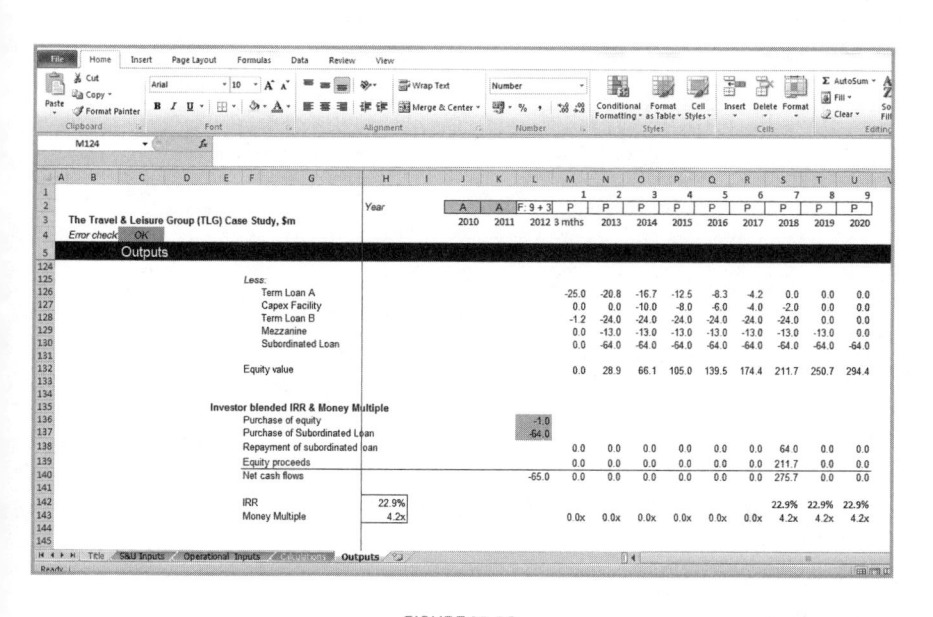

FIGURE 10.38

Finally, we show the Exit Sensitivity Analysis in Figure 10.39.

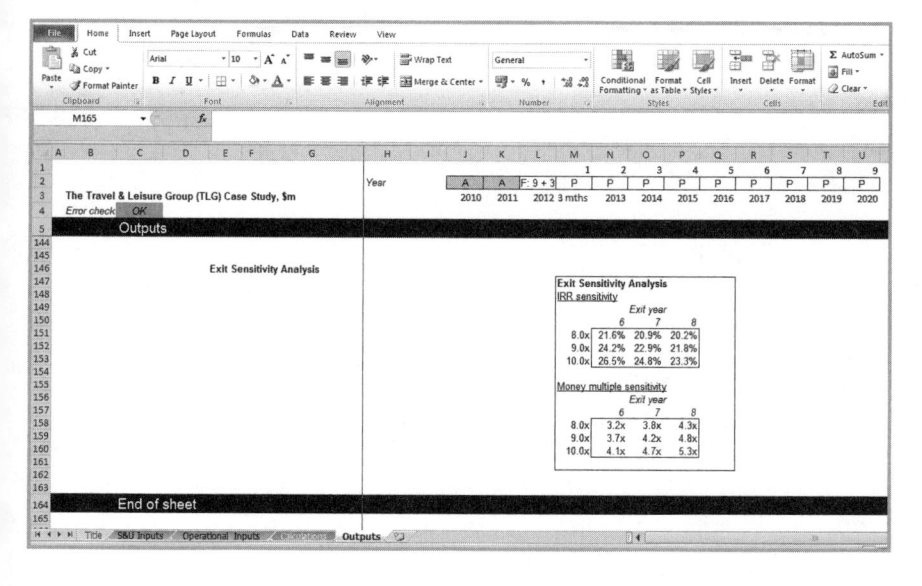

FIGURE 10.39

CHAPTER ELEVEN

Other Tricky Modeling Case Studies

In this chapter, we introduce a number of advanced modeling topics that you might encounter in deal structuring. We have already introduced some tricky topics in previous chapters. For example:

- Modeling a stub year across the profit and loss statement, balance sheet, and cash flow statement (see Case Study 5)
- Conditional formatting (see Case Studies 1, 3, 4, and 5)
- Modeling PIK (payment in kind) loans, that is, loans where the interest is rolled into the principal amount (see Case Study 1)
- Forecasting the completion or postdeal balance sheet (see Case Studies 4 and 5)
- Modeling semiannual and annual financials simultaneously (see Case Study 1)

Here we will cover the following additional topics: data validation for switches, cash sweep, and share buyback. These topics will be discussed using a variety of small stand-alone case studies that can be added to existing models.

11.1 CASH SWEEP CASE STUDY

A cash sweep is a means by which one can accelerate the repayment of a loan. Cash sweep structures are often encountered in project finance or leveraged finance transactions. In a cash sweep structure, the borrower uses any excess cash available to repay a loan, over and beyond the scheduled debt amortization plan. The cash sweep results in the loan's being repaid sooner than originally scheduled, thus resulting in a shorter loan life.

Since the idea of a cash sweep is to get the borrower to accelerate the repayment of a loan, cash sweep analysis essentially indicates refinancing risk and repayment ability. The refinancing risk is the net debt amount outstanding at the end of the loan maturity.

However, such an analysis of refinancing risk and repayment ability can be achieved without modeling a cash sweep. Looking at projected net debt (that is, debt minus cash) to see what the refinancing risk is (if any) will be sufficient. For this reason, cash sweeps are not always featured in financial models.

In this case study, we will model a simple cash sweep to illustrate how it might work in simple terms. In practice, modeling a cash sweep would require the complete interpretation of a term sheet cash sweep that is triggered by financial covenants, margin ratchets, or something similar. Yet the cash sweep model here still provides comparable levels of analysis.

11.1.1 Cash Sweep Steps

Let us assume a term loan A for which there is a cash sweep. The first step in modeling the cash sweep is to determine how much cash is available for sweeping. To this end, we start with the cash flow available for debt service (CFADS) and deduct from it the interest on term loan A. This gives us the cash flow available for principal (CFAP). If the term loan A were not subject to cash sweep, we would then deduct the debt repayment amount from the cash flow available for principal. However, since we are trying to repay as much of the term loan as possible under the cash sweep, we will calculate the amount to be swept as equal to the CFAP (provided that CFADS is positive and provided that we are not overpaying the term loan, beyond the amount needed to settle the loan).

To add a small complication, we will also include a *deminimus* in the cash sweep. The deminimus is a small amount of cash that we exclude from the sweep; in other words, we can sweep only the excess of CFAP over the deminimus.

11.1.2 Cash Sweep Modeling Specifications

Inputs

- Cash flow available for debt service
- Opening cash balance = 0
- Term loan A amortization schedule
- Opening term loan A balance = $25 million
- Term loan A interest rate: 8 percent
- Opening interest rate balance = 0
- Deminimus = $1 million

Cash Flow Module

- Cash flow available for debt service_t is given as an input.
- Term loan A interest_t will be calculated from the term loan A control account.
- Cash flow available for principal_t = cash flow available for debt service_t minus term loan A interest_t. (Term loan A interest is entered as a negative number, as it represents a cash outflow.)
- Term loan A repayment_t will be calculated from the term loan A control account.
- Free cash flow_t = cash flow available for principal_t minus term loan A interest_t minus term loan A repayment_t.
- Cash balance b/f_t = cash balance c/f_t–1 with cash balance b/f in year 1 equal to the opening cash balance.
- Cash balance c/f_t = cash balance b/f_t plus free cash flow_t.
- Term loan A balance c/f_t will be calculated from the term loan A control account.

Workings

We will run two control accounts for term loan A, one without cash sweep and one with cash sweep. For this reason, we will also have a switch button to select whether we want to run the control account with or without cash sweep.

Control Account Without Cash Sweep

The term loan A debt control account without cash sweep will be calculated as follows:

- Term loan A debt opening balance_t = term loan A debt closing balance_t–1, with term loan A debt opening balance_year 1 = opening term loan A balance.

- Term loan A debt drawdown_t = 0.
- Term loan A debt repayment_t is given by the amortization schedule in the inputs.
- Term loan A debt closing balance_t = term loan A debt opening balance_t plus term loan A debt drawdown_t plus term loan A debt repayment_t.

Control Account with Cash Sweep

The term loan A debt control account with cash sweep will be calculated as follows:

- Term loan A debt opening balance_t = term loan A debt closing balance_t–1, with term loan A debt opening balance_year 1 = opening term loan A balance.
- Term loan A debt drawdown_t = 0.
- Term loan A debt repayment_t = min(max0, cash flow available for principal_t minus deminimus), term loan A debt opening balance_t.
- Term loan A debt closing balance_t = term loan A debt opening balance_t plus term loan A debt drawdown_t plus term loan A debt repayment_t.

Term Loan A Interest Control Account

The term loan A interest control account will be calculated as follows:

- Term loan A interest opening balance_t = term loan A interest closing balance_t–1, with term loan A interest opening balance _year 1 = 0.
- Term loan A interest charge_t = term loan A interest rate times (no cash sweep term loan A debt opening balance_t plus term loan A debt drawdown_t) if no cash sweep; otherwise, term loan A interest charge_t = term loan A interest rate times (with cash sweep term loan A debt opening balance_t plus term loan A debt drawdown_t).
- Term loan A interest paid_t = – term loan A interest charge_t.
- Term loan A interest closing balance_t = term loan A interest opening balance_t plus term loan A interest charge_t plus term loan A interest paid_t.
- Cash flow available for debt service_t is given as an input.

- Term loan A interest_t will be calculated from the term loan A control account.
- Cash flow available for principal_t = cash flow available for debt service_t minus term loan A interest_t. (Term loan A interest is entered as a negative number, as it represents a cash outflow.)
- Term loan A repayment_t will be calculated from the term loan A control account.
- Free cash flow_t = cash flow available for principal_t minus term loan A interest_t minus term loan A repayment_t.
- Cash balance b/f_t = cash balance c/f_t −1, with cash balance b/f in year 1 = opening cash balance.
- Cash balance c/f_t = cash balance b/f_t plus free cash flow_t.

11.1.3 Building the Cash Sweep Model

We can build the cash sweep model in a new Microsoft Excel sheet. This will be a seven-year model.

11.1.3.1 Building a Switch in Microsoft Excel Using the Data Validation Tool

First let us build a cash sweep switch. The switch will have two possible values: 0 and 1, where *0* will indicate that the cash sweep option is disabled or is *off* and *1* will indicate that the cash sweep option is enabled or is *on*. We can build the cash switch using Excel's Data Validation tool. We will put the switch in cell C4 as follows.

The Data Validation tool is available under the Data tab within the ribbon (see Figure 11.1).

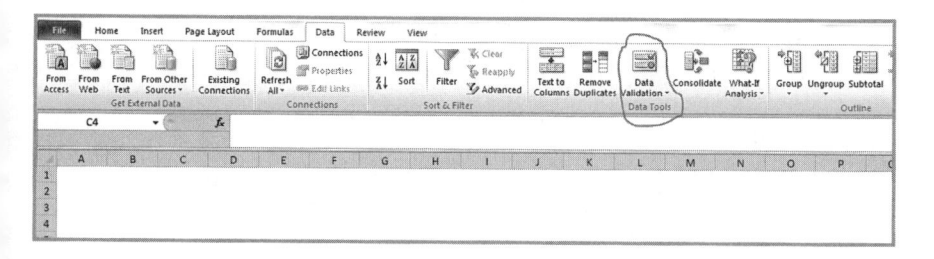

FIGURE 11.1

- Click on Data Validation and select Data Validation. The window shown in Figure 11.2 will pop up.

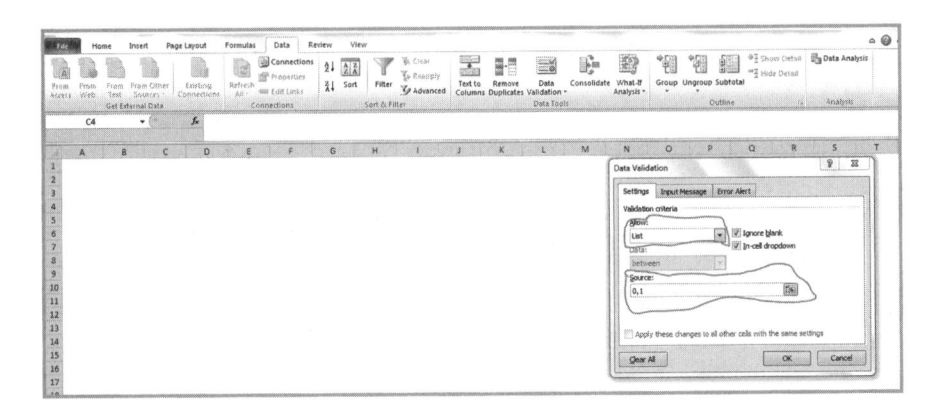

FIGURE 11.2

- Under the Allow category, select List.
- Then under Source, enter "0, 1", the two values that the cash switch can take.
- Click OK.
- Whenever cell C4 is selected, a small triangle appears.
- By clicking on the triangle, you can change the value of cell C4 to either 1 (meaning that the cash sweep is on) or 0 (meaning that the cash sweep is off).

11.1.3.2 Building the Cash Flow Module

We can build the Cash Flow module from row 7 as follows.

Cash flow available for debt service

- This is an input, and we assume that it is $10 million. Thus, we write the number 10 in cells I7 to O7.

Term loan A interest

- We leave block I8:O8 empty for now. Once the term loan A control account has been completed, we can then come back to complete the term loan A interest.

Cash flow available for principal

- In cell I9, we can write the formula "=SUM(I7:I8)", which calculates cash flow available for principal as cash flow available for debt service plus term loan A interest.

Term loan A repayment

- We leave block I10:O10 empty for now. Once the term loan A control account has been completed, we can then come back to complete the term loan A repayment.

Free cash flow

- In cell I11, we can write the formula "=SUM(I9:I10)", which calculates free cash flow as the sum of cash flow available for principal and term loan A repayment.

Cash balance b/f

- In cell I12, we can write the formula "=IF(I5=1,0,H13)", which basically means that if we are in Year 1, then cash balance brought forward = 0; otherwise, cash balance brought forward = cash balance carried forward in the previous year.

Cash balance c/f

- In cell I13, we can write the formula "=SUM(I11:I12)", which calculates cash balance carried forward as the sum of cash balance brought forward (in cell I12) and free cash flow (in cell I11).

Copy the block I7:I13 and paste it into the block I7:O13.

11.1.3.3 Building the Balance Sheet Module

We will show only the term loan A balance in this module.

Term loan A balance

- We leave block I16:O16 empty for now. Once the term loan A control account has been completed, we can then come back to complete the term loan A balance.

11.1.3.4 Building the Assumptions Module

We will show only the deminimus here.

Deminimus

- In cell K19, we write the figure 1, which represents the $1 million deminimus figure.

11.1.3.5 Building the Workings Module

Here we will include two term loan A control accounts, one with no cash sweep, and one with cash sweep.

Term Loan A Debt Control Account—No Sweep

Debt balance b/f

- In cell I24, we can write the formula "=H26", which basically means that term loan A debt brought forward is equal to term loan A debt carried forward from the previous year.

Debt repayment

- This is an input, and we assume that the debt is scheduled to be repaid in five equal installments. Thus, in each cell in the block I25:M25, we write the formula "=-$H$26/5".

Debt balance c/f

- In cell H26, we write the term loan A opening balance, which is $25 million. Then in cell I26, we write the formula"=SUM(I24 :I25)", which calculates the debt balance carried forward as the sum of the debt balance brought forward and debt repayment.

Copy cells I24:I26 and paste them into the block I24:O26.

Term Loan A Debt Control Account—With Cash Sweep

Debt balance b/f

- In cell I32, we can write the formula "=H32", which basically means that term loan A debt brought forward is equal to term loan A debt carried forward from the previous year.

Debt repayment

- In cell I31, we can write the formula "=-MIN(I30,MAX (0,I9-$K$19))", which means that debt repayment equals the lower of term loan A outstanding and (cash flow available for principal minus deminimus), provided that (cash flow available for principal minus deminimus} is positive.

Debt balance c/f

- In cell H32, we write the formula "=IF(H5>=1,SUM(H30 :H31),H26)", which means that from Year 1 onward, the debt balance carried forward is the sum of the debt balance brought forward and debt repayment; otherwise, debt balance carried forward is equal to term loan A opening balance.

Copy cell H32 and paste it into the block H32:O32. Copy cells I30:I31 and paste them into the block I30:O31.

Term Loan A Interest Control Account

Interest rate

- In cell G35, we write the interest rate on term loan A, which is assumed to be 8 percent.

Interest b/f

- In cell I38, we can write the formula "=H41", which basically means that term loan A interest brought forward is equal to term loan A interest carried forward from the previous year.

Interest charge

- In cell I39, we can write the formula "=$G$35*IF($C$4=0, I24,I30)", which calculates the term loan A interest charge as being equal to the annual interest rate (which is in cell G35) times (no cash sweep term loan A debt balance brought forward if the cash sweep switch is 0, or cash sweep term loan A debt balance brought forward if the cash sweep switch is 1).

Interest paid (or interest repayment)

- In cell I40, we can write the formula "=–I39", which reflects the assumption that interest charged (or incurred) is paid in the same year.

Interest c/f

- In cell I41, we can write the formula "=SUM(I38:I40)", which basically calculates interest carried forward as being equal to interest brought forward plus interest charge less interest paid.

Copy cells I38:I41 and paste them into the block I38:O41.

We can then go back to the cash flow module and complete the term loan A interest and term loan A repayment as follows.

Term loan A interest

- In cell I8, we write the formula "=I40", which picks up the interest from the term loan A control account.

Copy cell I8 and paste it into the block I8:O8.

Term loan A repayment

- In cell I10, we write the formula "=IF($C$4=1,I31,I25)", which means that the term loan A repayment is the term loan A repayment from the no cash sweep term loan A control account if the switch is 0; otherwise, term loan A repayment is the term loan A repayment from the cash sweep term loan A control account.

Copy cell I10 and paste it into the block I10:O10.

We can then also go back to the Balance Sheet module and complete the term loan A balance as follows.

Term loan A balance

- In cell I16, we write the formula "=IF($C$4=1,I32,I26)", which picks up the term loan A balance from the cash sweep term loan A control account if the cash sweep switch is enabled; otherwise, the term loan A balance is picked up from the no cash sweep term loan A control account.

Copy cell I16 and paste it into the block I16:O16.

The cash sweep model is illustrated in Figures 11.3 to 11.5.

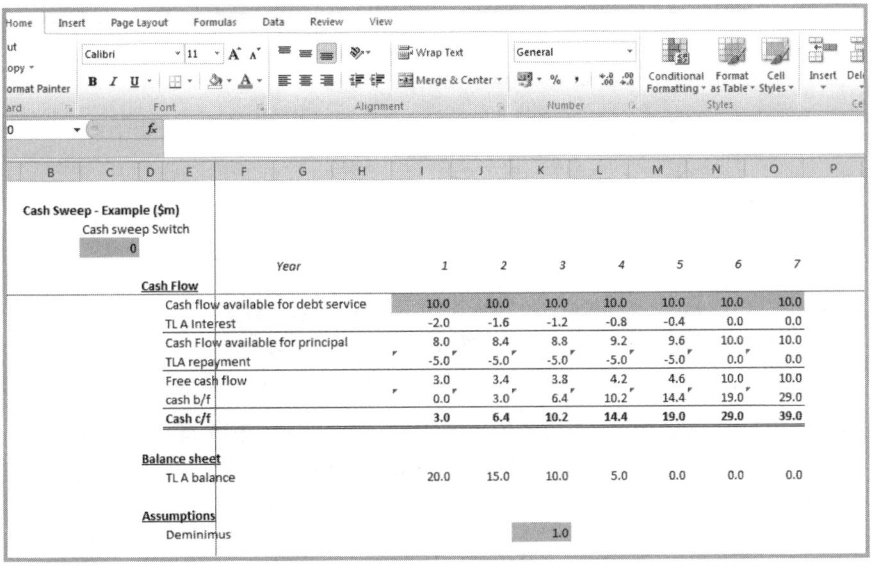

FIGURE 11.3

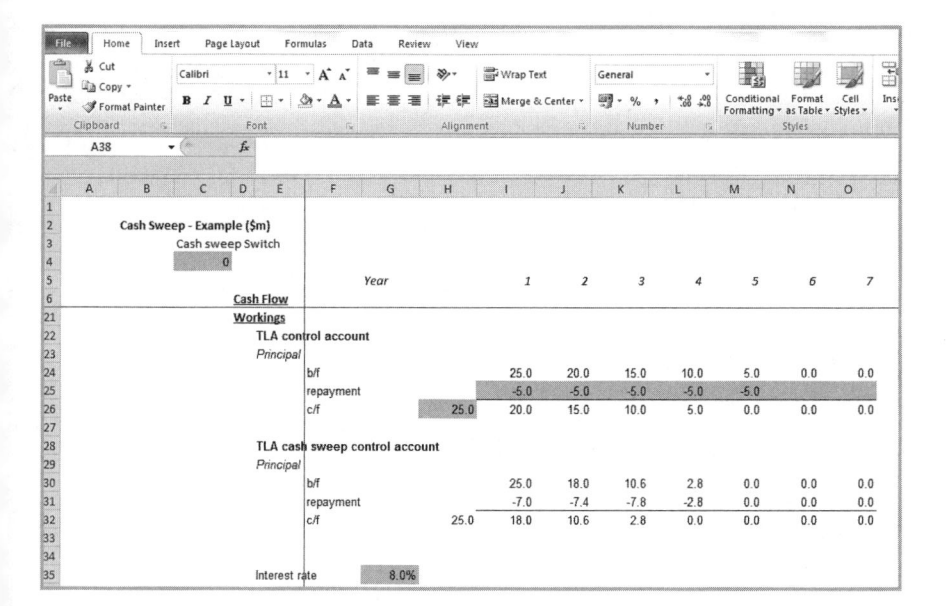

FIGURE 11.4

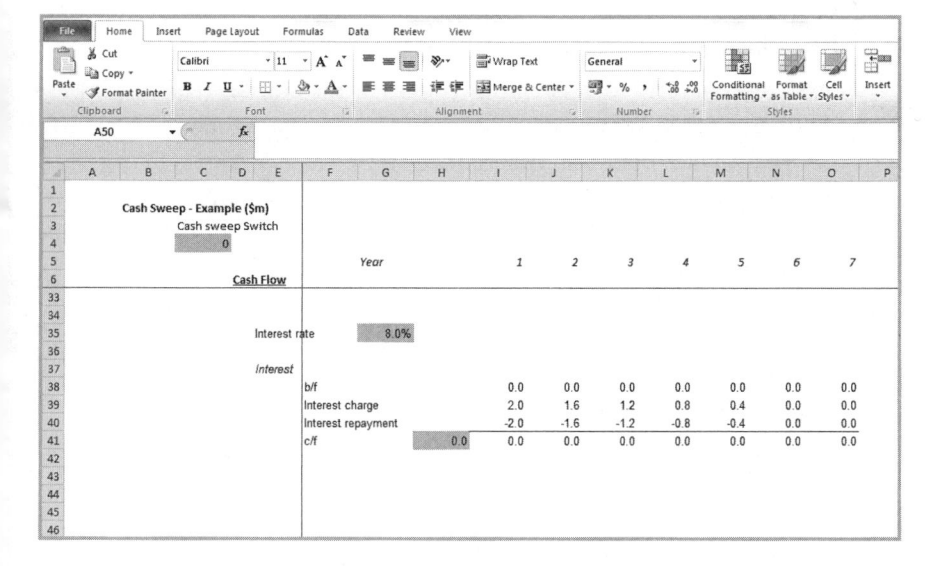

FIGURE 11.5

Please note that the switch in these figures is set to 0. Therefore, the cash flow shown does not reflect the effect of cash sweep. Figure 11.6 shows the cash flow with the cash sweep switch in the 1 position.

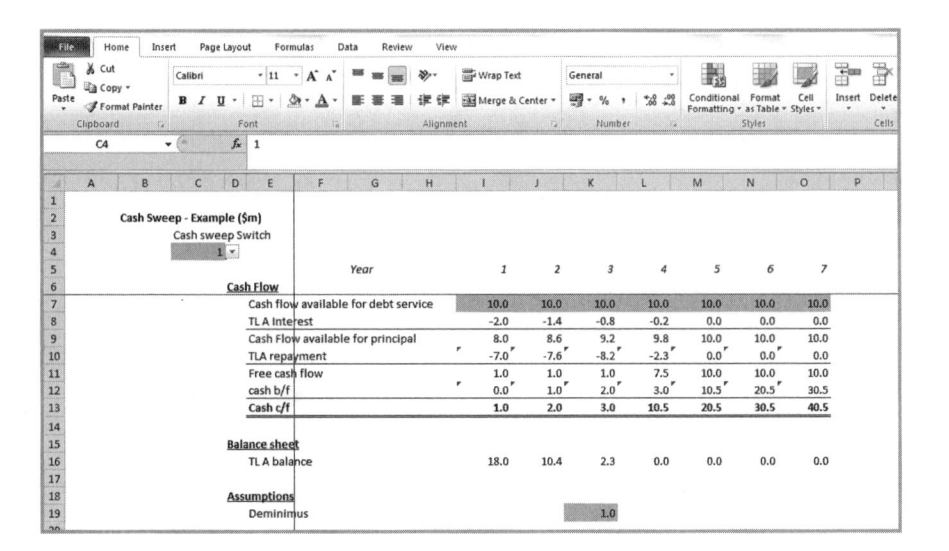

FIGURE 11.6

Analysis and Sense Check

- With the cash sweep switch enabled, we can see on row 16 that term loan A is fully repaid at the end of Year 4, whereas without cash sweep, term loan A is fully repaid at the end of Year 5.
- Under the cash sweep scenario, the company pays total interest of $4.5 million over the four years of term loan A, representing a saving of $1.5 million compared to the interest it would pay without cash sweep ($6 million).
- This saving of $1.5 million is reflected in the closing cash balance at the end of Year 7 of $40.5 million (compared to a closing cash balance at the end of Year 7 of $39 million without cash sweep).
- We can also see that the deminimus of $1 million is excluded from the amount of cash swept; for example, in each of Years 1, 2, and 3, the term loan A repayment is $1 million less than the cash flow available for principal. In Year 4, the amount needed to fully repay term loan A is $2.3 million, and so even though the cash flow available for principal in Year 4 is $9.8 million, only $2.3 million is used to repay term loan A.

11.2 SHARE BUYBACK CASE STUDY

We stick with the cash sweep case study just given. This time we will model a scenario involving the company buying back its own shares. Such a transaction is the reverse of the company issuing new shares. In a share issue scenario, the company receives cash for the new shares it has issued to the shareholders. In a share buyback, the company pays cash in exchange for redeeming shares.

We will add a share buyback component to the cash sweep model. The key to understanding the major steps involved in a share buyback is to build the share capital control account. There are two areas where the impact of the transaction will be reflected in an integrated financial model.

- *Cash flow impact.* As shares are bought back, cash is leaving the company to pay for those shares. There will therefore be a cash outflow shown in the Cash Flow module. Such an outflow will happen below the debt repayment line, reflecting the fact that the company will be able to spend money buying back shares only if it has repaid its debt, term loan A. Here we will assume that 50 percent of the free cash flow can be used to buy back shares.
- *Balance sheet impact.* Once the shares have been bought back, the value of the share capital will decrease by the value of the shares bought back. Here we will assume, however, that the company must maintain a minimum amount of share capital, say $30 million (for example, to comply with a covenant), assuming that the opening share capital is $40 million.

The following are the specifications, which are taken from the cash sweep module and adapted to include the buyback transaction.

Cash Flow Module
- Cash flow available for debt service_t is given as an input.
- Term loan A interest_t will be calculated from the term loan A control account.
- Cash flow available for principal_t = cash flow available for debt service_t minus term loan A interest_t. (Term loan A interest is entered as a negative number, as it represents a cash outflow.)
- Term loan A repayment_t will be calculated from the term loan A control account.
- Free cash flow_t = cash flow available for principal_t minus term loan A interest_t minus term loan A repayment_t.

- Share buyback_t will be calculated from the share capital control account.
- Net cash flow_t = free cash flow_t minus share buyback.
- Cash balance b/f_t = cash balance c/f_t–1, with cash balance b/f in year 1 = opening cash balance.
- Cash balance c/f_t = cash balance b/f_t + net cash flow_t.
- Term loan A balance c/f_t will be calculated from the term loan A control account.
- Share capital c/f_t will be calculated from the share capital control account.

Workings

We will keep the two control accounts for term loan A as before and add a share capital control account.

The share capital control account will be calculated as follows:

- Share capital opening balance_t = share capital closing balance_t–1, with share capital opening balance_year 1 = opening share capital, which is assumed to be $40 million.
- Share issue_t = 0.
- Share redemption _t = min(50% of free cash flow, share capital opening balance_t minus minimum share capital amount), provided that free cash flow is positive.
- Share capital closing balance_t = share capital opening balance_t plus share issue_t plus share redemption_t.

11.2.1 Building the Cash Flow Module

We will build the share buyback into the cash sweep model. To this end, create a copy of the cash sweep sheet.

The Cash Flow module starts on row 7.

After row 12 (that is, below the free cash flow line), we insert two new rows.

Share buyback

- We leave this row, row 12, empty for now.

Net cash flow

- In cell I13, we can write the formula "=SUM(I11:I12)", which calculates net cash flow as the sum of free cash flow (cell I11) and share buyback (cell I12).

Cash balance b/f

- In cell I14, we can write the formula "=IF(I5=1,0,H15)", which basically means that if we are in Year 1, then cash balance brought forward equals 0; otherwise, cash balance brought forward is equal to cash balance carried forward in the previous year.

Cash balance c/f

- In cell I15, we can write the formula "=SUM(I13:I14)", which calculates cash balance carried forward as the sum of cash balance brought forward (in cell I14) and net cash flow (in cell I13).

Copy the block I7:I15 and paste it into the block I7:O15.

11.2.2 Building the Balance Sheet Module

In addition to showing the term loan A balance, we will also show the share capital balance in this module.

Insert a new row after row 18; we will then show the share capital balance in row 19.

Share capital balance

- We leave the block I19:O19 empty for now. Once the share capital control account has been completed, we can then come back and complete the share capital balance.

11.2.3 Building the Assumptions Module

In addition to showing the deminimus, we will also include the percentage of free cash flow available for share buyback and the target minimum share capital.

Insert two new rows after row 21.

% of free cash flow available for share buyback

- In cell K22, we write the figure 50%, representing the 50 percent of free cash flow that is available for share buyback.

Target minimum share capital

- In cell K23, we write the figure 30, representing the minimum share capital of $30 million.

Deminimus

- This is left as it was in cell K19 of the previous model; that is, the figure 1 represents the $1 million deminimus figure.

11.2.4 Building the Workings Module

We leave the term loan A control accounts unchanged: one with no cash sweep and one with cash sweep. We will then add the share capital control account from row 49 as follows:

Share Capital Control Account

Share capital balance b/f

- In cell I50, we can write the formula "=H53", which basically means that share capital brought forward equals share capital carried forward from the previous year.

Share issue

- We are not modeling a share issue here, and so we leave this row empty.

Share redemption

- In cell I52, we write the formula "=–MIN(MAX(0,$K$22*I11), I50–$K$23)", which calculates share redemption as the lower of 50 percent of free cash flow and (share capital opening balance minus minimum share capital amount).

Share capital balance c/f

- In cell H53, we write the opening share capital balance, which is assumed to be equal to $40 million.
- Then in cell I53, we write the formula "=SUM(I50:I52)", which calculates the share capital balance carried forward as the sum of the share capital balance brought forward, share issue, and share redemption.

Copy cells I50:I53 and paste them into the block I50:O53.

We can then go back to the Cash Flow module and complete the share buyback line as follows:

Share buyback

- In cell I12, we write the formula "=I52", which picks up share buyback from the share capital control account.

Copy cell I12 and paste it into the block I12:O12.

We can then also go back to the Balance Sheet module and complete the share capital balance as follows:

Share capital balance

- In cell I19, we write the formula "=I53", which picks up the share capital balance from the share capital control account.

Copy cell I19 and paste it into the block I19:O19.

The combined cash sweep and share buyback model is illustrated in Figures 11.7 to 11.9.

			Year	1	2	3	4	5	6	7
2	Share buyback – Example ($m)									
3		Cash sweep Switch								
4		1								
5			Year	1	2	3	4	5	6	7
6		**Cash Flow**								
7		Cash flow available for debt service		10.0	10.0	10.0	10.0	10.0	10.0	10.0
8		TL A Interest		-2.0	-1.4	-0.8	-0.2	0.0	0.0	0.0
9		Cash Flow available for principal		8.0	8.6	9.2	9.8	10.0	10.0	10.0
10		TLA repayment		-7.0	-7.6	-8.2	-2.3	0.0	0.0	0.0
11		Free cash flow		1.0	1.0	1.0	7.5	10.0	10.0	10.0
12		Share buyback		-0.5	-0.5	-0.5	-3.8	-4.7	0.0	0.0
13		Net cash flow		0.5	0.5	0.5	3.8	5.3	10.0	10.0
14		cash b/f		0.0	0.5	1.0	1.5	5.3	10.5	20.5
15		Cash c/f		0.5	1.0	1.5	5.3	10.5	20.5	30.5
16										
17		**Balance sheet**								
18		TL A balance		18.0	10.4	2.3	0.0	0.0	0.0	0.0
19		Share capital		39.5	39.0	38.5	34.7	30.0	30.0	30.0
20										
21		**Assumptions**								
22		% of free cash flow available for share buyback		50%						
23		Target minimum share capital		30.0						
24		Deminimus		1.0						

FIGURE 11.7

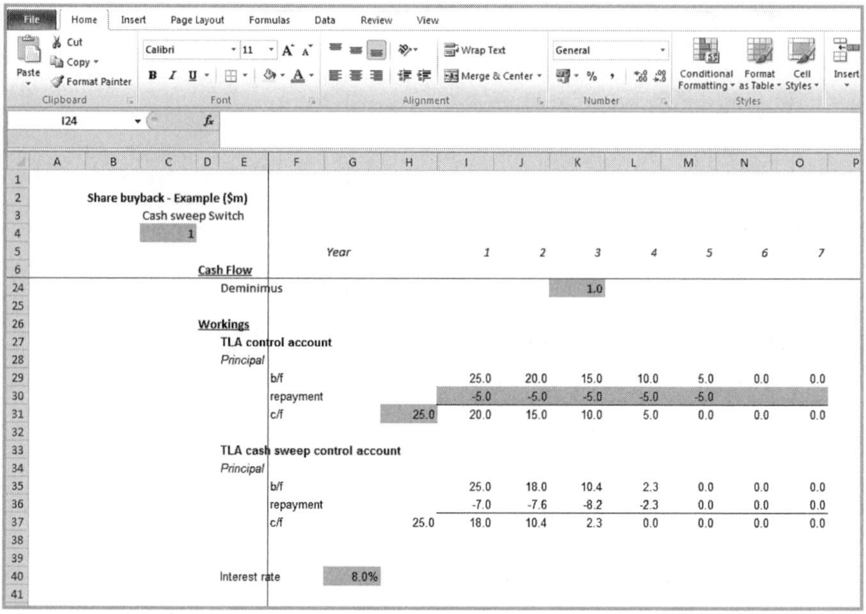

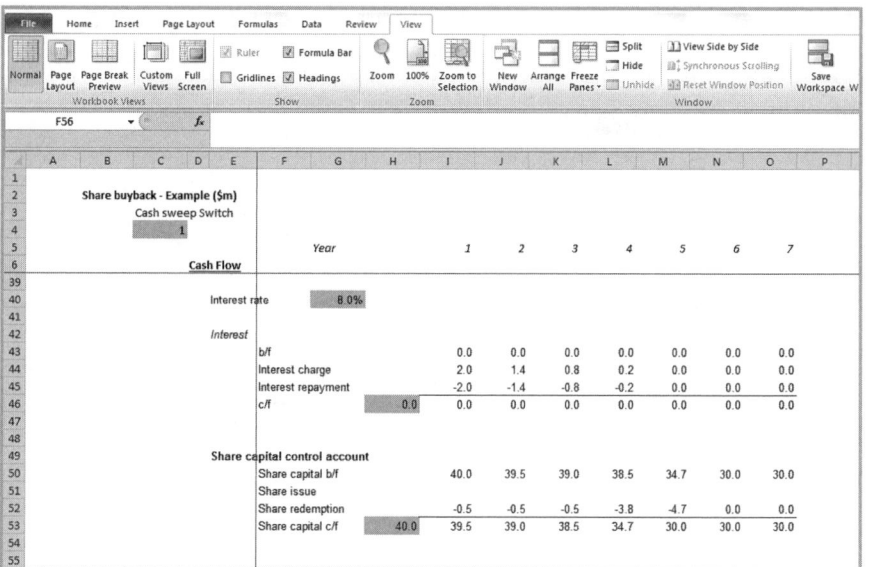

FIGURE 11.8

FIGURE 11.9

Analysis and Sense Check

- As can be seen in the free cash flow module, the cash spent on share buyback in each of Years 1 to 4 is half of the free cash flow, which is consistent with the assumption that 50 percent of the free cash flow is available for share buyback.
- However, we must also maintain a minimum balance of $30 million in share capital. And for this reason, in Year 5, even though up to $5 million, or 50 percent of $10 million free cash flow, can be spent buying back shares, we spend only $4.7 million on share buyback, as any buyback beyond $4.7 million will result in the share capital falling below the $30 million minimum share capital balance.

Part 4

Modeling Practice— Model Audit

CHAPTER TWELVE

Checking for and Fixing Modeling Errors

So far, this book has focused on learning to design and build models. However, it would be incomplete without a chapter that discusses checking for errors. As illustrated in the case studies presented in this book, financial models are often used to assist in decision making (for example, whether to invest or not, whether to sell or not to sell, and so on). These decisions typically involve large sums of money, and it is extremely important that the model be free from errors. For this reason, it is always safer to assume that models contain errors, and the question is how to minimize the chances of errors occurring in your model.

Errors can be grouped into two categories: those that have an impact on the model (that is, the model's output is incorrect) and those that have no impact (the model's output is correct in spite of the error).

In this chapter, we will present a number of practical tips for checking for possible errors in models. We will start with tools that exist within Excel, and then we will build our own error checks.

12.1 BUILDING CELL MAPS IN MICROSOFT EXCEL SPREADSHEETS

There is a tool in Microsoft Excel, often referred to as Cell Map, that (as the name suggests) gives the financial analyst a visual map of any selected area of the financial model. Cell Map works by scanning large areas of cells to check for formula consistency. The Cell Map tool compares the patterns of formulas cell by cell and highlights any cells that do not have a consistent formula pattern. Cell Map can be a very useful tool for identifying errors such as hard-coded cells in the middle of formulas or instances in which a block of cells contains a formula that has not been copied over correctly.

You can check for errors along the row or down the column. To illustrate the use of the Cell Map tool, we will build a small spreadsheet.

Let us open a blank spreadsheet in which we will write the following formulas:

- In cell F4, we write the formula "=+4+1".
- In cell F5, we write the formula "=F4*2".
- In cell F6, we write the formula "=F5–F4".
- In cell F7, we write the formula "=F6+3".
- Copy the block F4:F7 and paste it into the block F4:J7.

Our spreadsheet is illustrated in Figure 12.1.

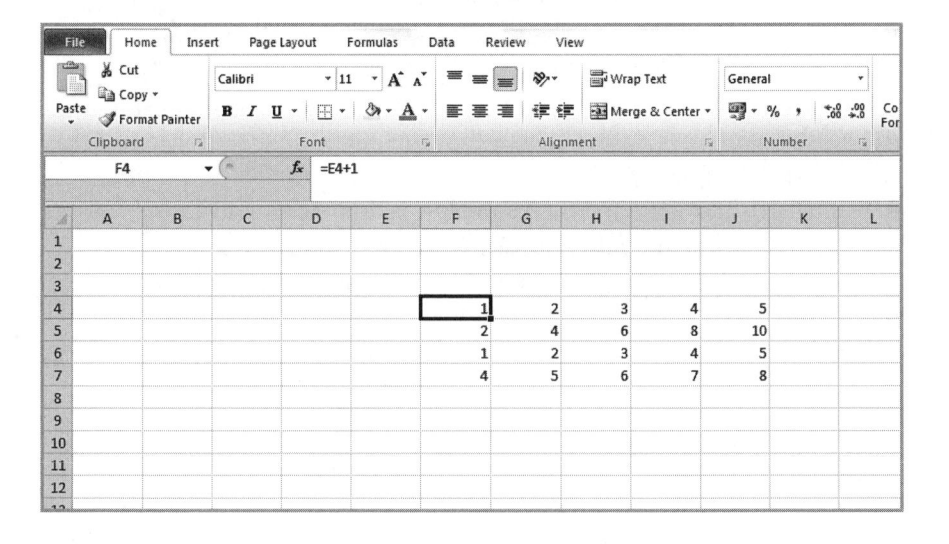

FIGURE 12.1

12.1.1 Detecting Hard-Coded Cells in a Block of Formulas

To illustrate the use of Cell Map, we will deliberately hard-code two randomly picked cells, say G5 and I6. We will put 0 in each of these cells. Then we will select the block F4:J7 (see Figure 12.2).

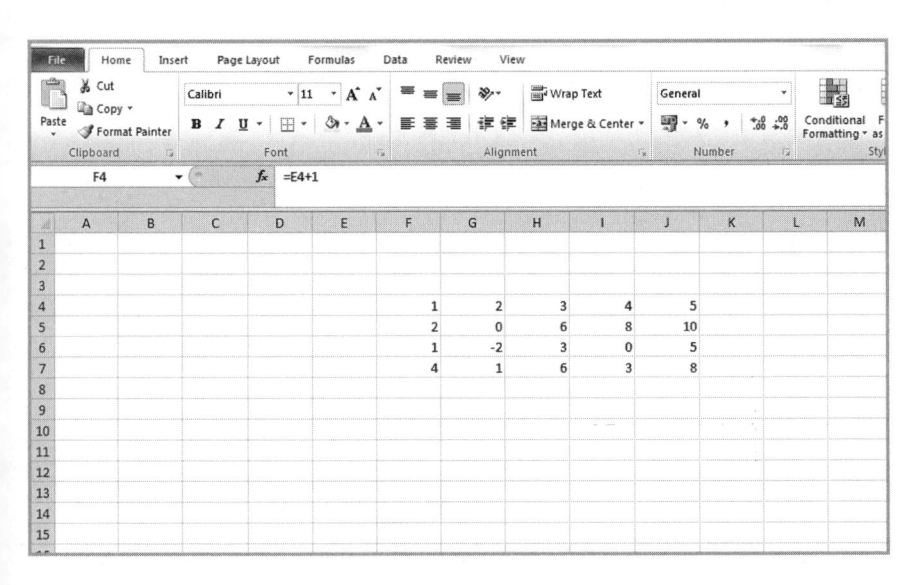

FIGURE 12.2

Now let us use the Cell Map feature to check for consistency along the row. In the Home ribbon, click on the Find & Select button. From the pop-up menu, choose the Go To Special option, tick the radio button Row differences, and click OK (see Figure 12.3).

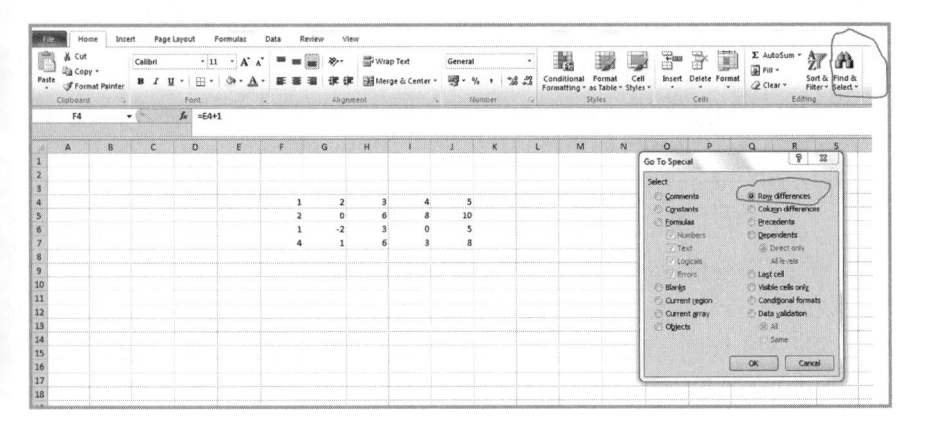

FIGURE 12.3

Microsoft Excel highlights cells G5 and I6. These are the two cells where Microsoft Excel has identified an inconsistency. These two cells contain hard-coded numbers, whereas all the other cells in the block F4:J7 contain formulas. The result from the Microsoft Excel Row difference is illustrated in Figure 12.4.

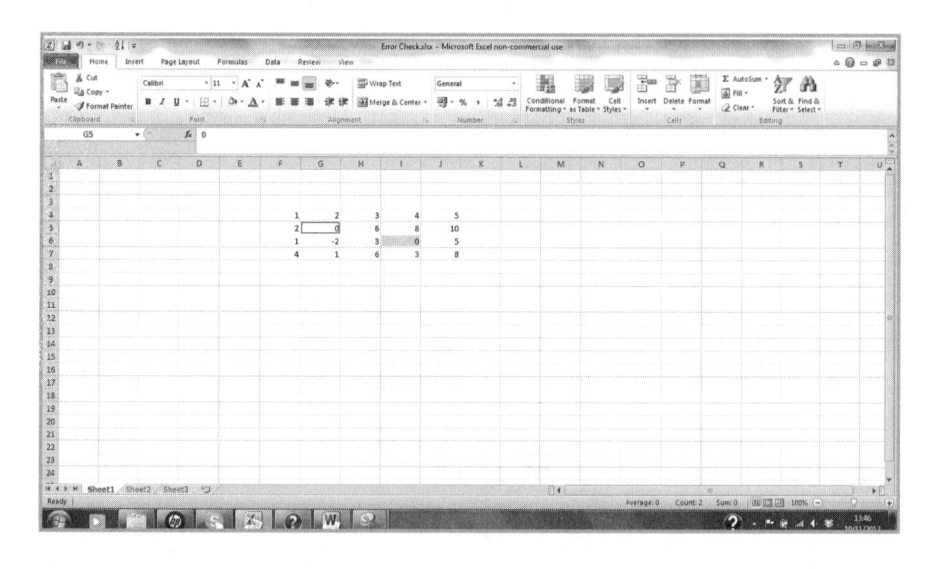

FIGURE 12.4

12.1.2 Detecting Cells with an Inconsistent Formula

Instead of hard-coding cells G5 and I6, let us now type into each of these two cells a formula that is different from the other formulas in that row.

- The formula in row 5 is "2 × row 4". But in cell G5, let us deliberately write a different formula, say "=G4*3".
- The formula in row 6 is "row 5 – row 4". But in cell I6, let us deliberately write a different formula, say "=I5+I4".

Let us rerun the Cell Map. First we select block F4:J7.

In the Home ribbon, click on the Find & Select button. From the pop-up menu, choose the Go To Special option, tick the radio button Row differences, and click OK.

Microsoft Excel again highlights cells G5 and I6. These are the two cells where Microsoft Excel has identified an inconsistency. This time, cells G5 and I6 are not hard-coded, but they contain a formula that is inconsistent with the formula in their row. The result from the Microsoft Excel Row difference is illustrated in Figure 12.5.

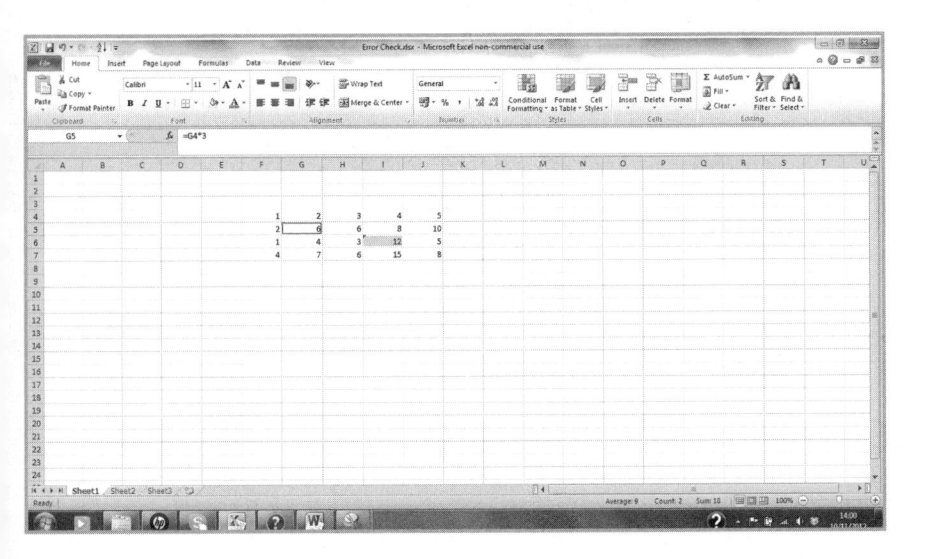

FIGURE 12.5

Note that there is another way of detecting inconsistent formulas. Microsoft Excel automatically highlights cells G5 and I6 by showing a small triangle at the top left-hand side, as shown in Figure 12.6 (in general, Microsoft Excel shows such a triangle in any cell containing an error). If you select cell G5 or I6, an exclamation mark appears, and hovering the mouse over the exclamation mark prompts the following message: "The formula in this cell differs from the formulas in this area of the spreadsheet".

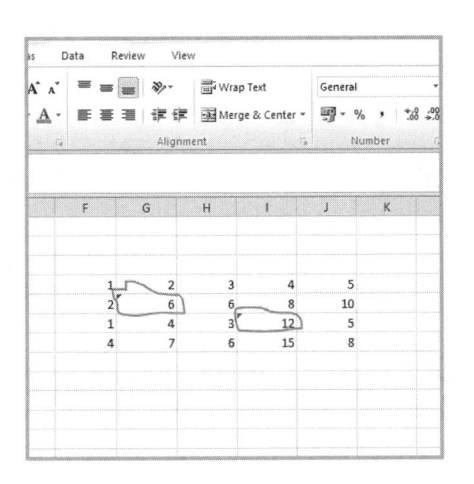

FIGURE 12.6

If the data were arranged in columns, then we could highlight the selected area and click the Column differences radio button in the Go To Special dialogue box. For example, let us create a block of formulas written down the columns as follows:

- In cell L10, we write the formula "=L9+1".
- In cell M10, we write the formula "=L10+2".
- In cell N10, we write the formula "=M10–L10".
- Copy the block L10:N10 and paste it into the block L10:N18.

Our spreadsheet is illustrated in Figure 12.7.

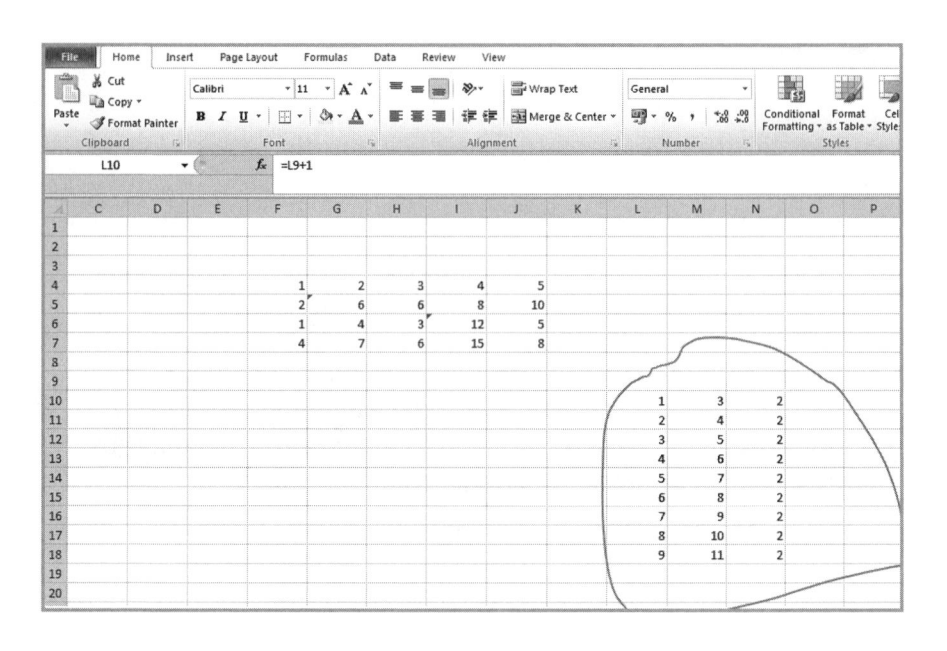

FIGURE 12.7

- The formula in column M is "column L + 2". But in cell M13, let us deliberately hard-code the number 4.
- The formula in column N is "column M – column L". But in cell N16, let us deliberately hard-code the number 4.

Let us rerun the cell map as before. First we select the block L10:M18.

In the Home ribbon, click on the Find & Select button. From the pop-up menu, choose the Go To Special option, tick the radio button Column differences, and click OK.

Microsoft Excel highlights cells M13 and N16. These are the two cells where Microsoft Excel has identified an inconsistency. The cells M13 and N16 are hard-coded, which is inconsistent with the formula in their respective columns. The result from the Microsoft Excel Column difference is illustrated in Figure 12.8.

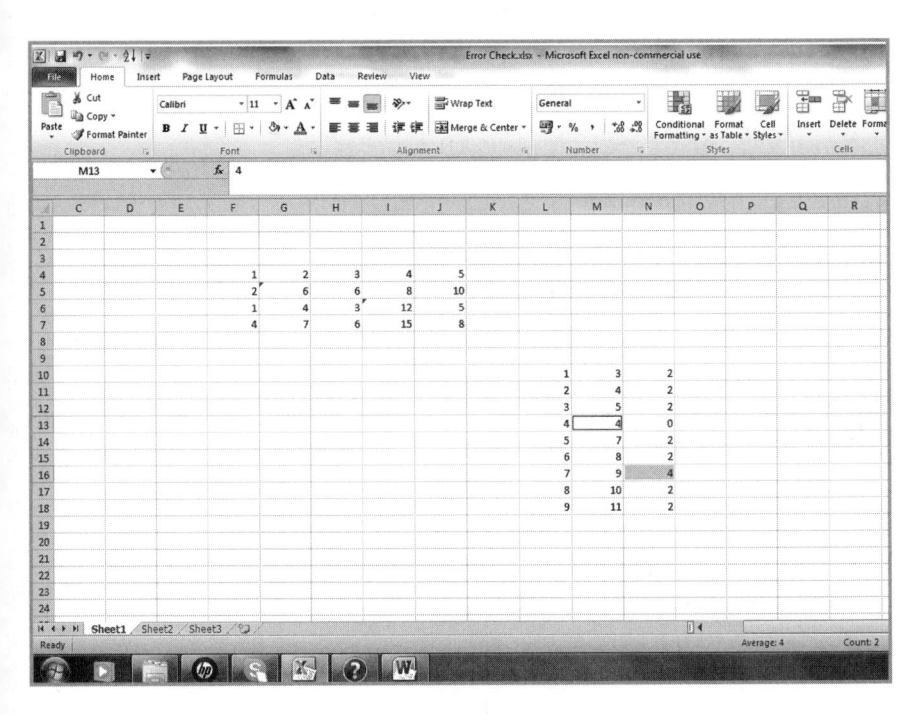

FIGURE 12.8

The Row differences, Column differences and, more generally, the Go To Special dialogue box are often overlooked even by advanced Microsoft Excel users. Yet it is worth looking at the various useful options these tools contain.

12.2 USE OF HISTORICAL DATA

As we learned in previous chapters, a financial model takes inputs, processes these inputs, and produces an output. It is thus possible to test the logic of a financial model by using actual historical data as the data input. For example, in an annual budget planning model, it is often possible to feed actual historical numbers into the model and see whether the results from the model coincide with those that actually occurred. If they do, the financial model is likely to be functioning as intended. For example, if after we feed the historical cost of sales into the financial model, the gross profit number (defined as revenue less cost of sales) that we get in the model is equal to that in the historical account, then we are likely to be on the right track.

12.3 CHECK LOGIC BY SELECTING CELL PRECEDENTS AND DEPENDENTS

Another useful audit tool is Excel's Formula Auditing features. These tools are available in the Formula tab of the ribbon under Formula Auditing. For example, you can use the buttons in the Formula Auditing section to display arrows connecting the active cell to related cells. In Figure 12.9, cell I4 contains the number 4, cell J3 contains the formula "=I4+2", and cell K5 contains the formula "=J3*2".

- With cell K5 active, we can click on the Trace Precedent icon. This will display a blue arrow from cell J3 to cell K5.
- With cell I4 active, we can click on the Trace Dependent icon. This will display a blue arrow from cell I4 to cell J3.

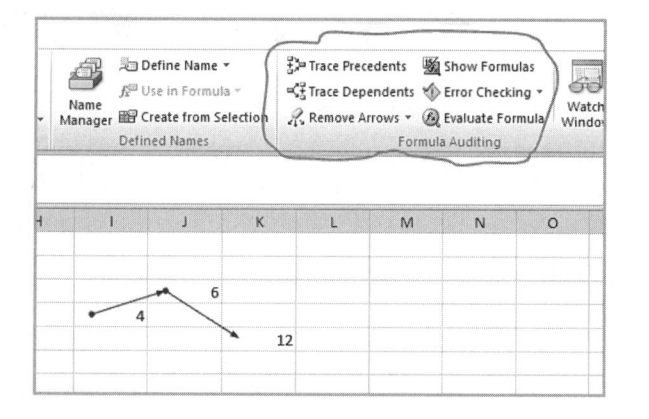

FIGURE 12.9

References to other sheets can be traced in a similar manner by double-clicking on the arrow.

12.4 TRACE ERRORS USING THE TRACE ERROR BUTTON WHENEVER MICROSOFT EXCEL REPORTS AN ERROR _____

You may have come across cells that display an error value, such as #NAME?, #N/A, #####, #REF!, #DIV/0!, #NULL!, #NUM!, or #VALUE! Each type of error has different causes and different solutions. Furthermore, the cell containing the error will have a small triangle in the top left-hand corner.

In error situations such as these, you can use the Trace Error button to help you trace the errors. The Trace Error button is within the Formula Auditing section in the Formula tab (see Figure 12.9). See Excel's Help for further details.

12.5 PROTECT CELLS CONTAINING A FORMULA _____

To help preserve the integrity of your model, you can protect cells containing formulas so that such cells are not inadvertently modified. To achieve cell protection, you need to complete three steps: (1) select the cells that need to be protected (for example, cells L10:N18), (2) lock the cell, then (3) protect the sheet in which the cell is.

- *Lock cells.* First, you need to lock the cell. This can be done by selecting the cell or block of cells, right-button clicking, and clicking on Format Cells. A pop-up window appears. In it, select the Protection tab and tick Locked. Then click OK. See Figure 12.10.

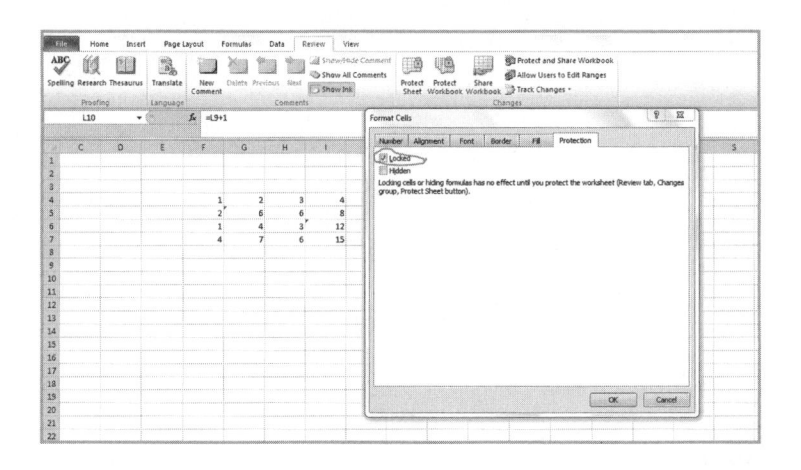

FIGURE 12.10

- *Protect the sheet in which the locked cell is.* To protect the sheet, go to the Review tab of the ribbon, then click on Protect Sheet. This will bring up a pop-up window, as shown in Figure 12.11.

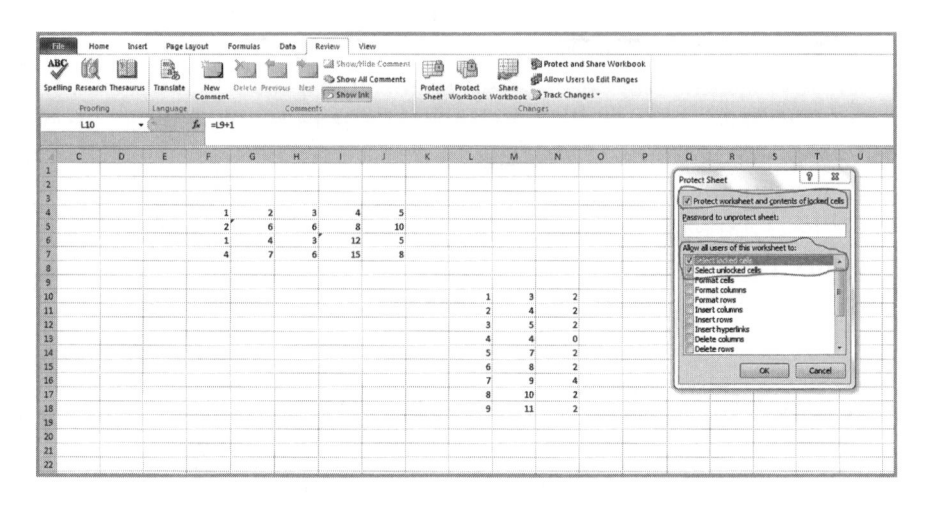

FIGURE 12.11

- Tick "Protect worksheet and contents of locked cells". Also, under "Allow all users of this worksheet to:", tick both "Select locked cells" and "Select unlocked cells". Then click OK.
- If you try to write in any cell in block L10:N18, you will get the error message shown in Figure 12.12 from Excel.

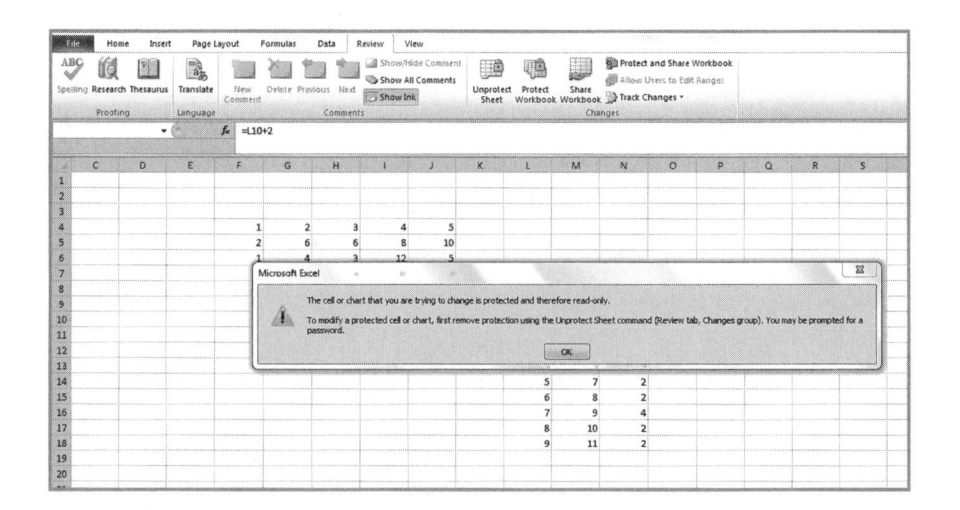

FIGURE 12.12

Some best practice tips:

- If you protect all the cells in your model, this will make it quite inconvenient to change the contents of input cells. To avoid this inconvenience, lock only the calculation cells, that is, cells that contain formulas, and leave input cells unlocked. That way, once the sheet is protected, it will not be possible for users to accidentally override cells containing formulas. But it will be possible for users to run different versions of the model by changing the input cells.
- Also, you will notice that in the sheet protection step, we did not provide a password for unprotecting the sheet. Of course, providing a password adds further protection, but it also means having to remember the password and having to share it with others who might be involved in developing the model further. So you will need to balance the need to preserve the integrity of the model with the cost of maintaining such integrity.

12.6 USE DATA VALIDATION

We have already used an example of data validation in the previous chapter. Data validation allows the user to control the type of data or the values that users enter into a cell. For example, you may want to restrict the data entered by users of your financial model to a certain range of dates, to limit their choices by using a list (such as in the previous chapter), or simply to ensure that only positive integer (that is, whole) numbers are entered.

See Excel's Help for further details.

12.7 IRR CALCULATIONS

Enter 0 instead of leaving cells empty when you are calculating the IRR for a given series of cash flows over a time period. Consider the following example. An investor buys an equity stake for $5 million, holds the stock for four years, and sells the stock at the end of Year 4 for $20 million. The IRR of this investment is 41 percent. However, to get the right result in Microsoft Excel, you will need to enter 0 for the cash flow in each of Years 1, 2, and 3. If you leave these cells empty, then the IRR will be calculated as 300 percent, which is the IRR of buying the stock for $5 million and selling it at $20 million at the end of Year 1 (see Figure 12.13).

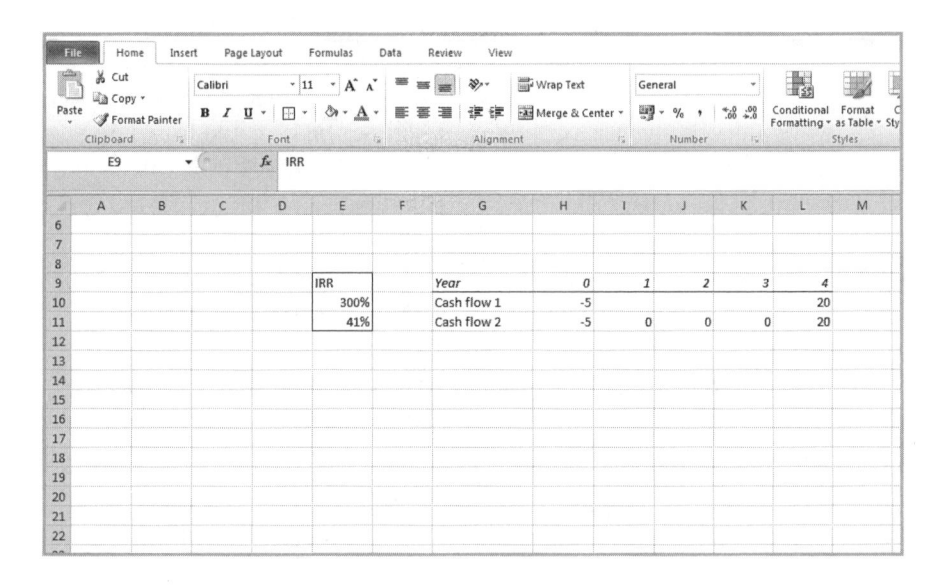

FIGURE 12.13

12.8 BUILDING YOUR OWN ERROR-CHECKING TOOLS

A good financial modeler will probably use the Microsoft Excel built-in error auditing and testing tools such as the ones described in this chapter. It simply makes sense to do so, as these tools can help minimize the chances of errors occurring in the model. That said, even using all these built-in tools, there are certain types of errors that cannot be picked up unless the user builds his own error-checking tools. For example, users should include check-sums, balance sheet balance checks, sources and uses of funds checks, opening balance sheet checks, and the good old-fashioned sense check.

Incorporating error checks into a financial model is best practice and will help to bulletproof and preserve the integrity and value of the financial model for the benefit of the user. To this end, it is good practice to bring together all the error checks across a financial model into a summary where these individual error checks are aggregated into one overall error check status. The overall error check status can then be displayed in all the sheets within the financial model (by linking each sheet to the overall error check status) so that it is not necessary to navigate out of the current sheet to check the overall error check status.

It is important to distinguish between errors that have no impact on the financial model and errors that do have an impact on it. An example of an error with no impact was presented in the previous chapter. When the cash sweep switch is disabled, but we are working on a model that uses a cash sweep, we won't realize that there is an error. An example of an error with impact can also be found in the share buyback case study in the previous chapter. In that case study, share capital must be >= $30 million in the share buyback model. Likewise, cash flow available for principal_t minus term loan A repayment_t >= deminimus_t in the cash sweep module. If either of these conditions is not met, then the impact will be felt across the model (for example, share capital will be less than $30 million when it should be at least $30 million, or the cash flow available after the cash sweep for term loan A will be less than the deminimus when it should be greater than the deminimus).

Based on the case studies presented in previous chapters of this book, examples of your own Error checks could include the following:

- *Check that sources = uses.* Check that the sum of all sources of funds equals the sum of all uses of funds.
- *Check that predeal and postdeal balance sheets balance.* The predeal and postdeal balance sheets drive the projected balance sheet in LBO models. It is best practice to check that net assets = shareholders' funds (or total assets = total liabilities).
- *Check that all uses and all sources have been applied to the predeal balance sheet.* This is important to ensure that no item in the sources of funds and no item in the uses of funds has been left out of the predeal balance sheet.
- *Check projected balance sheet balances.* Once the opening balance sheet balances, it is important to check that the balance sheet continues to balance at the end of each projected period. In this context, the balance sheet check could be based on calculating the difference between net assets and shareholders' funds. The result tells us by how much (if any) the balance sheet is unbalanced. Fixing the imbalance starts with the earliest period where the imbalance occurs. Key to fixing the balance sheet is having in mind the relationship among the profit and loss statement, the balance sheet, and the cash flow statement (see Figure 8.5).

- *Term loan A repayment.* Check that the sum of all installments on an amortizing loan equals the original amount of the amortizing loan.

12.9 SOME ERRORS TO AVOID

We refer the reader to the Chapter 2 discussion on best practice in financial modeling for further details. In the meantime, here is a list of typical errors to avoid:

- *Omitting the executive summary.* All financial models should display an executive summary that gives a synopsis of the key results from the model.
- *Avoid intertwining assumptions and calculations.* There should be a clear separation between assumptions and calculations.
- *Avoid rows containing more than one unique formula.* Otherwise, reviewing the model becomes much more difficult and costly.
- *Avoid VBA.* Financial models must be simple and easy to use. For this reason, it is recommended that you avoid (or minimize) the use of Visual Basic if possible.
- *Avoid long calculations.* Ideally, no formula should be longer than half the length of the Microsoft Excel formula bar.

Part 5

Conclusion

CHAPTER THIRTEEN

Conclusion

As can be seen throughout the book, building financial models requires multiple skills.

- First and foremost, it requires logical and analytical reasoning to gain a good understanding of the requirements for a financial model. Put simply, you cannot model what you do not understand.
- Then, based on an understanding of what is required, the model should be designed and the project scoped out to reflect the requirements of the model.
- Finally, some knowledge of spreadsheet software is required in order to develop the model in the selected software (in this case, Microsoft Excel). You do not need to be an expert in Microsoft Excel to build good financial models. Knowledge of Microsoft Excel functions can be acquired gradually over time, as and when their use is required. The Microsoft Excel Help menu is a useful information resource on how to use Microsoft Excel functions. There are also a number of online forums for users of Excel.

Throughout the book, we have used a variety of case studies as a learning platform for building financial models following best practice principles.

In particular, the following modeling concepts have been covered:

- Best practice principles
- Use of flags
- Modeling fixed versus variable costs
- Modeling inflation
- Financial ratios
- The use of multiple sheets in Excel
- Formatting cells and sheets to enhance the user-friendliness of models
- Modeling interest and debt repayments
- Control account mechanisms
- Debt and equity investing
- IRR and XIRR
- Aggregating more granular data (for example, semiannual data) into less granular data (for example, annual data)
- Conditional formatting
- The use of Goal Seek
- Data Validation
- Modeling cash sweeps
- Modeling share buybacks
- Building Cell Maps
- Error-checking techniques
- Sources and uses of funds
- Calculating the postdeal balance sheet
- Growth capital modeling
- LBO modeling
- Credit statistics

This case study approach to learning gives readers the potential to build advanced financial models once they have completed the learning in this book.

Modeling is a decision-making tool that is used in practically every sphere of business. It plays such a critical role in decision making that it is important to ensure that financial models are free from errors. This book has introduced a host of error-checking tools to help ensure that models do not contain errors. Ultimately, however, the best way to ensure that models are free from errors is to perform a sense check.

Notwithstanding the importance of modeling in decision making, it is important to keep in mind that in some cases, decision making cannot be based solely on models. Commercial judgment is required to support and complement numerical reasoning.

We believe that the best way to master financial modeling is through experience. The case studies presented in this book serve that purpose. Future editions of this book will include new case studies that will give readers further opportunities to develop more advanced financial models.

Index

About the Author

Eric Soubeiga is Investment Officer at the World Bank. His finance career spans private equity, investment banking, and transactional advisory gained in the City of London. Prior to his finance career, Eric worked in academia and was involved in research and teaching at the University of Nottingham (UK).